AF573958

Mabel's SANTA FE and TAOS

Mabel's SANTA FE and TAOS

Bohemian Legends
1900-1950

Elmo Baca

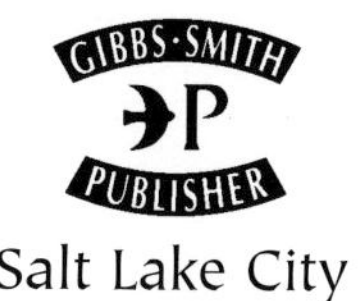

Salt Lake City

First Edition
02 01 00 4 3 2 1

Published by
Gibbs Smith, Publisher
P.O. Box 667
Layton, UT 84041

Orders: 1-800-748-5439
Website: *www.gibbs-smith.com*

Jacket designed by Fourth Gear Design
Interior designed by Trent Alvey Design
Edited by Gail Yngve
Printed and bound in China

Library of Congress Cataloging-in-Publication Data

Baca, Elmo.
Mabel's Santa Fe and Taos : Bohemian legends, 1900–1950 / Elmo Baca.
p. cm.
ISBN 0-87905-913-3
1. Artist colonies—New Mexico—Santa Fe. 2. Arts, American—New Mexico—Santa Fe. 3. Art, Modern—20th century—New Mexico—Santa Fe. 4. Arts, American—New Mexico—Taos. 5. Taos school of art. 6. Luhan, Mabel Dodge, 1879–1962—Homes and haunts—New Mexico—Taos. I. Title.

NX510.N43 B33 1999
700'.9789'53—dc21

99-016868

Contents

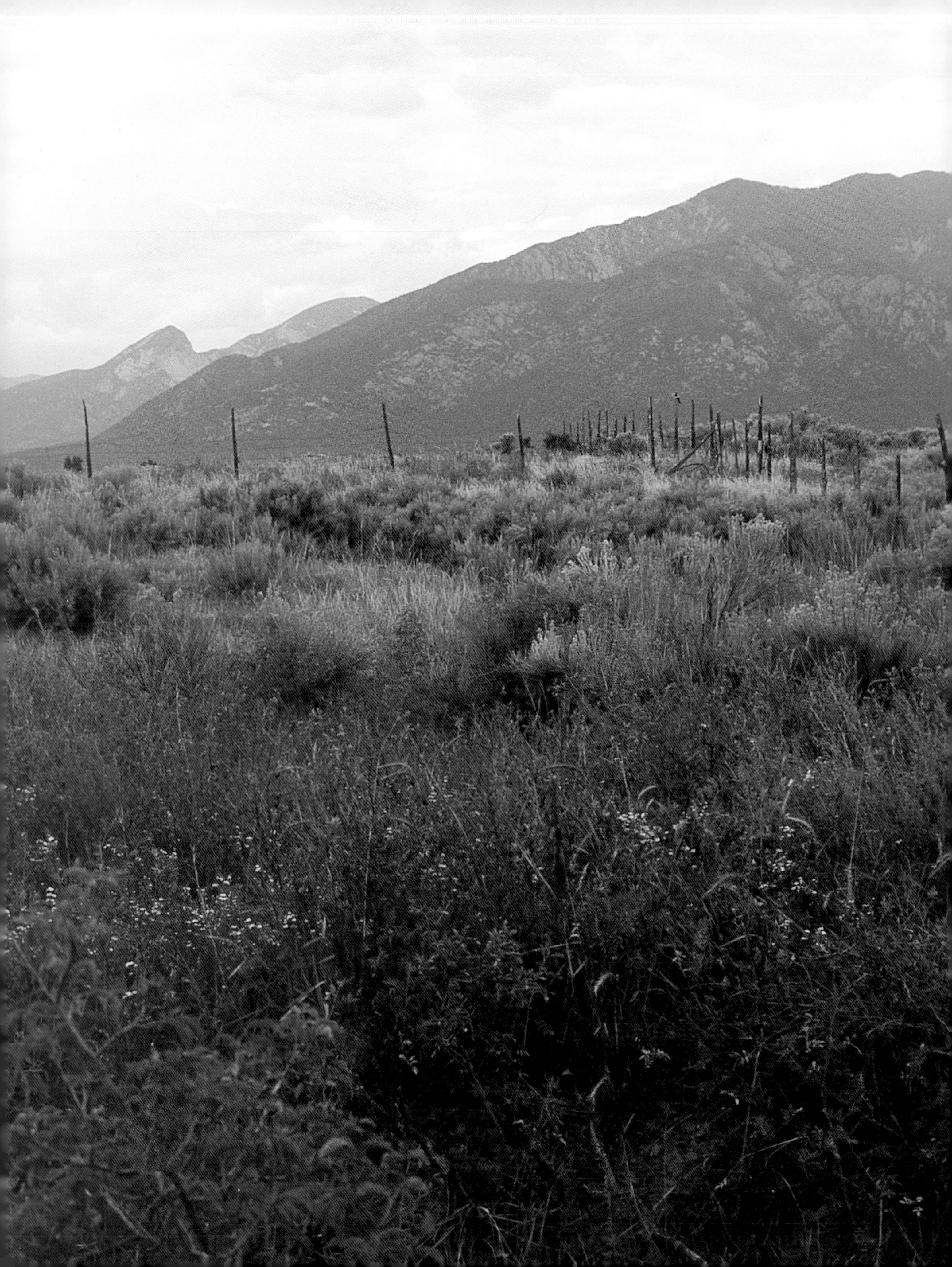

Taos Mountain and Taos Pueblo

Taos Mountain is eternal. The mountain dwells regally within its awesome valley, its rock heart a spiritual siren for an endless stream of worshippers. Like other famous mountains of the world, it is shrouded with many veils of mystery, love, power, legend, and symbolism.

Over eighty years ago, a remarkable woman chose to settle beneath the shade of Taos Mountain, to bask within its ineffable attraction. She was led there by luck and instinct, built a magnificent house—a Shangri-la—and, in turn, used the power of the mountain to attract some of the most fascinating minds and personalities.

Mabel Ganson Evans Dodge Sterne Luhan's path to Taos Mountain is a celebrated one—among the more improbable stories of the twentieth century. How did a wealthy socialite from Buffalo, New York, come to Taos Mountain and in her wake cut a swath through the fields of American art, literature, and cultural history?

After she became Mabel Dodge Luhan, she mused that followers of the ancient Chinese sage Lao-tzu, the mythical author of the *Tao Te Ching*, had wandered over the Siberian straits down to the great mountain, naming it "Taos," a variation of the Tao, or "the Way."

The Chinese mystical reference is not so farfetched. Many others, including such luminaries as psychologist Carl Jung and novelist D. H. Lawrence, have ascribed profound spiritual significance to Taos Mountain, not to mention the Taos Pueblo people themselves, who believe the mountain is the heart of the universe.

During Mabel's years in Taos (1917–62), an astonishing parade of creative spirits made the pilgrimage to her house and to the mountain, each drawing a measure of power and inspiration from the sacred landscape. In this way, the culture of Taos, New Mexico, and America were all influenced.

Mabel was also a student of the *I Ching*, or the *Book of Changes*, an ancient Chinese text of wisdom and divination. Ask the book a question, and it will respond by offering one or more of its sixty-four hexagrams to interpret. A primal symbol of meaning in the *Book of Changes* is the mountain, whose power along with heaven, earth, thunder, water, wind, fire, and lake acts to produce all of the phenomena of change in the cosmos.

According to the *I Ching*, keeping still is the major attribute of the mountain, which is the youngest son of heaven and earth. The *Book of Changes* tells us that the hexagram of the

Sangre de Cristo Mountains near Taos.

mountain (#52) "turns upon the problem of achieving a quiet heart. It is very difficult to bring quiet to the heart."

There beneath Taos Mountain, Mabel Dodge Luhan sought to quiet her raging heart. Whether she or anyone has truly found the stillness beneath Taos Mountain, we will never know, but we will always wonder.

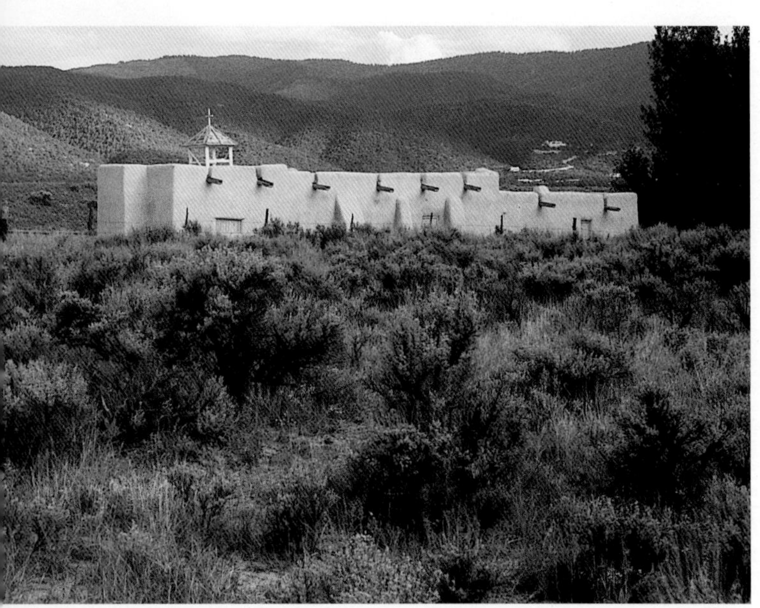

A former penitente morada, *or prayer chapel, near the Mabel Dodge Luhan estate in Taos.*

Carl Jung on Taos

It is the role of religious symbols to give a meaning to the life of man. The Pueblo Indians believe that they are the sons of Father Sun, and this belief endows their life with a perspective (and a goal) that goes far beyond their limited existence. It gives them ample space for the unfolding of personality and permits them a full life as complete persons. Their plight is infinitely more satisfactory than that of a man in our own civilization who knows that he is (and will remain) nothing more than an underdog with no inner meaning to his life.

—Man and His Symbols, *based on Jung's visit to Taos Pueblo, January 1925.*

The Allure of Taos

It is no wonder that so many sensitive and religiously minded people have fallen under Taos's spell. She gives the impression of being able to sustain a dialogue between heaven and earth that can make the sacraments real to men. At another level her secrecy, her disguises, and especially, her indefatigable trickery, intrigue our imagination as they suggest shamanistic styles of religious practice now normally unconscious or long gone.

—Vincent Scully, architectural historian, in Pueblo.

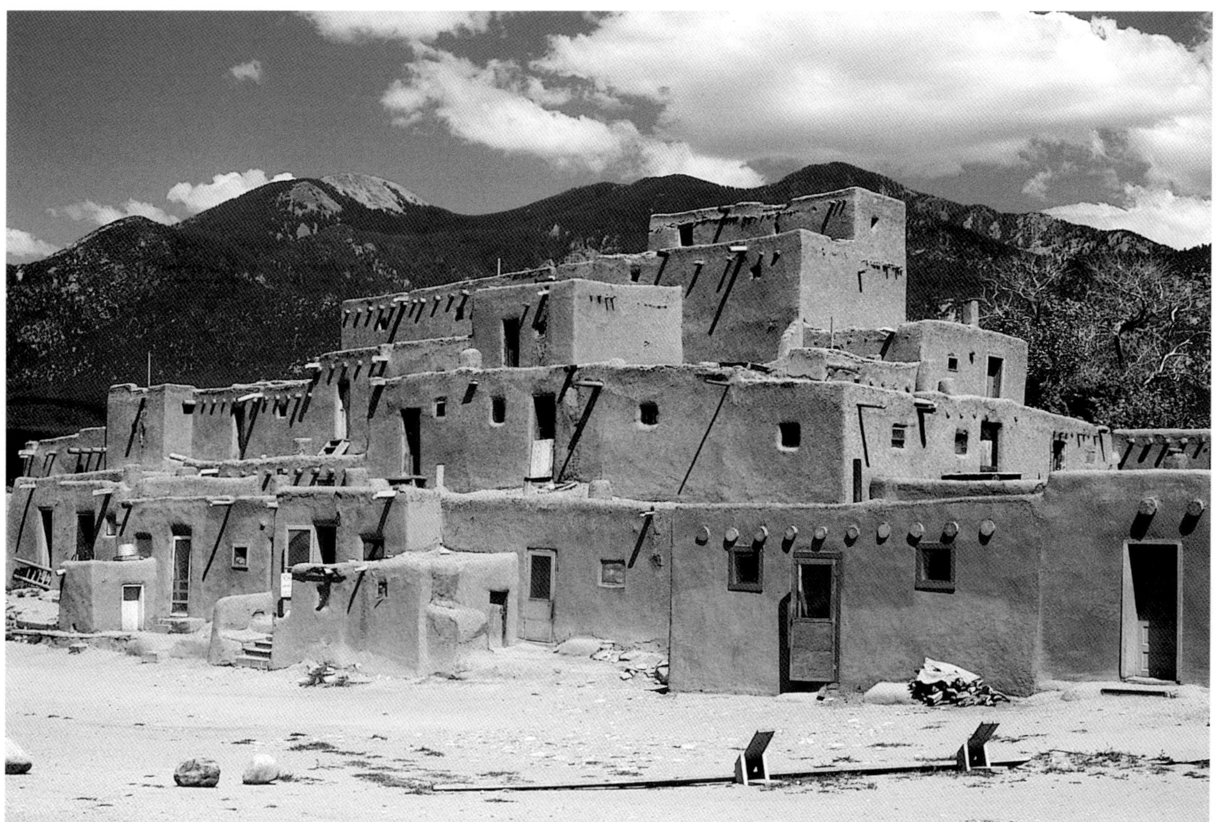

The north house of Taos Pueblo with the sacred mountain behind.

The Monastery and Taos

The Indians say Taos is the heart of the world. Their world, maybe. Some places seem temporary on the face of the earth: San Francisco, for example. Some places seem final. They have a true nodality. I never felt that so powerfully as years ago in London. The intense powerful nodality of that great heart of the world. And during the war that heart, for me, broke. So it is. Places can lose their living nodality. Rome to me has lost hers. In Venice one feels the magic of the glamorous old node that once united East and West, but it is the beauty of an afterlife. Taos Pueblo still retains its old nodality. Not like a great city. But in its way like one of the monasteries of Europe. You cannot come upon the ruins of the old great monasteries of England, beside their waters, in some lovely valley, now remote, without feeling that here is one of the choice spots of the earth, where the spirit dwelt. . . . Taos Pueblo affects me rather like one of the old monasteries. When you get there you feel something final. There is an arrival. The nodality still holds good.

—D. H. Lawrence in Taos, 1922.

Taos—A Eulogy

[The Indians] built their Pueblo beneath the mountains they call "Sacred," beside the creek that flows down from Blue Lake twelve thousand feet up in the hills. On either side of this stream they built the two large pyramidal community dwellings that have been called "the finest apartment houses in America," and they called themselves the "Summer People" and the "Winter People," for one group lay to the north and the other to the south of the stream. . . . The Indians, in their religious ceremonies, believe they "take care" of this earth. They take care of the sun, the running water, "Star Water," as they call Lucero Creek, and the life of this valley. Is it too much to believe that they really do, that they pour into this air we breathe some potent and quite magical power? Who, that has awakened early to see the morning star rise over the foothills and has heard in the dawn silence an unearthly music too delicate and too remote to define, doubts that there is a joyous, invisible genius loci presiding here? . . .

Said [D. H.] Lawrence: ". . . go to Taos Pueblo on some brilliant snowy morning, and see the white figures on the roof: or come riding through at dusk on some windy evening, when the black skirts of the women blow around the wide white boots, and you will feel the old, old root of human consciousness still reaching down to depths we know nothing of."

—Mabel Dodge Luhan, 1931

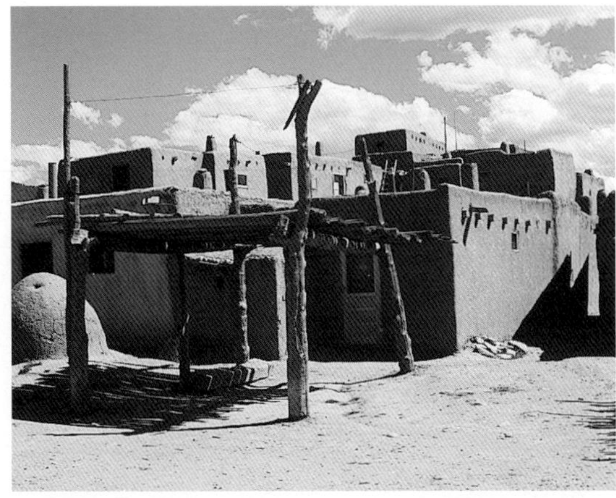

Taos Pueblo dwellings.

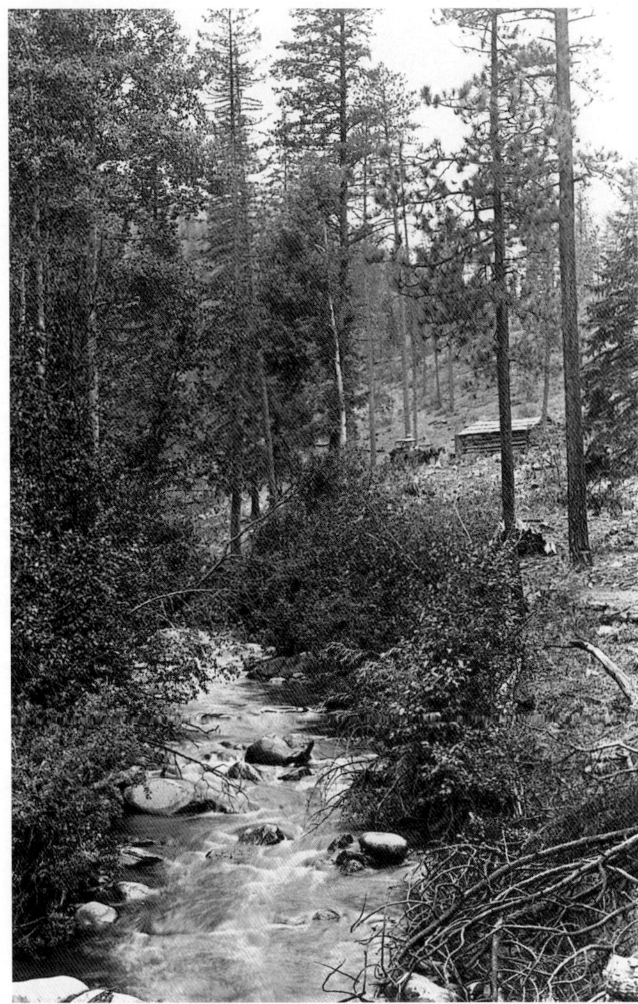

Creek in upper Gallinas Canyon north of Las Vegas, New Mexico.

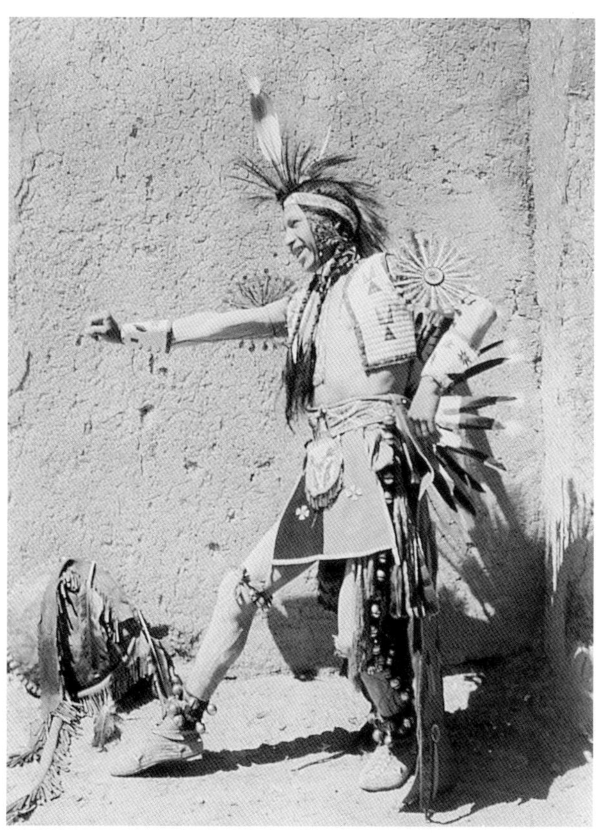

Pueblo ceremonial dancer.

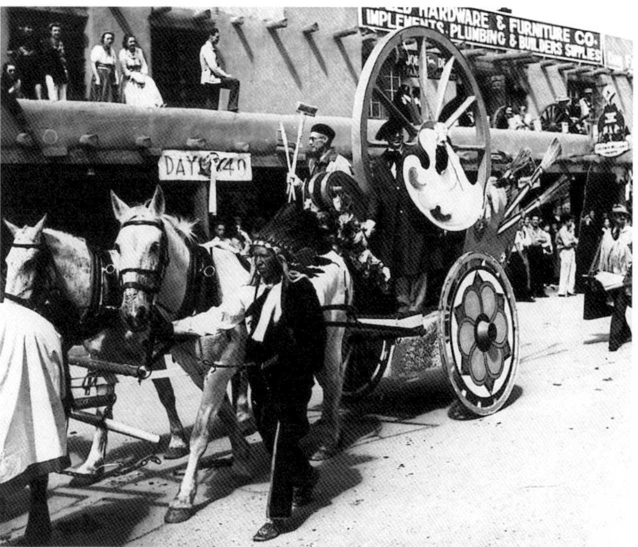

Ernest L. Blumenschein and Bert G. Phillips on "Broken Wheel" float, celebrating their fated discovery of Taos in the Taos Fiesta Parade, 1930s.

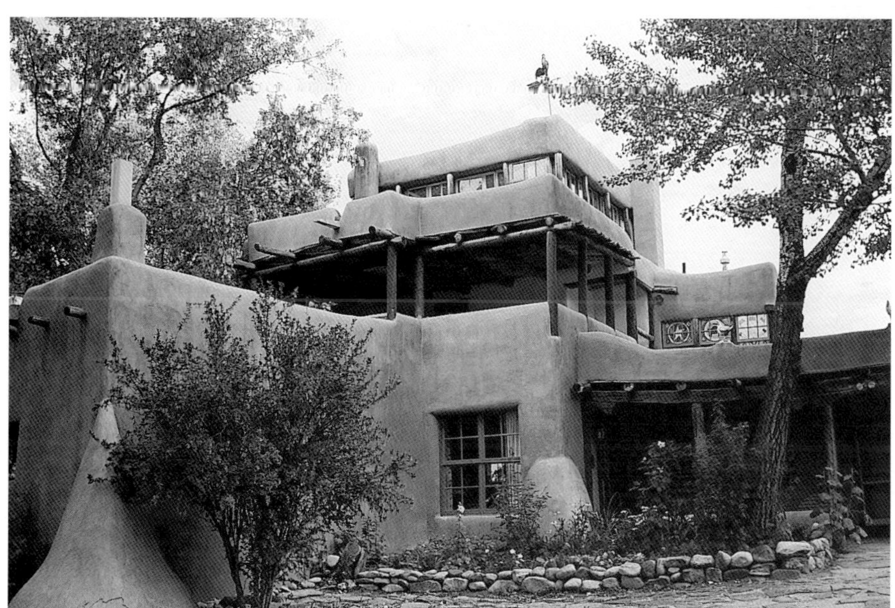

Contemporary view of the "big house," Mabel Dodge Luhan estate, Taos.

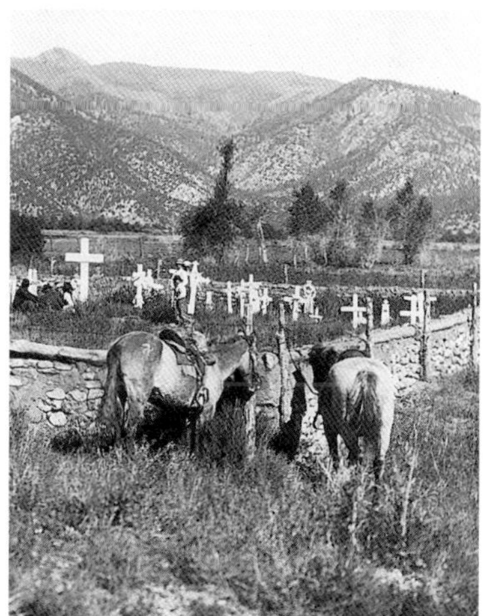

Camposanto, *or cemetery, near Taos, 1930s.*

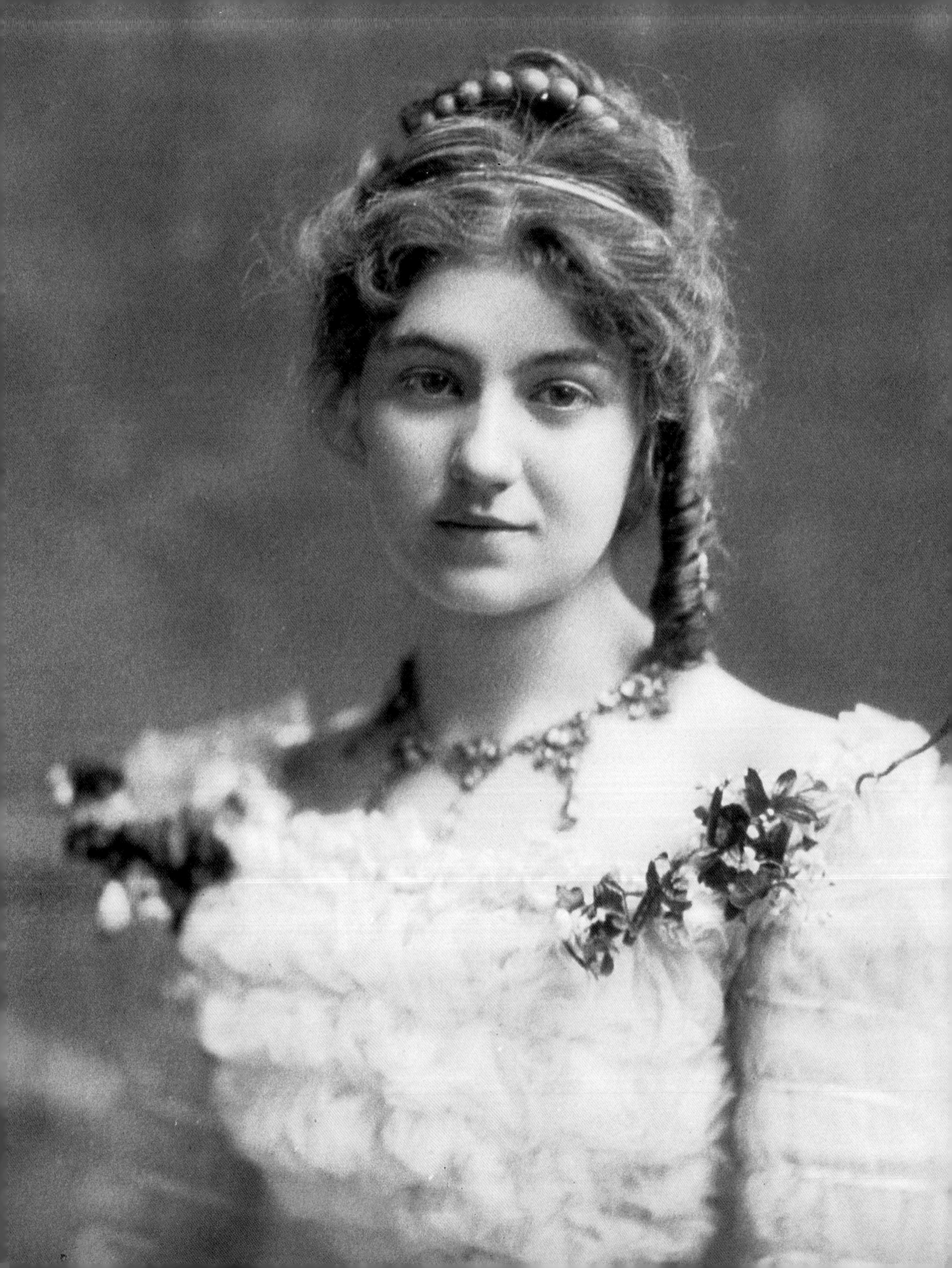

New Women of Modernism

Paris had Gertrude Stein. New York and Taos had Mabel Dodge Luhan. In the early decades of the twentieth century framed by the world wars, two powerful women embodied the hopes, yearnings, and failings of a generation of creative souls searching for a new reality, a new bridge to the infinite.

Rarely before had the world seen this kind of woman-muse, patroness, seductress, leader, author, salon keeper, collector of genius. Not until the early twentieth century had common women—albeit aristocratic ones—assumed the powerful role of cultural arbiter, which was usually the privilege of royal women such as England's Elizabeth I, or France's Marie d'Medici, or Spain's Isabella.

By the second decade of the twentieth century, societies on both sides of the Atlantic were finally emerging from the long domination of Victorian lifestyle and morality. The extravagance of "La Belle Epoque," perhaps best exemplified by the art of Henri de Toulouse-Lautrec and the novels of Henry James, was yielding to the frenzy and excitement of machine-age modernism.

The world was becoming faster now, hurried along by rapid advances in automobiles, communication devices such as telephones and telegraphs, motion pictures, and transoceanic travel epitomized by the launch of the *Titanic* in 1912. In Europe, such avant-garde artists and writers as the Italian Futurists contemplated the effects of speed and machines on social and cultural life.

In the early years of the twentieth century, young artists flocked to Paris—for at least two hundred years the world's art capital—still basking in the glory of the Impressionist movement. For these young bohemians, the potential of new expressions inspired by modern society in art, photography, filmmaking, and sculpture was nearly hypnotic. In addition, women were gradually emerging from traditional roles imposed upon them, determined to participate in the exhilarating revolution of "modernism."

Gertrude Stein and Mabel Dodge emerged—one by design, the other almost by accident—as leading female modernists of the new

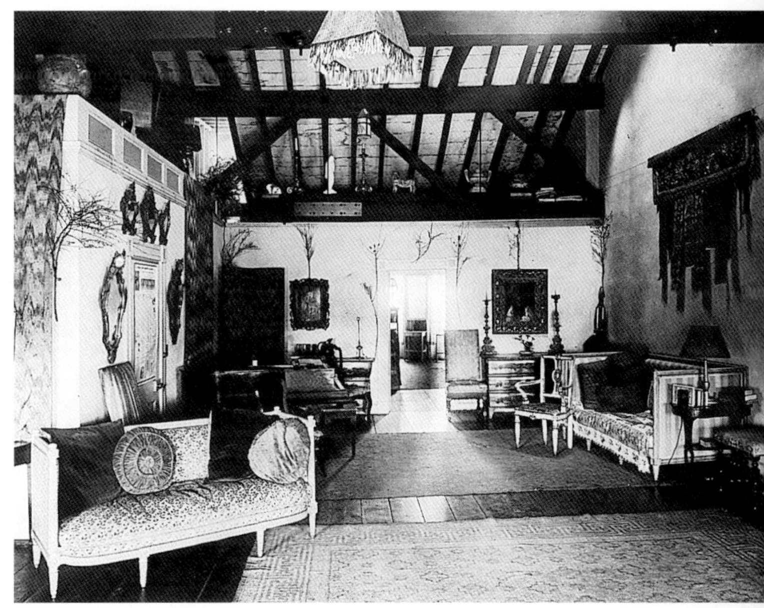

Mabel Dodge's salon on Washington Square in New York City's Greenwich Village, 1916.

Mabel Ganson (later Dodge), sixteen-year-old Buffalo, New York, debutante.

century. Yet their adventures and articulation of the new age would take radically different paths. For Gertrude Stein, the sophisticated cultural milieu of Paris fostered her own stream-of-consciousness experimentations with literature. Mabel Dodge would pursue a utopian dream of transcendent cultural consciousness among the Pueblo Indians of New Mexico.

Mabel and Gertrude

Mabel Dodge first met Gertrude Stein in Paris in 1911, and soon thereafter the two women became friends and correspondents, trading visits and letters. In the years before World War I, both Paris and New York were teeming with intellectual and artistic energy.

Arriving in Paris in 1905, Gertrude Stein and her brother Leo had championed the art of Cezanne, Gauguin, Picasso, Matisse, and Renoir, displaying the "radical" paintings on the walls of their home in the Montparnasse district. Their home soon became a favorite place for writers and poets to stop by on Saturday evenings for conversation, food and drink, art viewing, and gossip. These lively Parisian salons would later inspire Mabel's successful New York and Taos gatherings.

Mabel and her husband Edwin Dodge had also left America for Europe in 1905, settling in Florence, Italy, where Mabel quickly adopted a carefree lifestyle of aesthetics and sensuality. In her new home, the magnificent Villa Corunia, which had been built by the Medici in the fifteenth century, Mabel found an ideal playground to suit her many moods and whims and also to showcase her powerful sexuality.

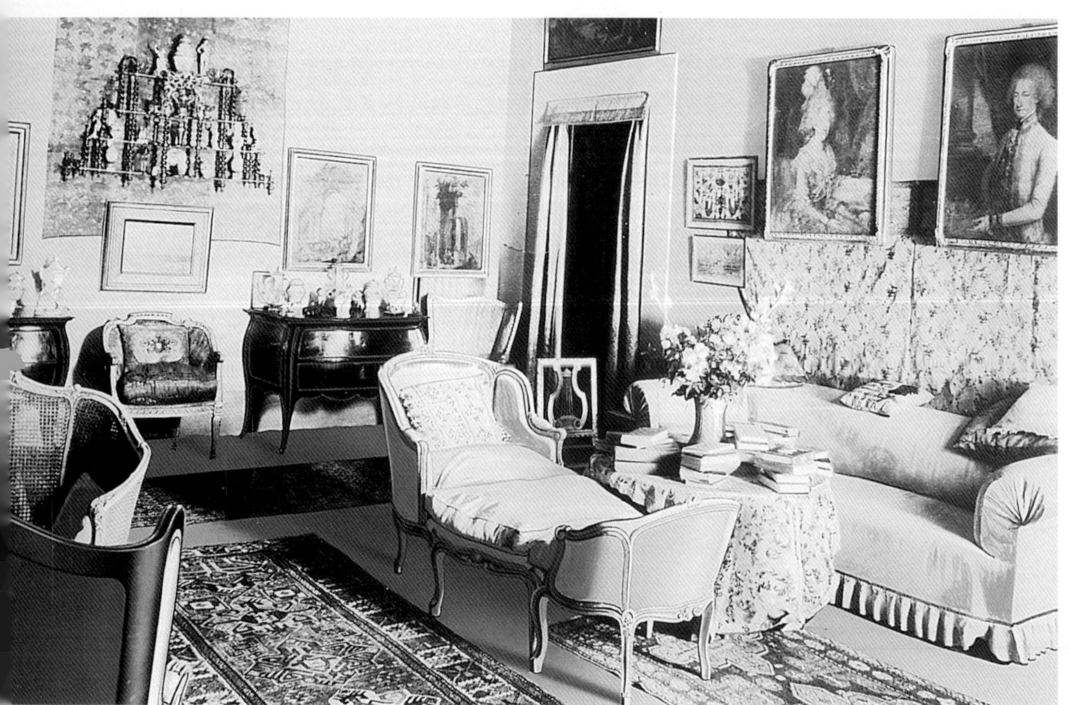

Mabel's study, the French neoclassical "Yellow Room," in the Villa Corunia near Florence, Italy.

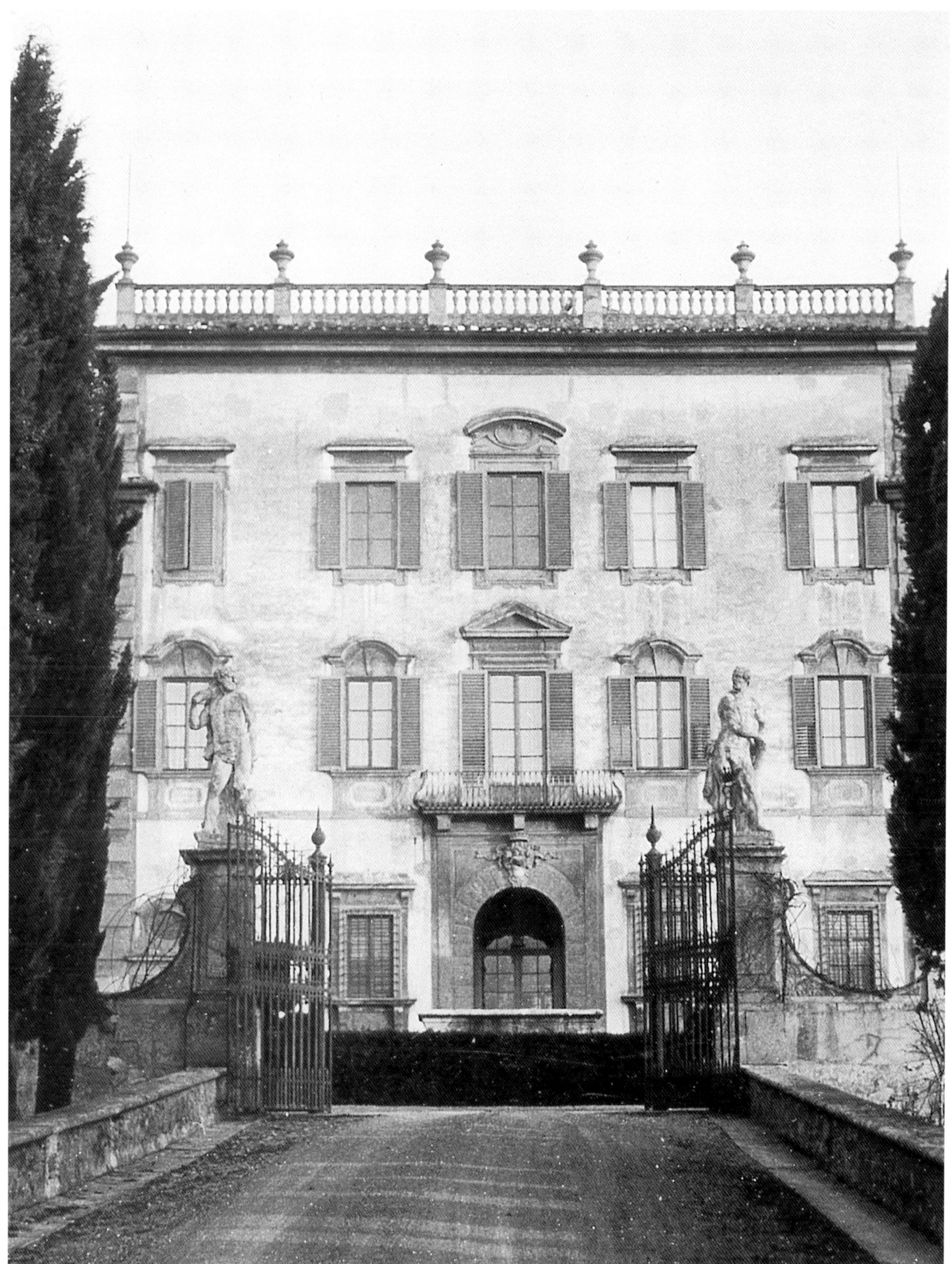

The grand cortile entrance of the Villa Corunia is an impressive example of classical proportions and renaissance grandeur.

In the Villa Corunia, Mabel began to fully develop the art of hospitality that would serve her so well in New York and Taos. Her sumptuous villa boasted exquisite Renaissance furniture, Venetian glassware, damasks, silks, and tapestries, creating romantic settings for her lavish parties. Pianist Arthur Rubinstein described one of these lively gatherings in *My Young Years:*

> *There was the art and music critic Carl Van Vechten, a genius at arguing; Robin de la Condanune, a charming, stuttering actor whom nobody had seen on stage . . . John Reed, a journalist and poet, and a militant Communist, was sullen and very aggressive. He was Mabel's choice companion. . . . We had Gertrude Stein, engaged in some interminable vocal battles with Van Vechten, Reed hating everything and everybody, Norman Douglas using with relish his most profane repertoire in swearing, and last but not least, myself, persistently jealous and irritable. Whenever and whatever I played, whether Beethoven or Stravinsky, some of those present would leave the room hating one or the other.*

These luxuries were not enough to satisfy Mabel's enormous appetites. Above all, she needed and craved the company of dynamic, creative people. At the time she met the Steins in 1911, she had already earned a reputation as one of Florence's leading hostesses.

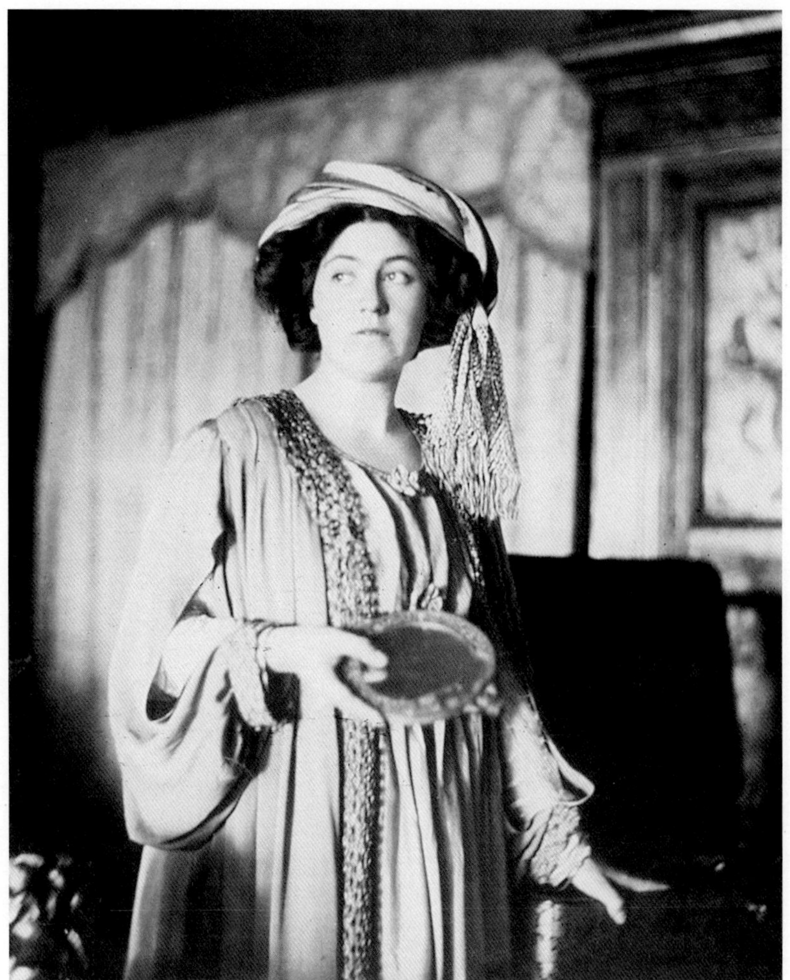

Mabel Dodge in Florentine costume at the Villa Corunia, 1911.

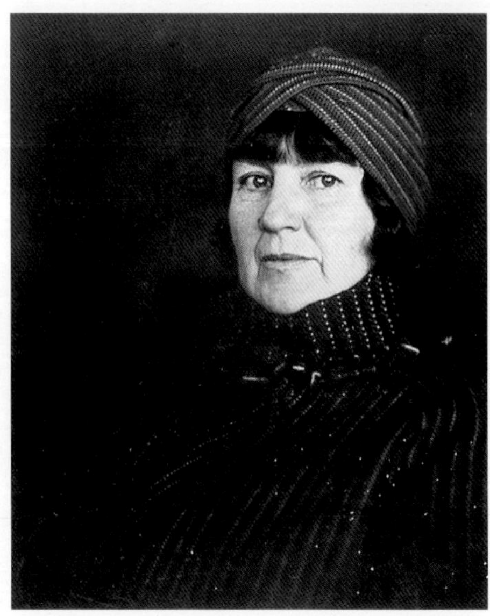

Portrait of Mabel Dodge Luhan by Edward Weston.

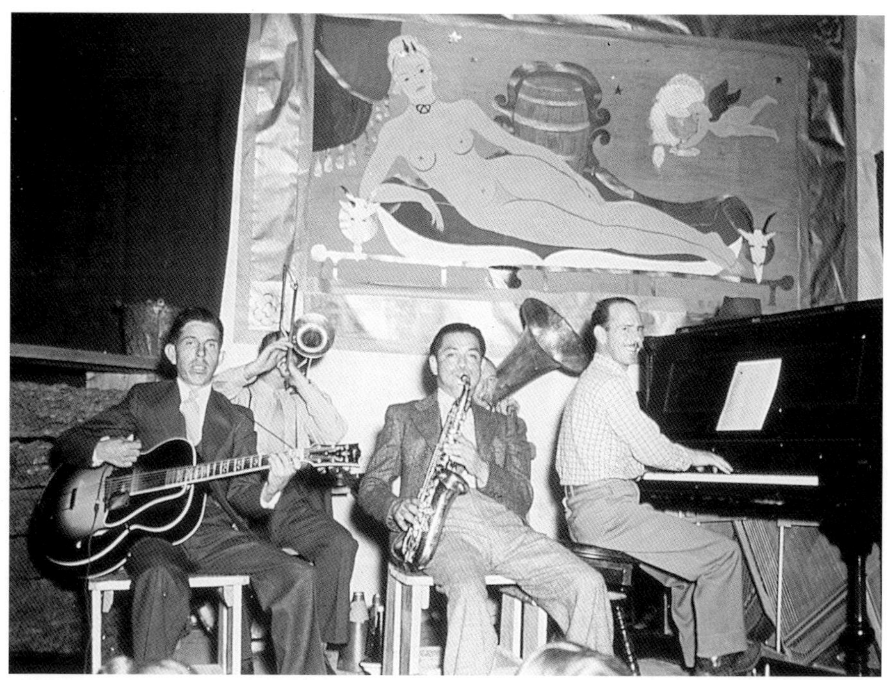

Taos party band, 1930s.

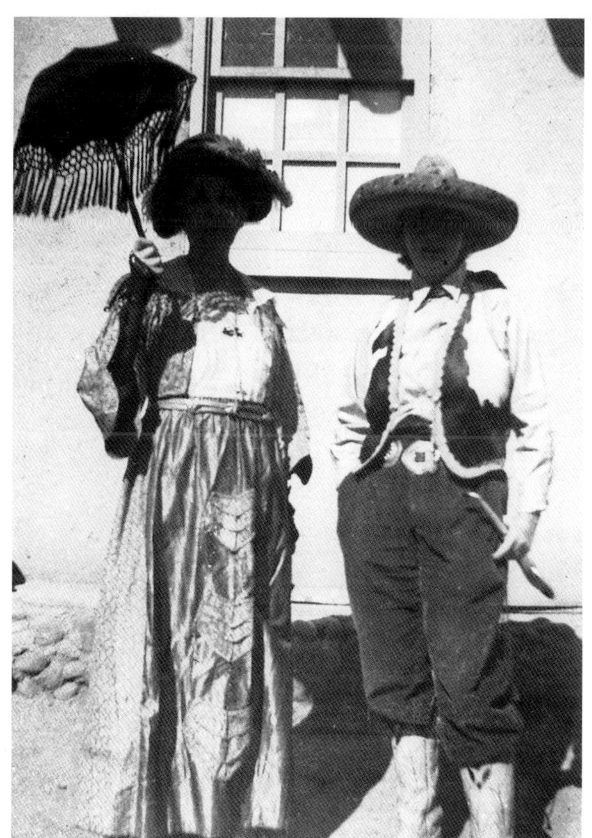

Artist Dorothy Brett (right) and unindentified friend in costume for the Taos fiestas.

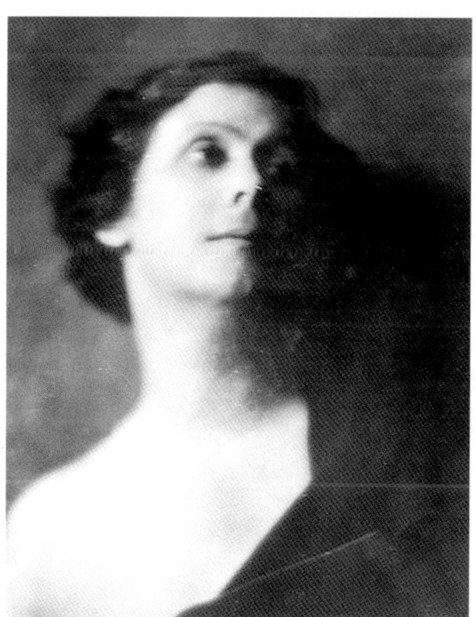

Modern dancer Isadora Duncan.

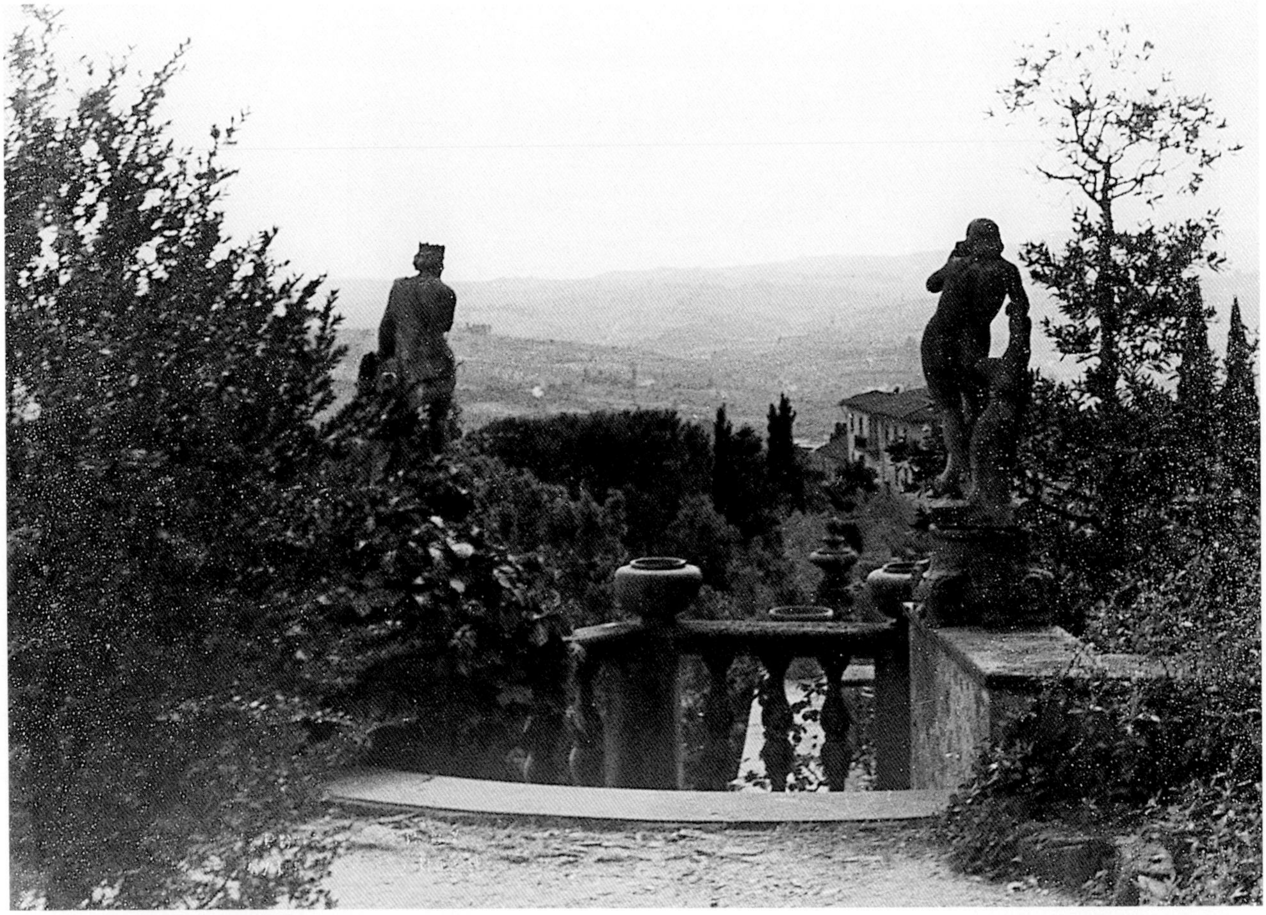

A view of the Tuscan countryside from the Villa Corunia.

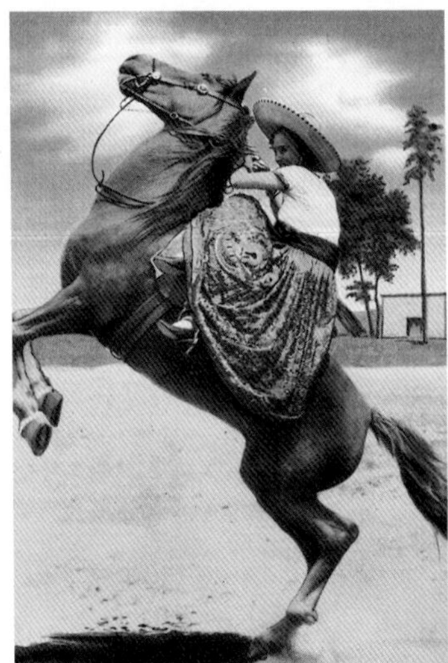

Postcard: "Queen of the Rancho."

In the fall of 1912, Mabel lured Gertrude Stein to the Villa Corunia. Gertrude Stein was at the vanguard of a powerful avant-garde artistic movement, which claimed that an artist's vision and imagination could equal or surpass perceived reality, a new consciousness that celebrated the supremacy of the ego. Her philosophy and influence would remain a basic element of Mabel's lifelong search for artistic and cultural utopia—a journey that would end in the mountains of northern New Mexico.

From the Steins, Mabel learned the power of the artist to invent a new reality, to overcome all limitations of life and circumstance, and to create a New World.

Mabel's profound belief that artists could restructure reality to influence society and culture would guide her existence in Taos, becoming a powerful magnetic attraction that would transform southwestern art and literature.

In Gertrude Stein, Mabel Dodge had found not only a mentor but also a cool and aloof friend. Yet Gertrude *painted* a word "Portrait of Mabel Dodge at the Villa Corunia in 1912." Its abstract, somewhat disjointed, stream-of-consciousness style has been compared as the literary form of cubism. In this excerpt, it is as much an intellectual exercise as it is a portrait of Mabel:

A walk that is not stepped where the floor is covered is not the place where the room is entered. The whole one is the same. There is not any stone. There is the wide door that is narrow on the floor. There is all that place. There is that desire and there is no pleasure and the place is filling the only space that is placed where all the piling is not adjoining. There is not that distraction. Praying has intention and relieving that situation is not solemn. There comes that way.

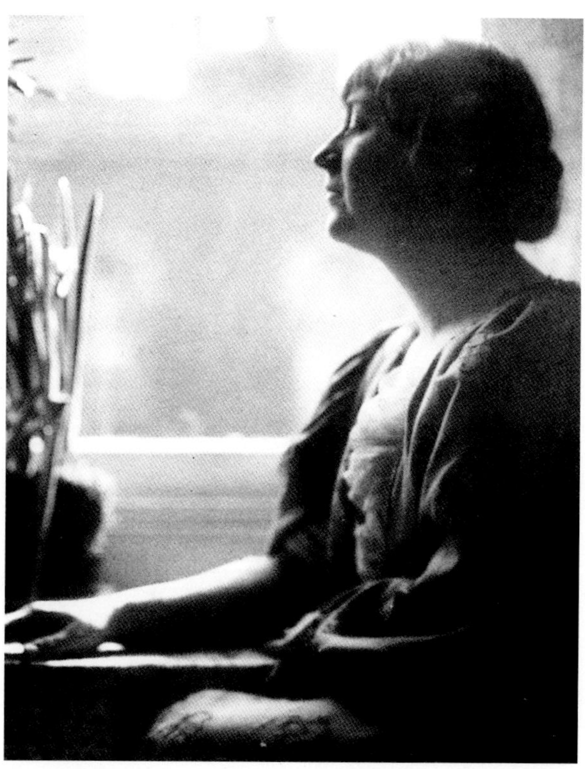

Mabel Dodge in 1912, the fateful year of her "portrait" by Gertrude Stein and arrival in New York City.

Mabel was thrilled with Gertrude's portrait of her, cloaked in the wordplay of modernism. At the end of 1912, Mabel and Edwin Dodge decided it was time to return to New York to save their faltering marriage. In Europe, Mabel had seen the new age and there was no turning back. She would bring Florence and Paris to New York and beyond—to Taos.

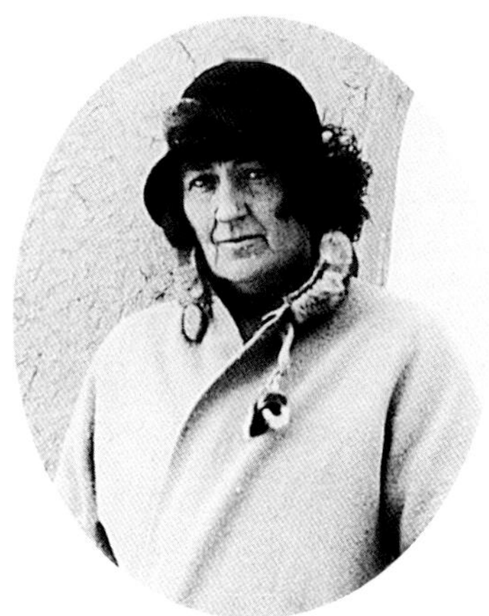

Detail of Irving Abbe's portrait of Mabel for Vogue *magazine, 1930s.*

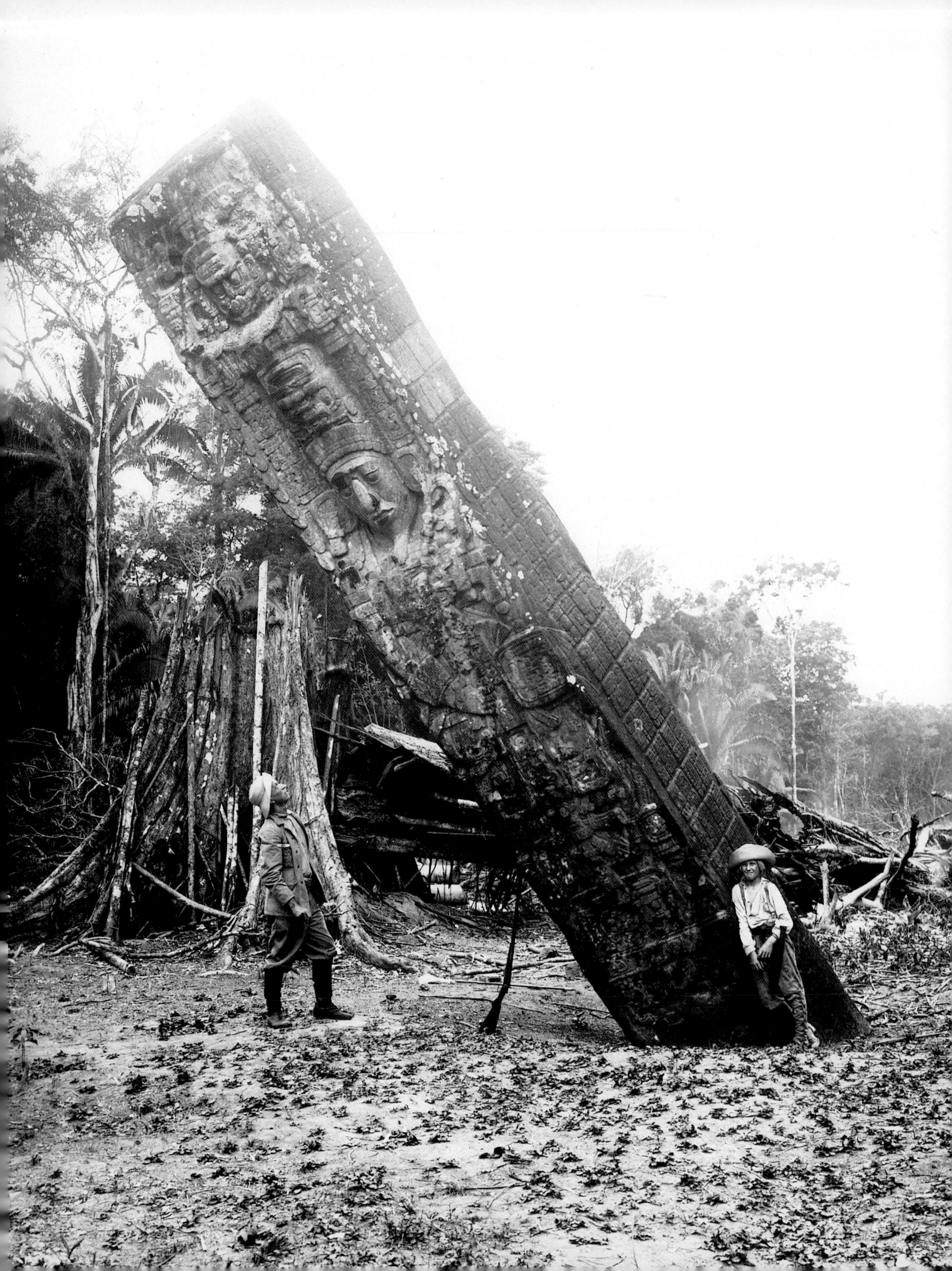

Rediscovery of an Ancient Land

It is safe to say that for all intents and purposes the real places of New Mexico and the greater Southwest were unknown to the world in 1900, existing primarily in the realm of the imagination. The name "Santa Fe" conjured up images of a dusty, forlorn, and lusty (immoral) oasis known to many Americans through improbable dime-novel romances and sometimes even more incredible true tales of Santa Fe Trail adventurers.

The mythical quality of New Mexico was further enhanced in 1884 by young Charlie Lummis's *Tramp Across the Continent*. In his trip from Ohio to Los Angeles, Lummis found succor and relaxation in the homes of generous Santa Feans after two-thirds of the strenuous hike. He delivered syndicated newspaper accounts of the exotic Native American and Hispanic cultures he encountered, captivating millions of readers. Lummis's exploits were a real-life Indiana Jones saga for the prim and proper Victorian reader. Lummis's own gifts of self-promotion and sensationalism would serve him well during his long career as the Southwest's first modern Renaissance man.

Charles Lummis's own remarkable career closely paralleled the emergence of the Southwest as America's cradle of civilization and focus of an exciting new school of American archaeology. While the ruins of Troy, Athens, Rome, and Cairo had captivated the attention of the world in preceding centuries and generations, America's prehistoric treasures lay concealed beneath layers of dirt, jungle, and memory in 1880.

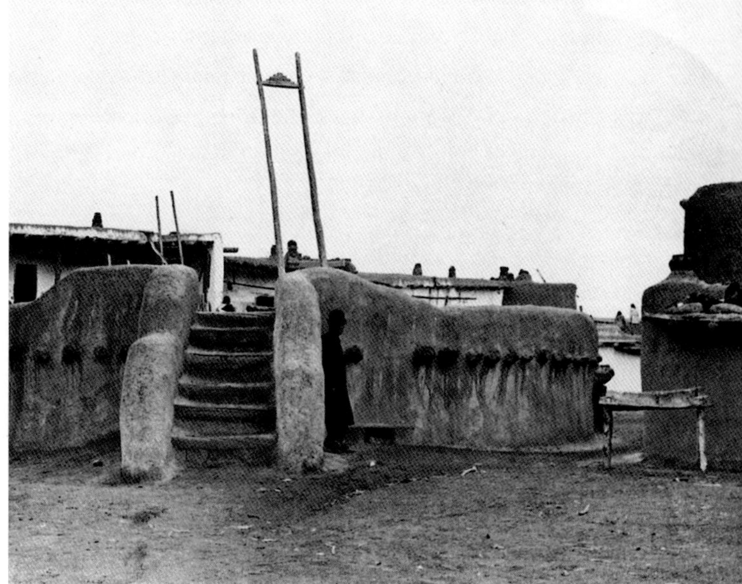

Pioneer Native American scholar Adolph Bandelier at a kiva, Santo Domingo Pueblo, October 1, 1880.

The wonders of the Southwest had been glimpsed by a few federally sponsored expeditions in the nineteenth century. Chaco Canyon and the ruins at Canyon de Chelly in northern Arizona had been spotted in 1849. William Henry Jackson and Timothy O'Sullivan had both photographed cliff ruins in the early 1870s. Jackson's models of cliff pueblos exhibited at Philadelphia's Centennial Exposition of 1876 fascinated the public. The scientific community was becoming convinced of the region's promise for serious study.

On August 23, 1880, forty-year-old Swiss scholar Adolph Bandelier arrived in Santa Fe. Bandelier was being sponsored by the newly formed Archaeological Institute of America on a yearly stipend of $1,200 to investigate the

Charles Lummis and his son Quimu at Stela E., Quirigua, Guatemala, 1911.

"aboriginal history of Spanish America."

Bandelier spent eight years in New Mexico, and his strenuous effort was amply rewarded—not in the riches he sought but in his discoveries for posterity. Today Bandelier National Monument on the Pajarito (Little Bird) Plateau between Santa Fe and Los Alamos is among America's most popular archaeological sites. When Adolph first saw the ruined pueblo of Tyuonyi, he wrote the following description:

Bunches of tall grass, low shrubbery, and cactus grow in the open spaces between the rocky debris fallen from above. They also cover in part low mounds of rubbish, and ruins of a large pentagonal building erected formerly at the foot of a slope leading to the cliffs. In the cliffs themselves, for a distance of about two miles, numerous caves dug out by the hand of men are visible. Some of these are yet perfect; others have wholly crumbled away except the rear wall. From a distance the port-holes and indentations appear like so many pigeon's nests in the naked rock. Together with the cavities formed by amygdaloid chambers and crevices caused by erosion, they give the cliffs the appearance of a huge, irregular honeycomb.

Bandelier's studies and expeditions into the lost canyons of the Southwest had provided some of the earliest glimpses of the splendid and elegant culture of the ancestral Pueblo people—also popularly known as the Anasazi. Later, on a frigid December day in 1888, two Colorado cowboys tracked some lost cattle into a magical and sacred canyon of the Mancos River, beneath Mesa Verde. Light snow traced the broken geometry of a mud village tucked within a gigantic cavern, known to us now as Cliff Palace. America had found its Parthenon.

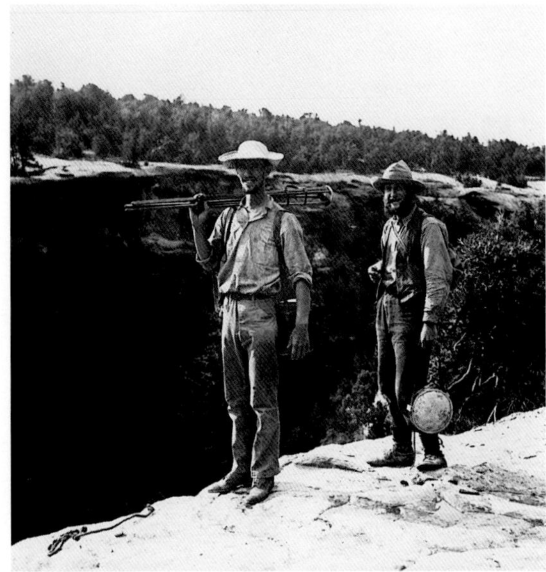

Photographer Jesse L. Nusbaum (left) and archaeologist Alfred Vincent Kidder at Mesa Verde, Colorado, 1908.

By 1907, Santa Fe had become the focal point of an intensive effort to excavate the archaeological ruins of southwestern Native American cultures as well as those of Mexico, Central America, and South America. The year 1907 welcomed the transfer of the beloved Palace of the Governors on the Plaza by the legislature to the newly formed Museum of New Mexico.

That year also witnessed the founding of the School of American Archaeology in Santa Fe by Edgar Lee Hewett, which evolved into the School of American Research. Along with Hewett, an entire generation of American archaeologists cut their professional teeth in the awesome ruins that surrounded Santa Fe and farther beyond. Scholar Sylvanus Morley pioneered the study of Mayan hieroglyphics from his home in Santa Fe and "restored" one of the city's first adobe structures in 1909. Archaeologists were active in the city's cultural life, helping to stage the annual historical pageants, or fiestas, and hoping to rival the Mardi Gras festivities of New Orleans.

But surely one of the crowning achievements of the growing collaboration between archaeologists and the swelling colony of artists was the New Mexico pavilion at San Diego's Panama-California Exposition of 1915. While artists such as Carlos Vierra and Gerald Cassidy painted murals for the *Science of Man* exhibits, archaeologists and architect I. H. Rapp fashioned a highly evocative exposition building that was a conglomeration of several outstanding features of New Mexico's mission churches. The New Mexico pavilion became the inspiration for the New Mexico Fine Arts Building of 1917 and, more importantly, helped launch the Santa Fe style of architecture.

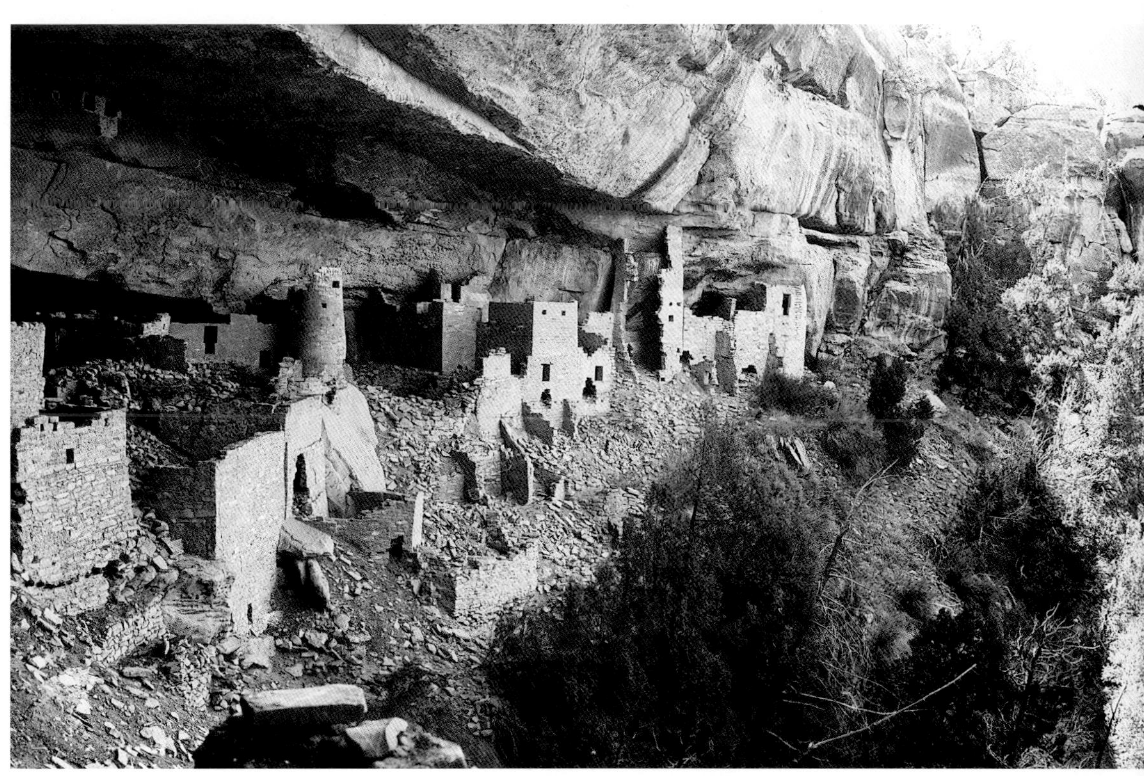

Cliff Palace before its restoration, circa 1907 (now Mesa Verde National Park, Colorado).

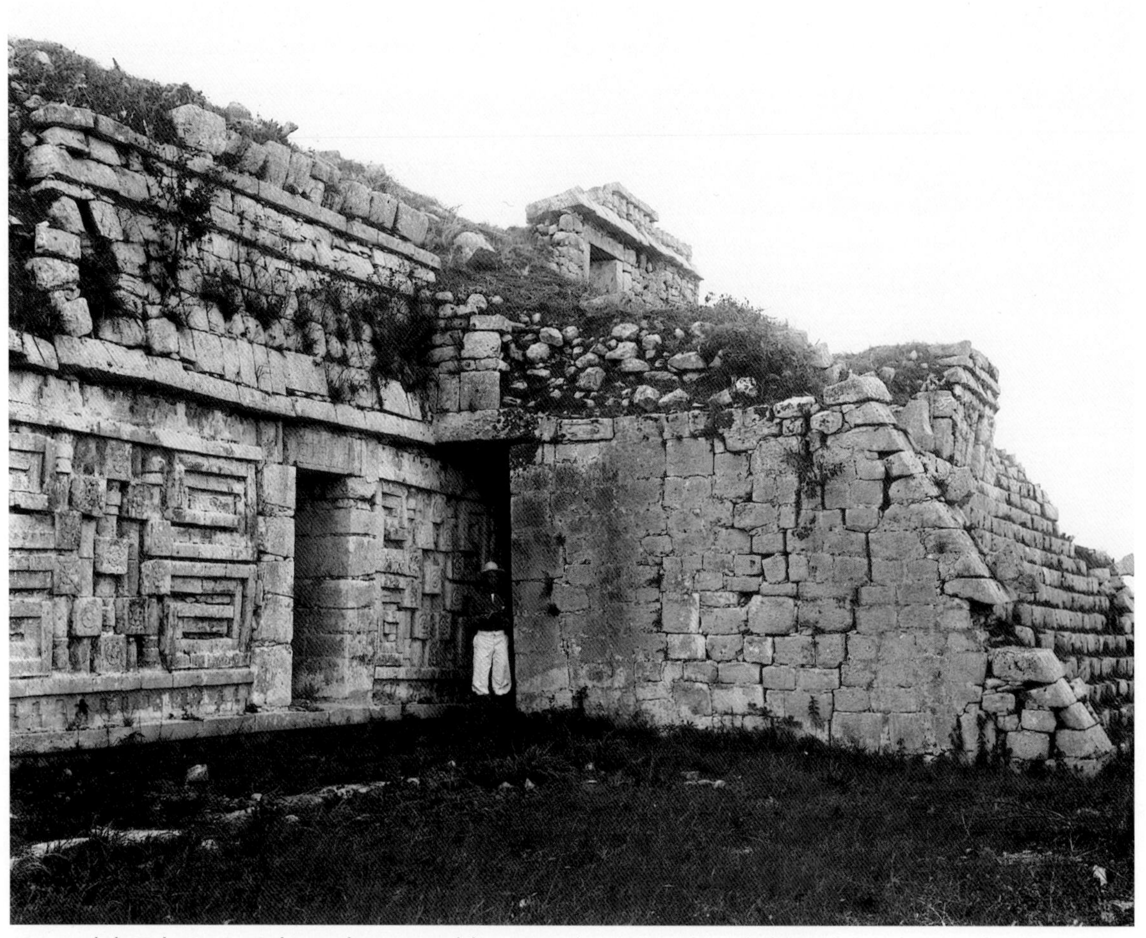

Mayan scholar Sylvanus G. Morley standing in ruin of the Nunnery ("Las Monjas"), at Chichén Itzá, Yucatán Peninsula, Mexico, 1910.

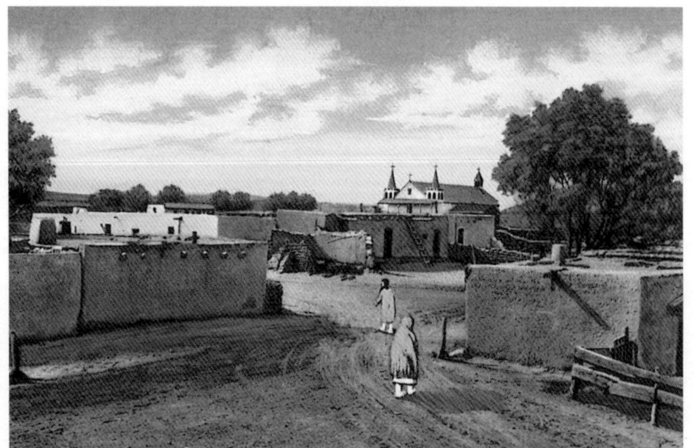

Historic postcard of Isleta Pueblo, south of Albuquerque, circa 1900.

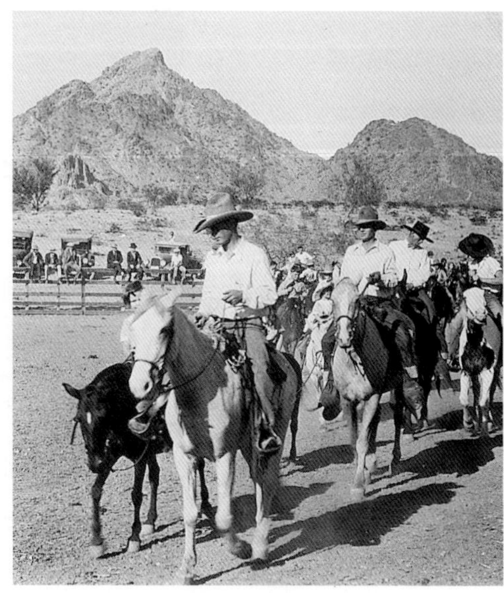

Arizona rodeo near Phoenix, circa 1930.

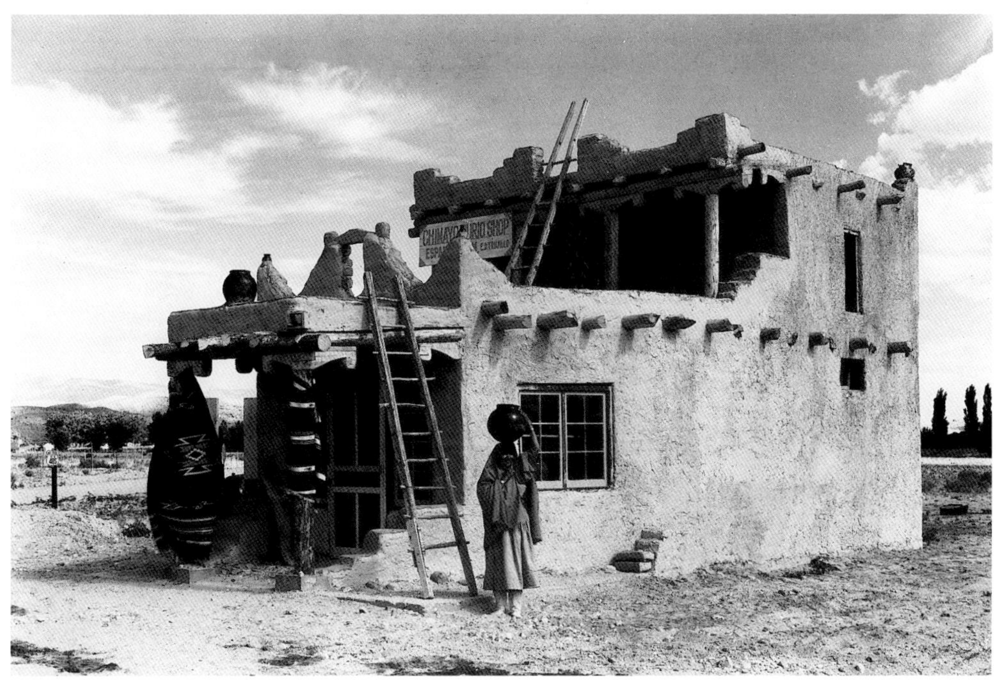

Chimayo Trading Post, Española, New Mexico, about 1925.

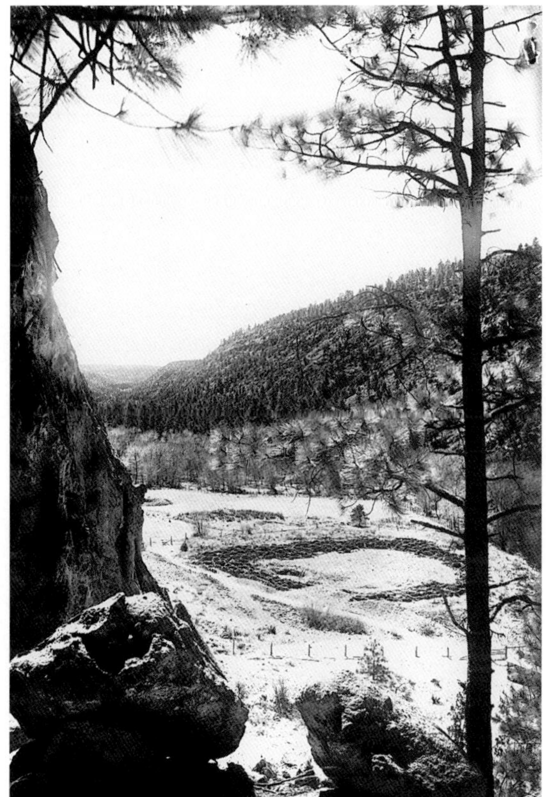

Tyuonyi Ruin, on the Rio de Los Frijoles, New Mexico, circa 1920 (now Bandelier National Monument, thirty miles north of Santa Fe).

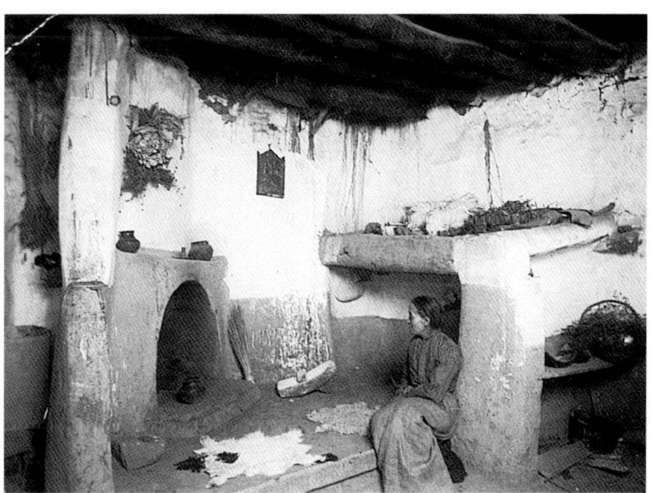

Dwelling interior, Taos Pueblo, 1920s.

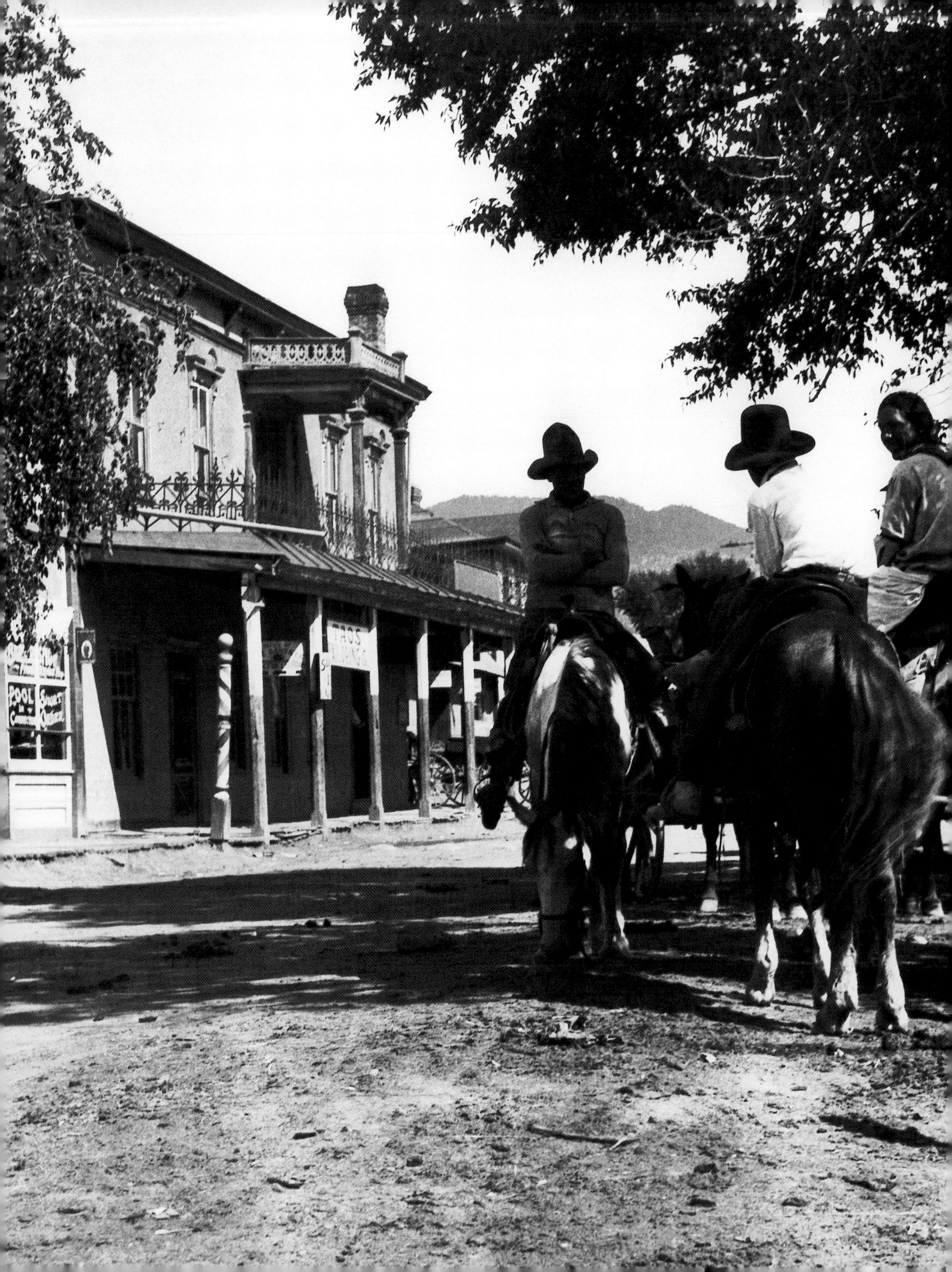
POOL
TAOS

An American Anomaly: New Mexico at the Turn of the Century

Within the bosom of a rising world power in 1900 lay the "anomaly of the Republic . . . the Great American Mystery—the National Rip Van Winkle—the United States which is not the United States," asserted Charlie Lummis. Of course, he was referring to New Mexico.

New Mexico had suffered a mean and undeserved prejudice in the eyes of its new American masters—because of its predominantly brown population, because of its ties to Mexico and Spain, and because of its isolation and poverty. Anti-Hispanic fervor fueled by the Spanish-American War of 1898 did not help, even though some of Colonel Theodore Roosevelt's cowboy soldiers hailed from New Mexico and bore Castilian surnames.

As much of America and Europe approached the twentieth century on the wave of modern miracles such as electricity, telephones, and motion pictures, New Mexico seemed mired in its past. But what a past it was!

From its earliest traces of human habitation, the Upper Rio Grande watershed had been a lost country, not even known long enough to be forgotten by most strangers. A strong sedentary culture had developed on the high mesas and within the canyon beds and cliffs. It was a far-flung clustering of Pueblo clans and somewhat recent nomadic newcomers—the Navajo and Apaches. For centuries, these southwestern people were on the remote fringes of such great societies as the Aztecs of central Mexico or even the English and French colonies far to the east. The Pueblos were lost beyond the high ridges of the Rocky Mountains, though they proved tenacious in the face of invaders and missionaries, surviving still.

The Pueblo world was shattered in the sixteenth century when armed expeditions of Spanish soldiers ventured north from Mexico, chasing the golden cities of a friar's overworked imagination. By 1610, a Spanish capital city of Nuestra Señora de Santa Fé (Our Lady of the Holy Faith) had been founded. The new Spanish villa grew upon the ruins of two pueblos built after A.D. 1200: Analco Pueblo and Kwapoge Pueblo. Upstream along the Rio Grande some seventy miles north, the Spanish established a village called San Gerónimo de Taos about 1615. Both communities were abandoned during the Pueblo Revolt of 1680

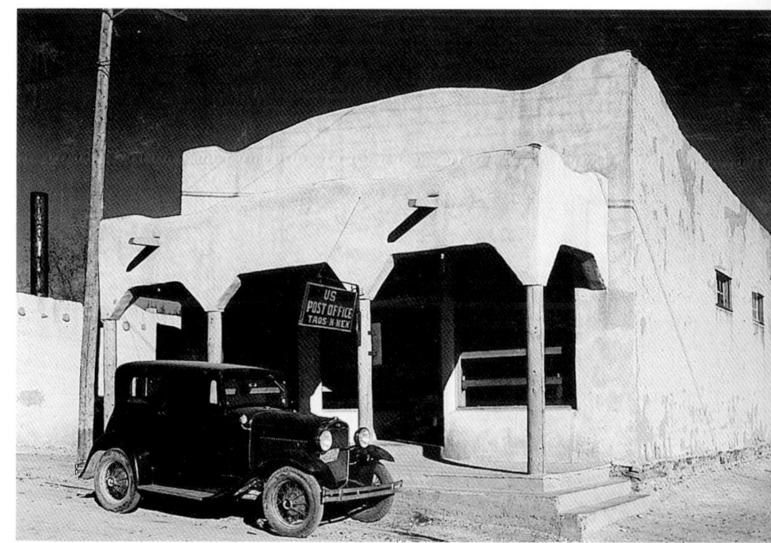

Taos Post Office, 1920s.

Taos Plaza, circa 1900.

and resettled early in the eighteenth century.

The Spanish colony in New Mexico grew slowly amid much hardship while the Age of Enlightenment, and later Napoleon's vanities, ruled Europe. For many of the tough Spanish colonists, New Mexico was synonymous with exile, but for others it was a place to redeem oneself, make a new start, and, most importantly, own land.

Spain guarded her borders zealously, and exaggerated accounts of Santa Fe's wealth sailed on invisible winds to the ears of such men as Zebulon Pike and Thomas Jefferson. After Mexico finally freed itself from the Spanish yoke in 1821, the first caravans of American traders were joyously ushered into the forbidden adobe stronghold.

For the next sixty years, until the Atchison, Topeka, and Santa Fe Railroad arrived in New Mexico in 1879, Santa Fe enjoyed a mythical reputation as a pleasure oasis on the Santa Fe Trail, a reward for the brave, lucky, or foolhardy adventurer strong enough to endure the arduous overland journey it took to get there.

Santa Fe reigned in many frontier minds as a woman—a beautiful if coquettish woman. Beneath her veil of juniper-laden hills and mountains lay the seductions of gambling halls, flirtatious women, all-night fandangos, and brandy. By day's light, her

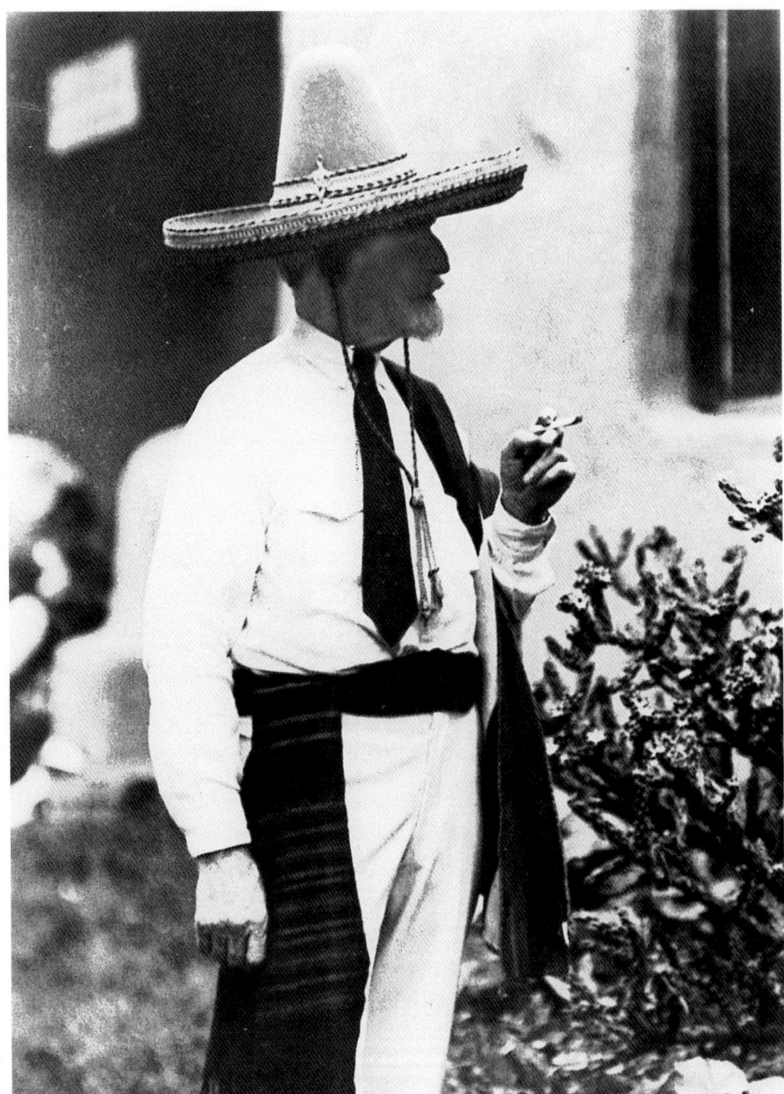

Santa Fe artist Sheldon Parsons dressed in costume for the Santa Fe fiesta, 1920s.

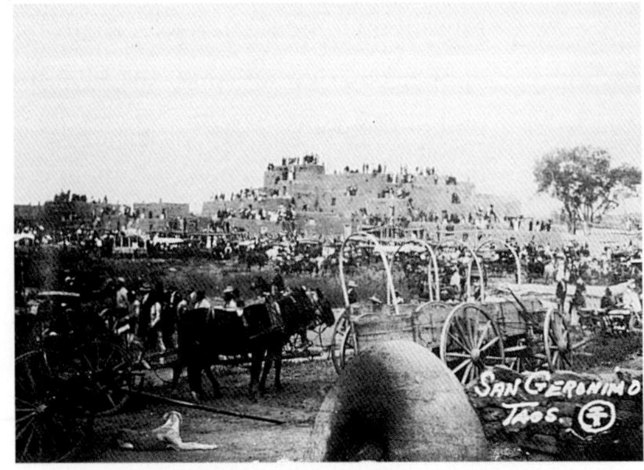

San Gerónimo Feast Day, Taos Pueblo, circa 1920.

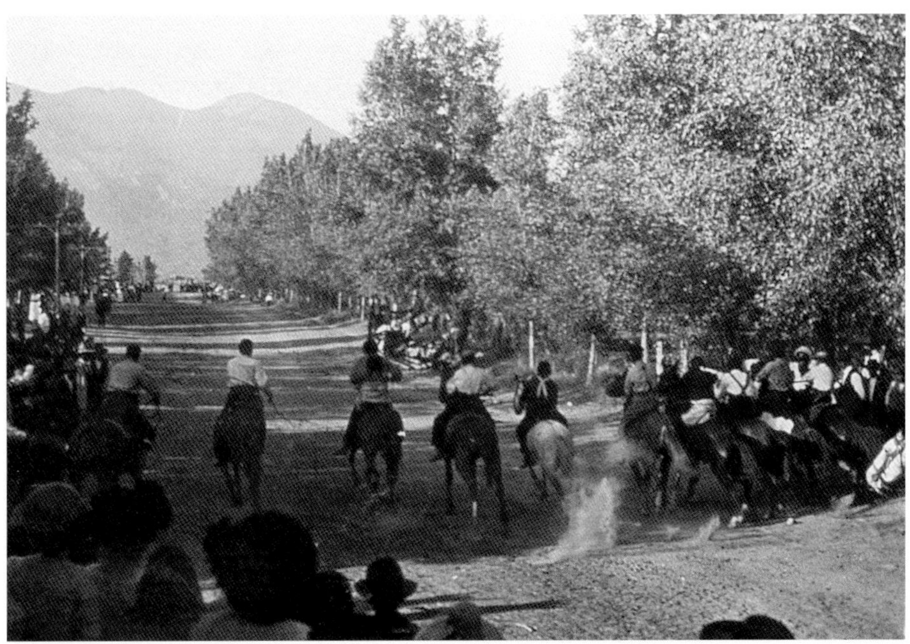

Indian horse race on Pueblo Road, San Gerónimo Feast Day, Taos, circa 1920.

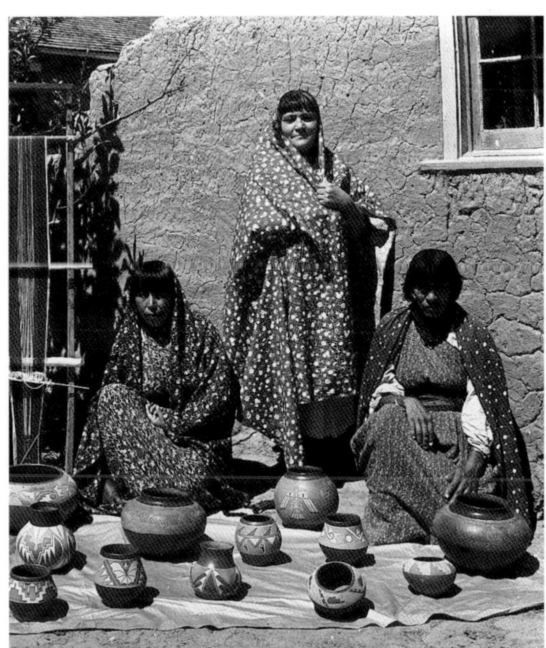

San Juan Pueblo women selling their pottery to tourists.

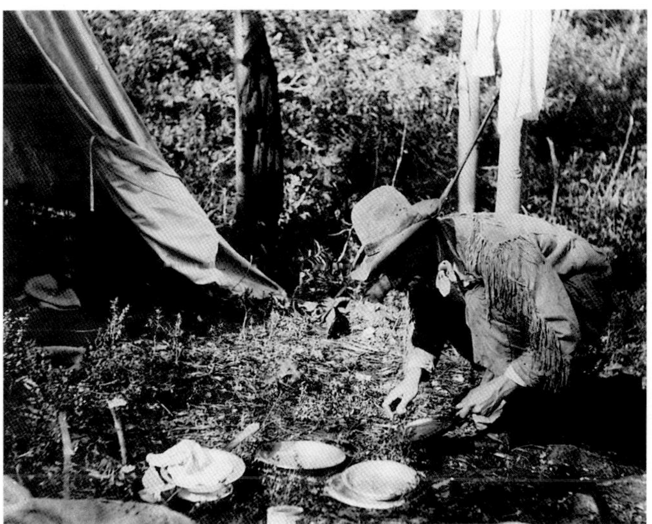

W. Herbert "Buck" Dunton, famed Taos cowboy artist, at camp.

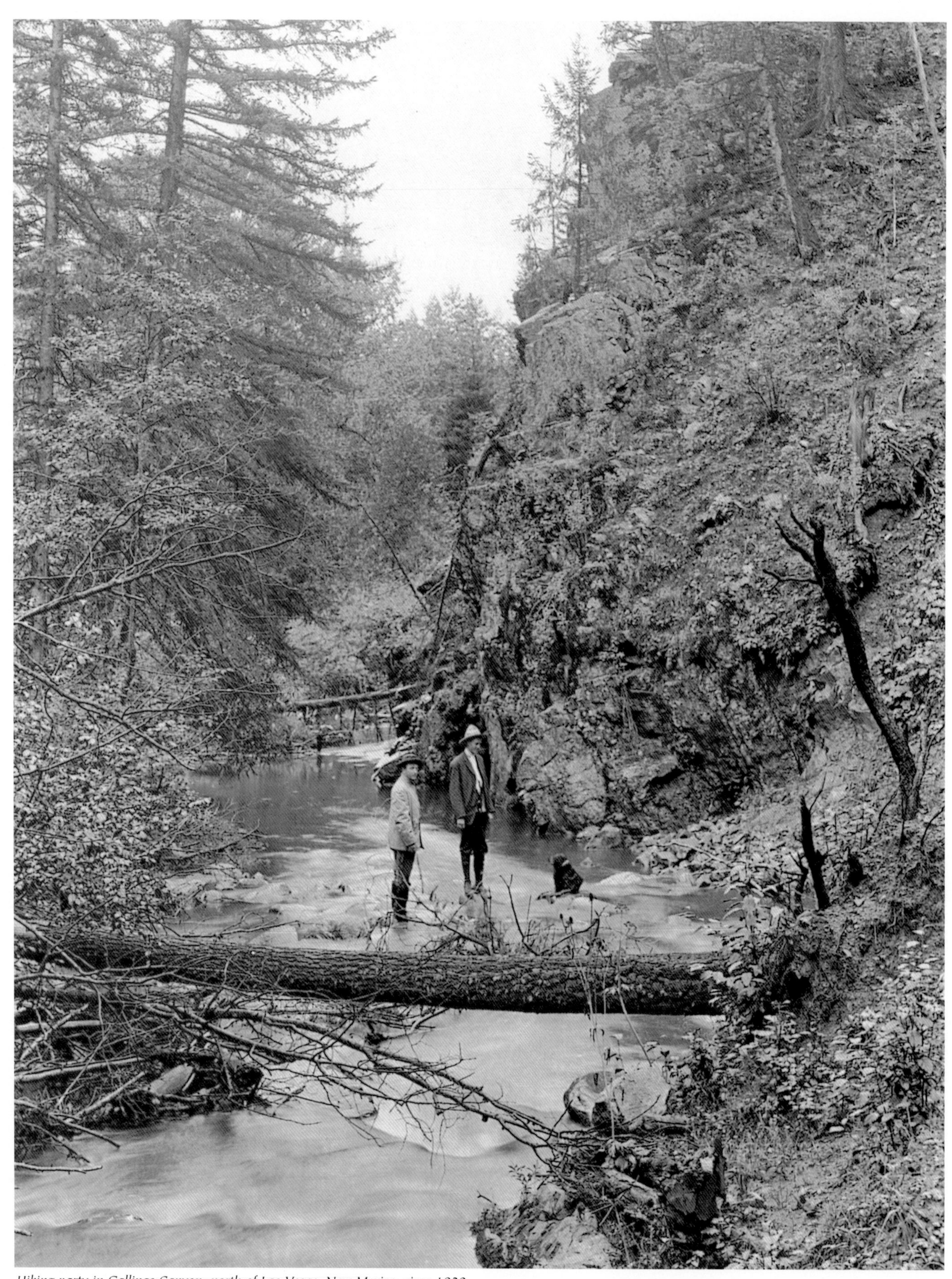

Hiking party in Gallinas Canyon, north of Las Vegas, New Mexico, circa 1920.

beauty seemed wholesome, tinged with the dazzling blue sky that reminded some of Persia or Morocco. Cheerful hollyhocks and rosebushes sang against the parchment-like earthen walls. But to others, these delights just masked an immoral and poverty-stricken society.

By 1900, Santa Fe and New Mexico had become a true multicultural society. The indigenous Native American tribes had survived (although with many casualties) the three centuries of Spanish and American colonizations. Spanish Americans and some Europeans lent an old-world aura to the region. Mexicans had begun to settle in the northern Rio Grande after Mexican Independence in 1821, and finally Americans had arrived in substantial numbers after General Steven Watts Kearny's invasion of 1846 that ignited the Mexican War.

The twenty years after the railroad first steamed into the New Mexico Territory transformed the old capital more so than the two centuries that preceded them. Factory-made building materials, paints, and tools began to change the looks of the streets and buildings. Brick homes and Victorian gingerbread trim dotted the hillsides and the plaza.

Yet despite the Americanization of New Mexico and the Southwest, Santa Fe and Taos still retained their timeless charms. It is difficult for us today, a century later, to visualize the tiny adobe communities that cast their spell on so many sensitive and creative men and women of genius. By all accounts, New Mexico had miraculously retained its integrity in the face of overwhelming forces of foreign cultures (including American) and machine-age progress. How and why it managed to do so fascinated the intellect of many outsiders while her abundant visual and sensual attractions tantalized the body.

In many ways New Mexico provided a perfect counterpoint to the artistic appeal of Paris during the early years of cubism and the Jazz Age. Paris was well known and famous as the world's art center; New Mexico was unknown and mysterious. Parisian culture was sophisticated and urbane; New Mexico was perceived as primitive and isolated. Paris's great boulevards were filled with classical and beaux-arts buildings; New Mexico's humble mud buildings faded into the landscape. Parisian

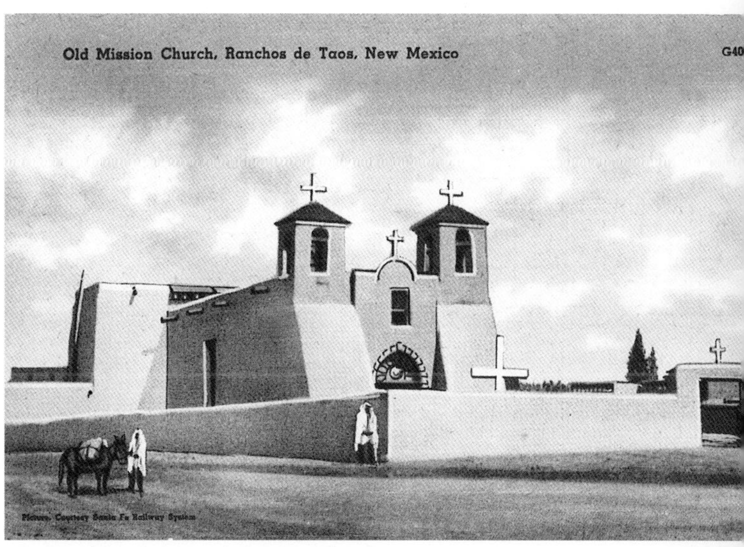

Mission of San Francisco de Asis, Ranchos de Taos, circa 1920.

authors wrote of angst and psychosexual nuances; New Mexican authors wrote of spiritual harmony and the inspirational power of the landscape.

Not unlike the mythical Tibetan valley in Frank Capra's 1937 film *Lost Horizon,* New Mexico seemed to appeal to the utopian fantasies in many artists and writers, who fought against time to capture its essence before it disappeared into the ether of memory. What survives in the paintings, writings, photographs, letters, and other mementos of the bohemian legends of New Mexico is a profound joy and wonderment in the face of the miraculous.

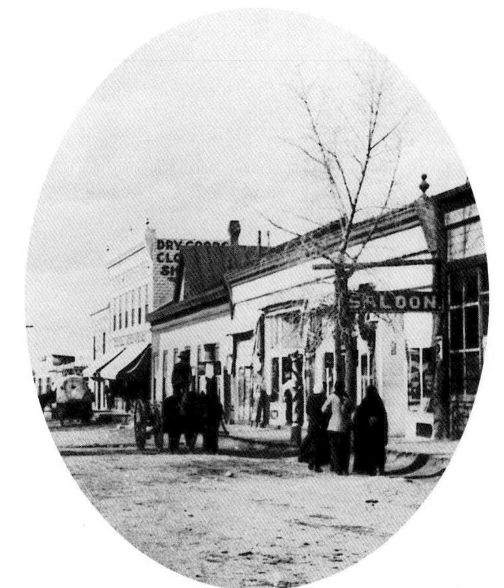

Taos Plaza, circa 1900.

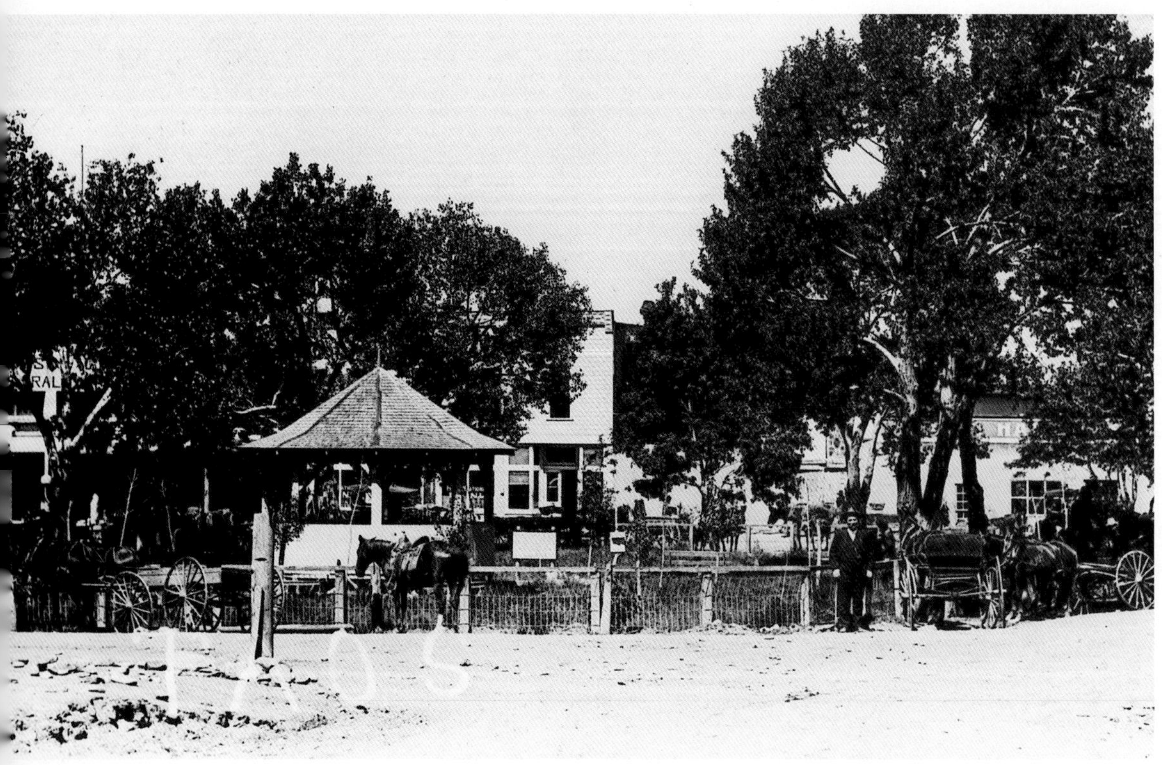

Taos Plaza, circa 1915.

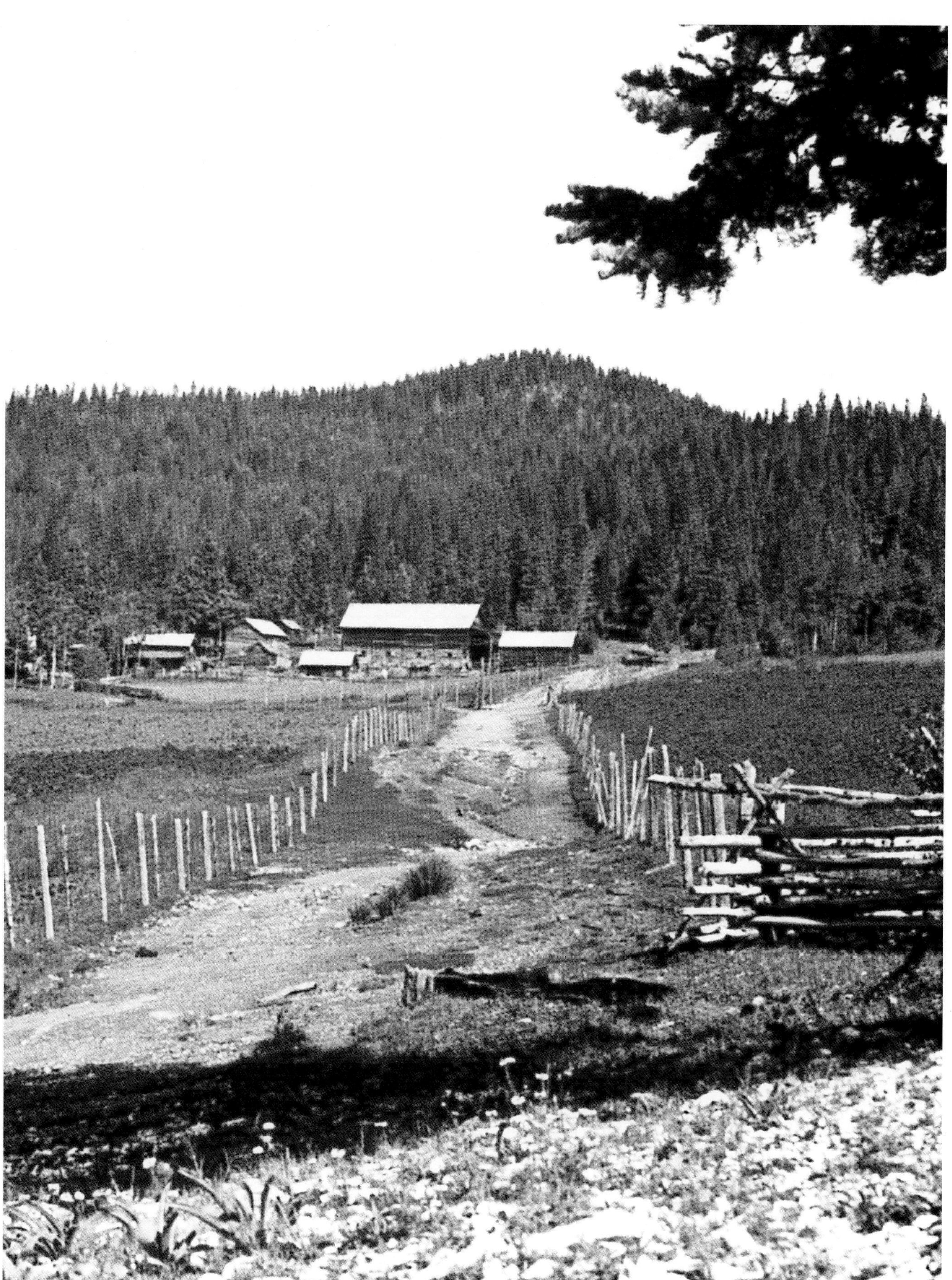

Ranch compound north of Las Vegas, New Mexico, circa 1920.

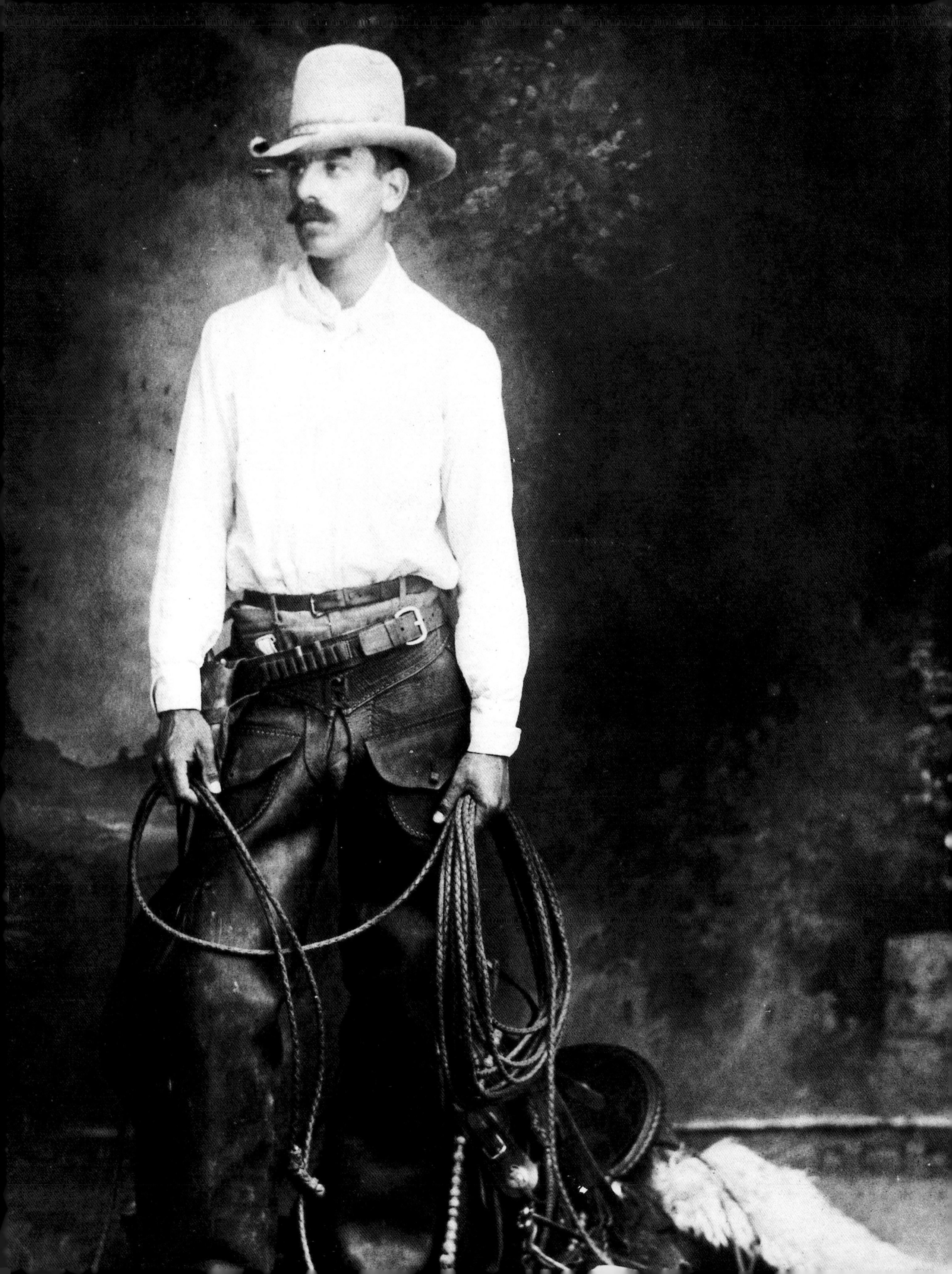

Los Ocho Pintores: The Taos Founders

Mabel Dodge Luhan was not the first urban sophisticate to bring a sense of Parisian aesthetics to New Mexico. In fact, a legendary group of artists schooled in the ateliers of the French capital had gravitated to Taos during the first two decades of the twentieth century. We know them as the Taos Society of Artists, but they informally called themselves *Los Ocho Pintores,* the Eight Painters.

By 1900, American artists had skillfully interpreted the West, mostly drawing and painting awesome landscapes and incredible human subjects in romantic dramas. Thomas Moran, Charles M. Russell, and Frederic Remington had become media superstars for their awe-inspiring illustrations of the primal beauty of the West. Yet by 1900, the vast frontier had already been transformed from a wilderness to a mecca for opportunists. Frederic Remington, who spent a good part of 1902 in Taos, had the tiny village in mind when he mourned that "Americans have gashed this country up so horribly with their axes, hammers, scrapers, and plows that I always like to see a place which they have overlooked; some place before they arrive with their heavy-handed God of Progress."

A sense of the exotic and the undiscovered inspired artists during the "gilded" years of Queen Victoria's reign, as if a primitive counterpoint to the opulence and exuberance of Paris. Paul Gauguin escaped to Tahiti; Eugene Delacroix savored the colors of Morocco; and in his Paris studio at the Académie Julien, Joseph Henry Sharp wistfully recalled the Taos Mountains where he had seen two young American artists, Ernest L. Blumenschein and Bert Greer Phillips.

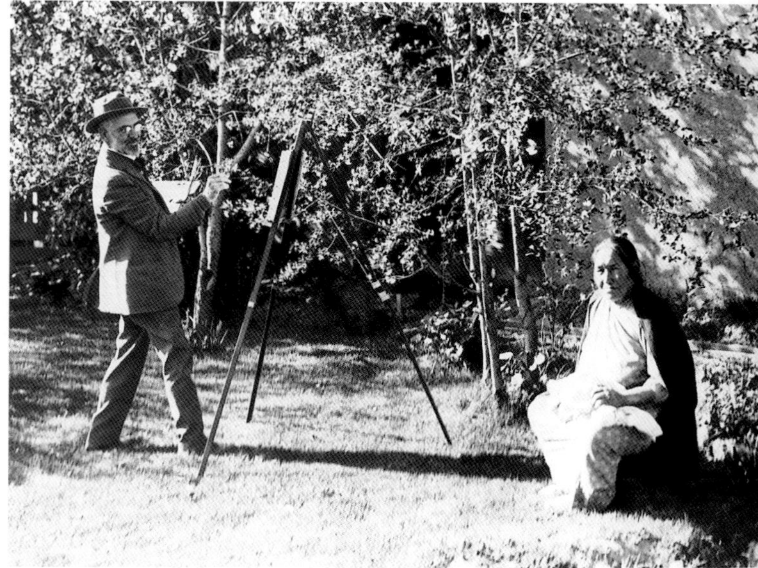

Joseph Henry Sharp painting in Taos, circa 1920.

Blumenschein and Phillips ventured to Colorado and New Mexico in 1898 (on an ill-conceived carriage ride from Denver to Mexico City) to see Taos for themselves. A broken

W. Herbert "Buck" Dunton in cowboy regalia.

wagon wheel and the September sunlight changed both men forever. In Blumenschein's words:

The beautiful Sangre de Cristo range to my left was quite different in character from the Colorado Mountains. Stretching away from the foot of the range was a vast plateau cut by the Rio Grande and the lesser gorges in which were located small villages of flat-roofed adobe houses built around a church and plaza, all fitting into the color scheme of the tawny surroundings. The sky was a clear, clean blue with sharp moving clouds. The color, the effective character of the landscape, the drama of the vast spaces, the superb beauty and serenity of the hills, stirred me deeply.

Phillips never left Taos. Blumenschein returned most summers in between stints in New York and Paris before he settled permanently in Taos in 1919.

With Sharp, Phillips, and Blumenschein as the nucleus, the colony grew steadily in the next few years to include Oscar E. Berninghaus from New York and Irving Couse from Michigan, who arrived in 1902. W. Herbert "Buck" Dunton, a Maine farm boy and gifted cowboy artist, came in 1912, followed by Indiana native Victor Higgins two years later. German American Walter Ufer rounded out Los Ocho Pintores by settling in Taos after 1914.

Los Ocho decided to formalize their group into the Taos Society of Artists in 1912, incorporated with bylaws to "develop a high standard of art among its members,

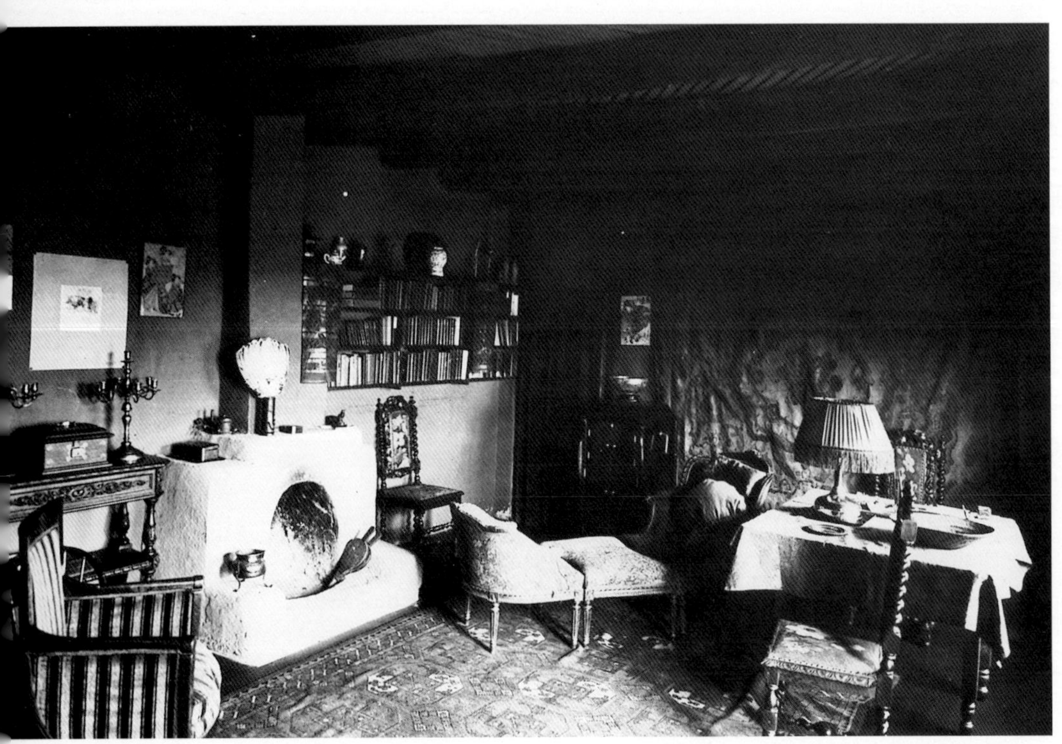

Interior, Ernest L. Blumenschein residence, Taos, circa 1920.

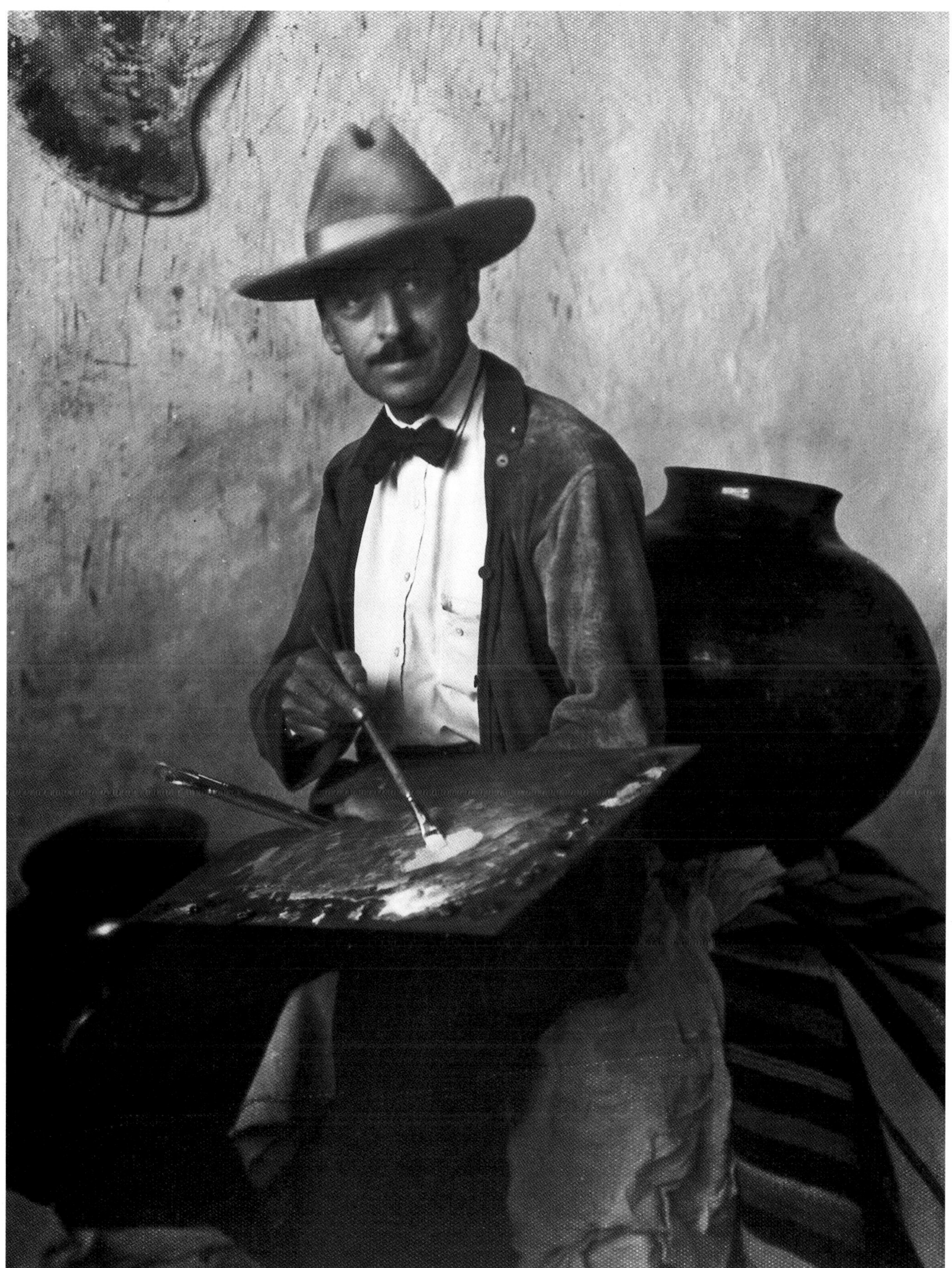

Victor Higgins in Taos, circa 1920.

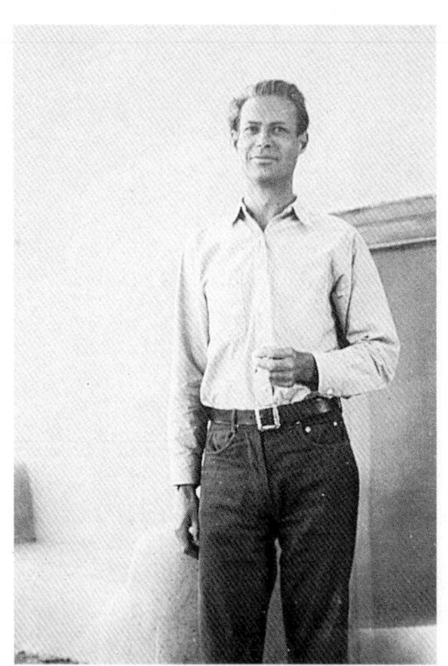

Author Frank Waters, circa 1940.

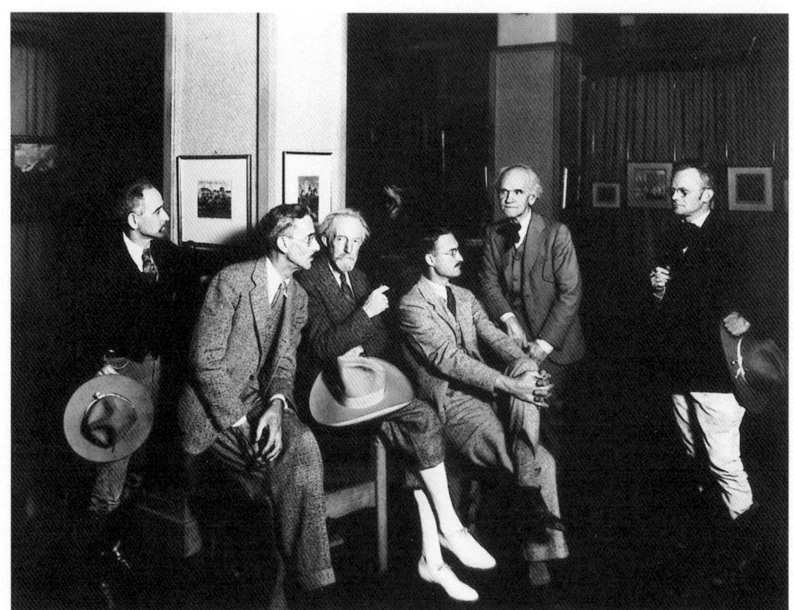

Santa Fe artists at La Fonda Hotel art gallery, 1933. From left to right: Carlos Vierra, Datus Myers, Sheldon Parsons, Theodore van Soelen, Gerald Cassidy, and William Shuster.

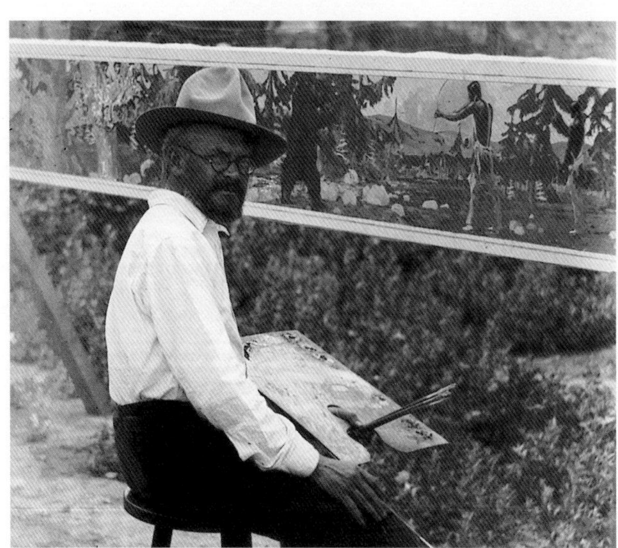

Walter Ufer, circa 1927.

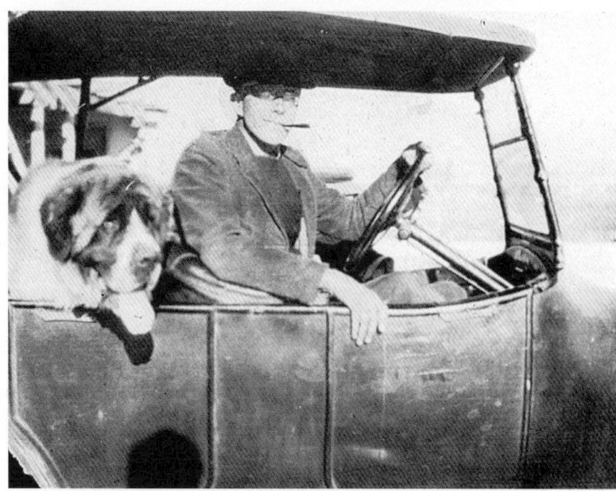

Gustave Baumann and his St. Bernard, circa 1930.

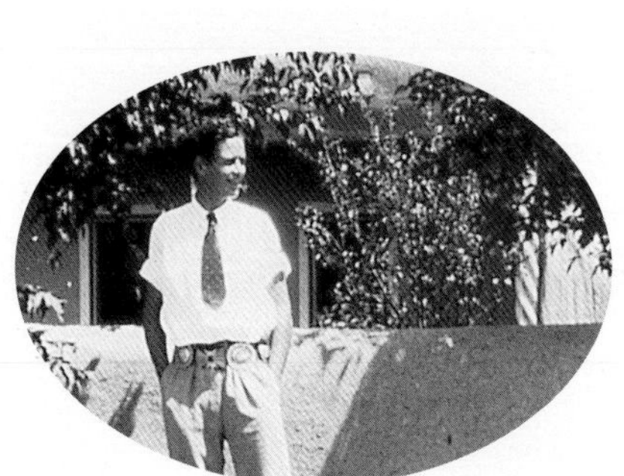

Author Frank Waters, late 1930s.

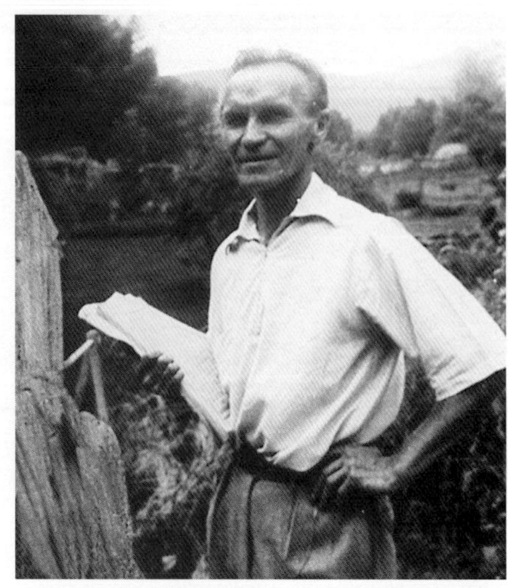

Taos artist Nicolai Fechin.

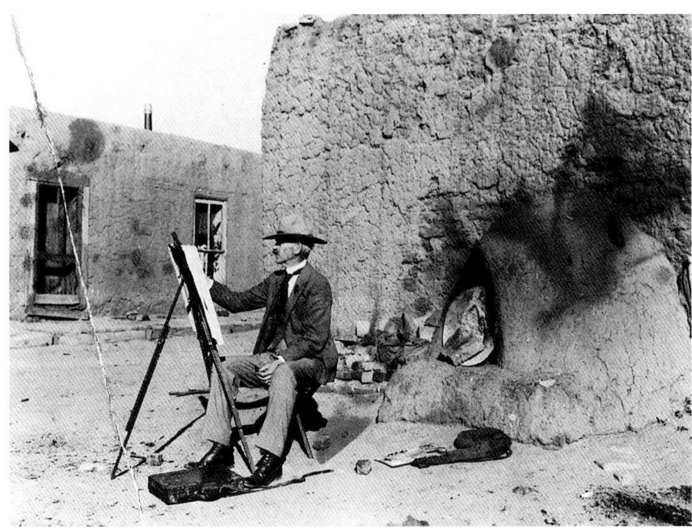

Santa Fe artist and architect William Penhallow Henderson, painting.

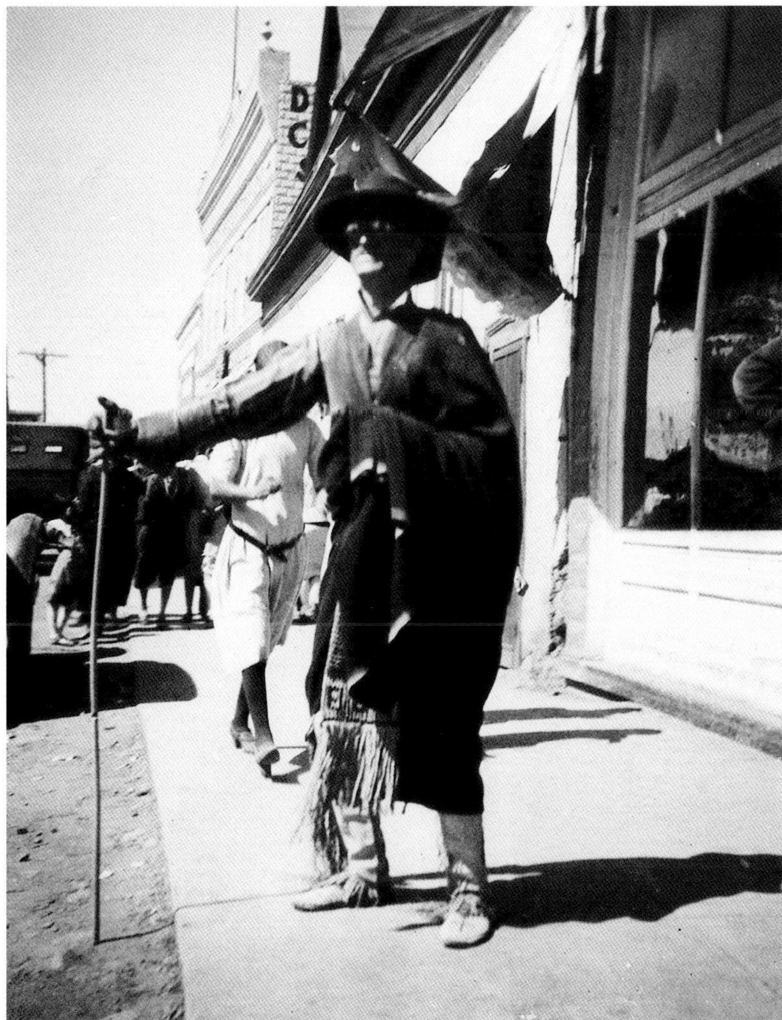

Ernest L. Blumenschein dressed as an Apache scout, Taos Fiesta, 1940s.

and to aid in the diffusion of taste for art in general." The group also sought to promote high standards in other arts and intellectual endeavors, including "sculpture, architecture, applied arts, music, literature, ethnology, and archaeology, solely as it pertains to New Mexico and the states adjoining."

Election to the group was according to simple but daunting requirements: residency in Taos for at least three years, receipt of a prize in a national exhibition, and a unanimous vote from the membership. E. Martin Hennings, Catherine C. Crichter, and Kenneth M. Adams were the only additional full members elected to the society.

As a group, the Taos Society of Artists was an instant success. Exhibitions of their work traveled nationally and internationally, garnering fame, sales, and commissions. By 1915, over one hundred artists had gravitated to Taos, and the vitality of one of America's great art colonies was insured.

In spirit and personality, the Taos Artists never acquired the bohemian habits of their New York and Paris counterparts. New Mexico was by definition rural, conservative, and poor and would not tolerate outlandish behavior. Above all, the Taos Artists worked hard and raised families in a rather primitive, challenging environment. (There was no electricity or plumbing in the remote village until the 1930s.)

The Taos Society of Artists succeeded in creating a mutual self-help and promotional organization, which was founded on excellence, mutual respect, and camaraderie. The artists were constantly pushing each other to produce work for their group shows. One member of the group had the thankless task of prodding his fellow artists to produce canvases. Kenneth M. Adams (last survivor of the Taos Society) recalled in 1966 a penciled note he received from Joseph Henry Sharp:

Dear Adams, you know the difficulties of the 1st Exhibition at Harwood's—1/2 the fellows not here and it throws more on the rest of us. I am depending on you to send us a couple good sized canvases and some drawings, etchings, lithos—what you may have with you that is representative. If you don't come through you can go plumb to hell and I'll set your hut on fire.

From Recuerdos: Early Days of the Blumenschein Family, *Helen Greene Blumenschein, 1979*

And Helen Greene Blumenschein wrote the following:

I don't believe the present generation realizes to what extent TV has invaded our lives. Like all human beings, we love to hear people talk or talk ourselves, and in the 1920s in Taos everyone became a proficient conversationalist. Mother [Mary Greene Blumenschein] welcomed the artists to her home of an evening, and many were the wonderful monologues we listened to after dinner. In the twenties, it was "Buck" Dunton who kept us on the edge of our chairs, telling of his hunting for "bahr" in his Maine nasal twang, or Walter Ufer who even gave the sound effects of a blacksmith blowing bellows while shoeing a horse with one of his tales.

From Recuerdos: Early Days of the Blumenschein Family, *Helen Greene Blumenschein, 1979*

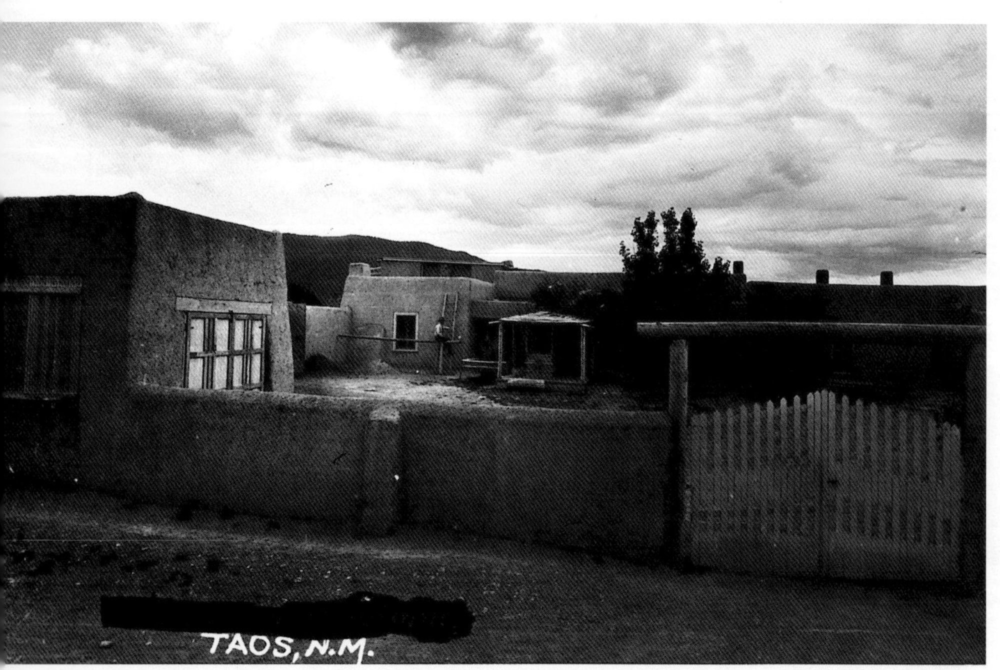

Ernest L. Blumenschein house and studio, Ledoux Street, Taos, circa 1930.

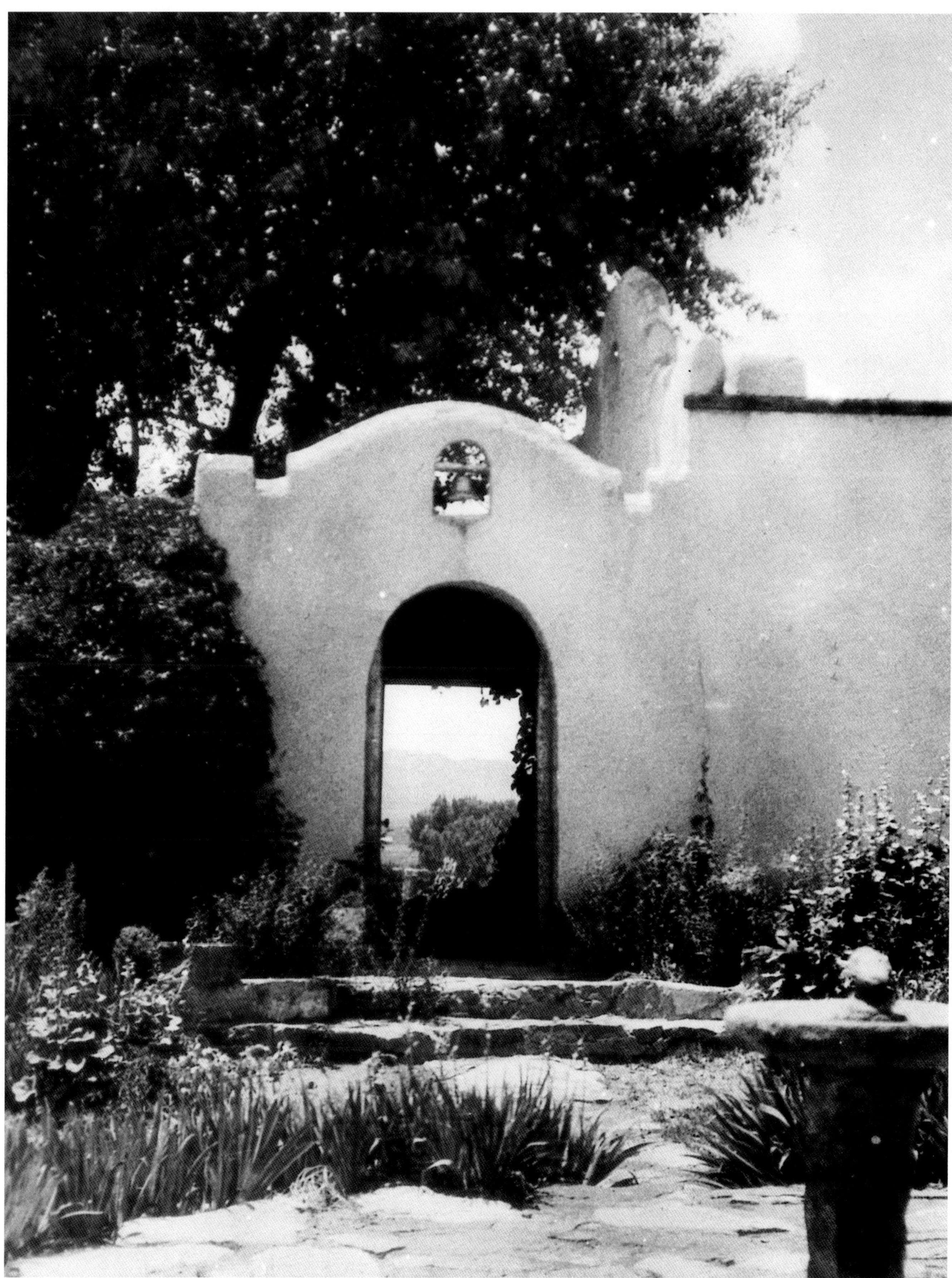

Irving Couse studio, Taos, circa 1920.

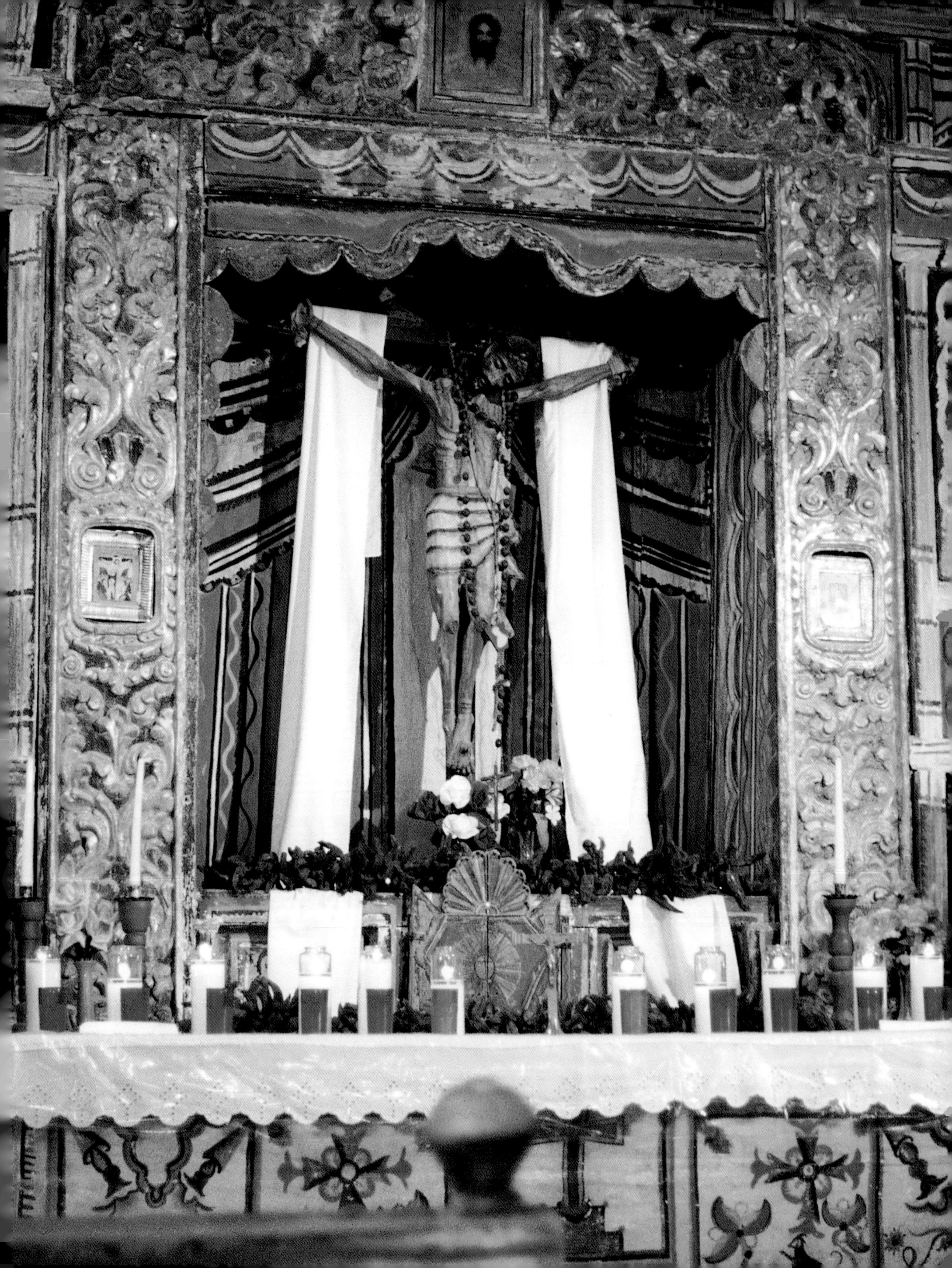

Ritual and Redemption: Power of the Land

From the earth we emerge, we are born into this world—she is our Mother. To the sun we must travel on this Road of Life—he is our Father. May our path to Father Sun be blessed with sacred cornmeal. May we walk in beauty always.

It is not at all apparent to anyone who has traveled to New Mexico that he or she has entered a land of power. The land and its people have nurtured manifestations of devotion and spirit that have enthralled all witnesses.

The artists' and writers' colonies of the twentieth century were by no means the first groups of interested observers to encounter the remarkable ceremonials of the Pueblo Indians. Nor were they the first to experience the intensity of Catholic devotion in New Mexico. In the nineteenth century, U.S. Army field reporters, Santa Fe Trail traders, pioneer photographers, writer Charles Lummis, and many others had attempted to capture in words or pictures the unbelievable religious choreography that was accepted as a normal way of life in New Mexico.

For the most part, Native American ceremonialism had been decimated by 1900, and accounts of Indian dances in various parts of America had been greatly sensationalized and exaggerated in books and other publications. But in New Mexico, ancient religious traditions, beliefs, and ritual ceremonials had survived in spite of intense persecution by Spanish missionaries and civil authorities. The sacred lifeways had not been broken.

From its earliest beginnings in the pithouse cultures of the ancient ancestors, Pueblo religion embodied the cosmic duality of male and female, light and dark, creative and receptive known as yin and yang by Oriental philosophers. A circular religious and community chamber known as a kiva was developed over a millennium ago, sunken in Mother Earth. The kiva provided a beautiful sculptural and architectural counterpoint and duality to the cubical dwelling spaces.

Out of the sunken kivas, climbing the angled, wooden ladders that pierced the world of men and animals, the gods would emerge, clothed in gorgeous woven kilts, animal skins,

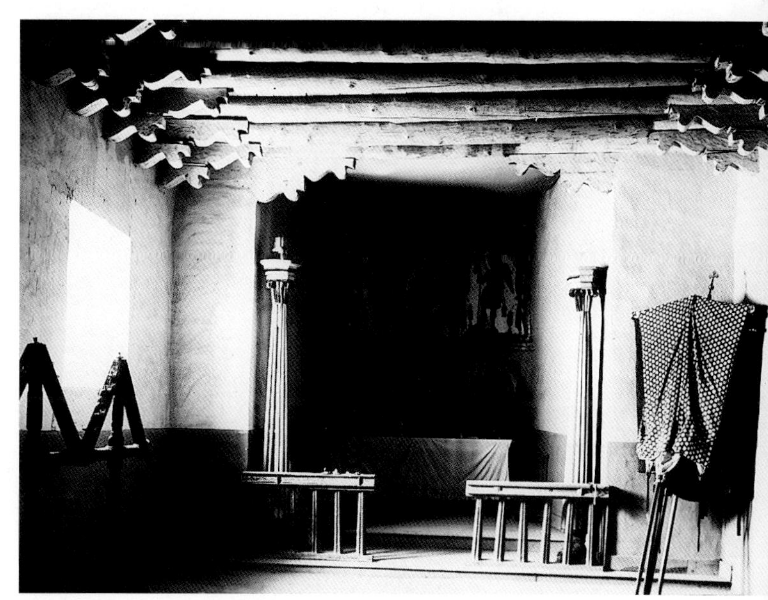

Church interior in Santa Cruz, New Mexico, circa 1900.

Altar at the Santuario de Chimayo, New Mexico.

and masked headdresses of the highest artistic value. Each pueblo developed its own dances to the gods, praying for a good harvest, or hunt, or good health for the people. Sacred power animals were celebrated and their powers invoked on behalf of the people. Thus, Zuñi Pueblo staged an elaborate "buffalo dance," Taos Pueblo became a multistoried amphitheater for the "deer dance," and the Hopis celebrated the "snake dance" by dancing with poisonous vipers in their mouths.

The deep and steady rhythms of the dancers and the drums pounded the mantra of the Pueblo's soul. All of the pageantry, all of the movement, all of the focused intensity reinforced the primal belief in man's harmony with nature, with Mother Earth. Over

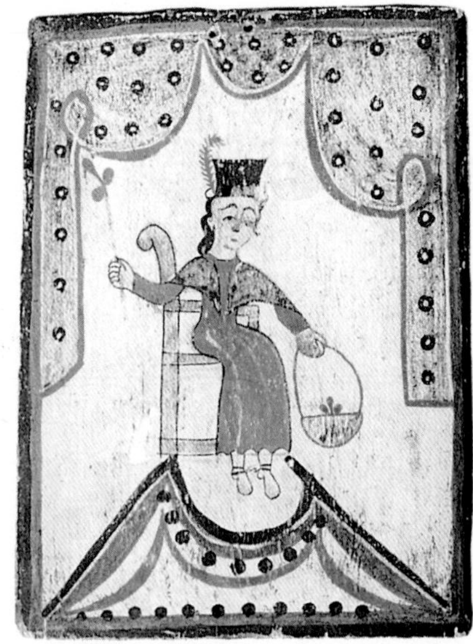

Santo Niño de Atocha.

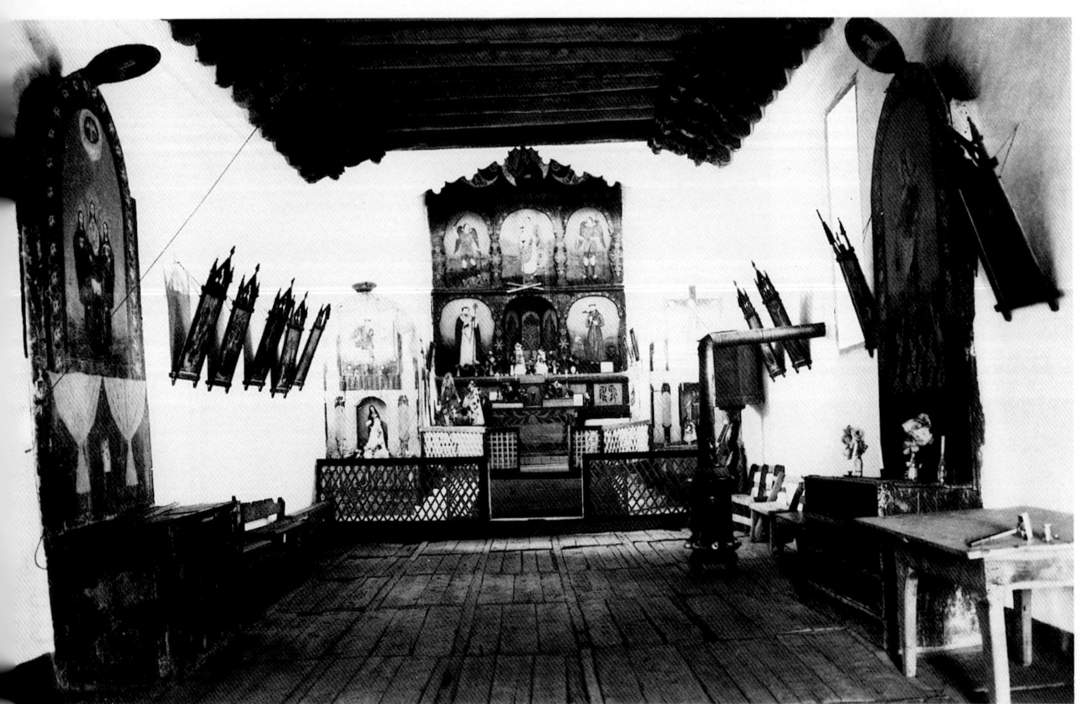

Interior, San Jose de Gracia Church, Las Trampas, New Mexico, circa 1900.

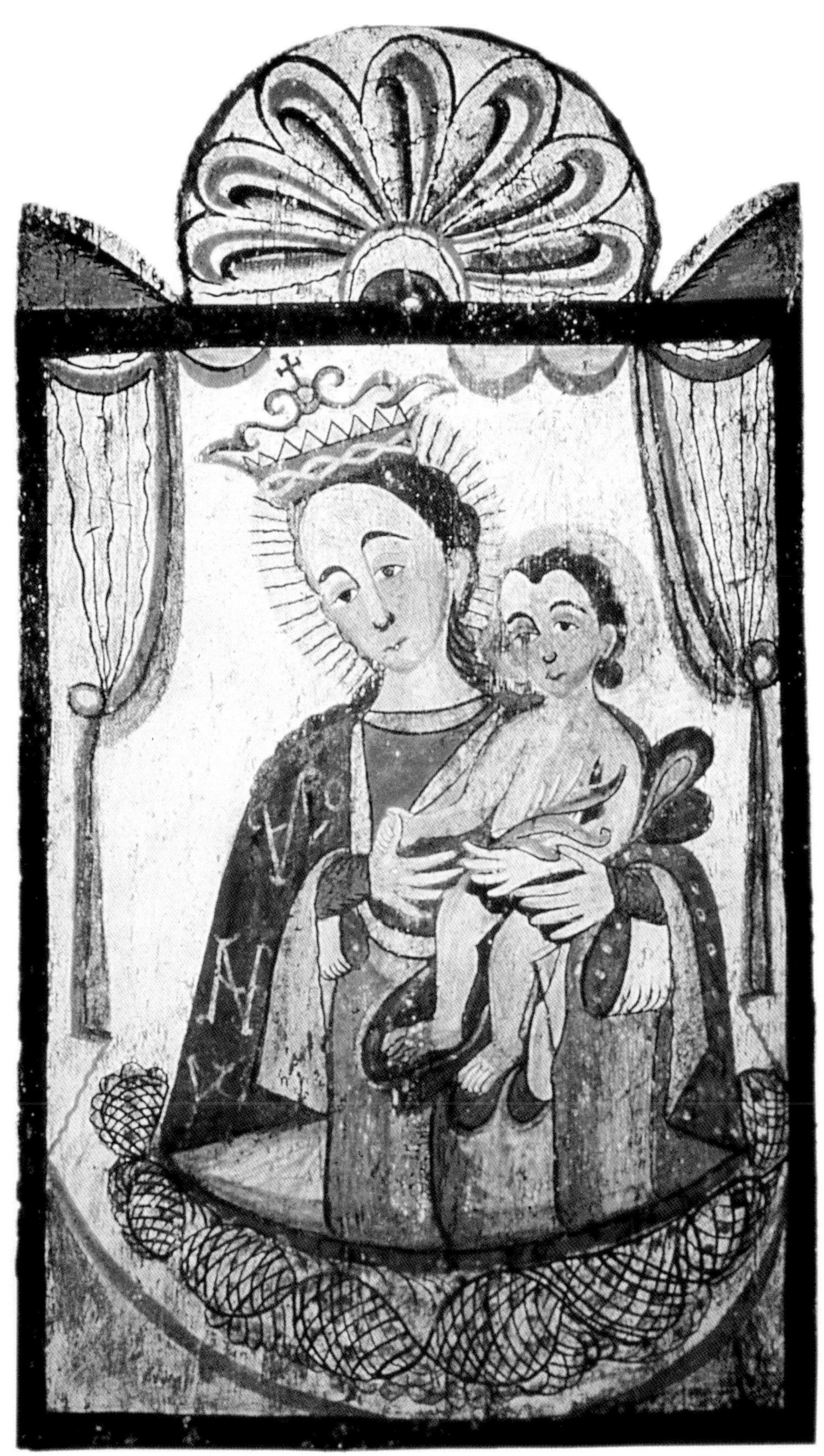

Virgin and Christ child, retablo by Jose Rafael Aragon, circa 1830.

the years, the centuries, and the millennium, Pueblo people pounded their prayers into the earth, and Earth has responded. For Frank Waters, describing the Taos deer dance: "It is a mystery play as old, as subtle and profound as were the ancient Greek Mysteries of Eleusis and the Egyptian mysteries at Sais. Its players are cosmic forces and it dramatizes the dualism of all life" (*Masked Gods*, 1950).

Along with the spectacular Pueblo ceremonials, New Mexico's Hispanic population also offered a profound vision of Catholic spirituality that had been transformed by the sheer isolation of the colony and its mountain communities. Churches, pews, religious art, chandeliers, and even musical instruments were all handcrafted lovingly and creatively. All furnishings and architectural elements of the New Mexican home were also fashioned painstakingly by hand. Even the crosses and gravestones of the *camposantos* that awaited the body's final demise were genuine expressions of folk art.

As New Mexico grew slowly in the nineteenth century, spawning tiny villages in remote canyons and valleys, priests became a rare commodity. Villagers often had to rely on each other for spiritual guidance. A lay brotherhood of religious devotees called *Los Penitentes* (the Penitent Ones) or *Los Hermanos* (the Brotherhood) evolved to serve their

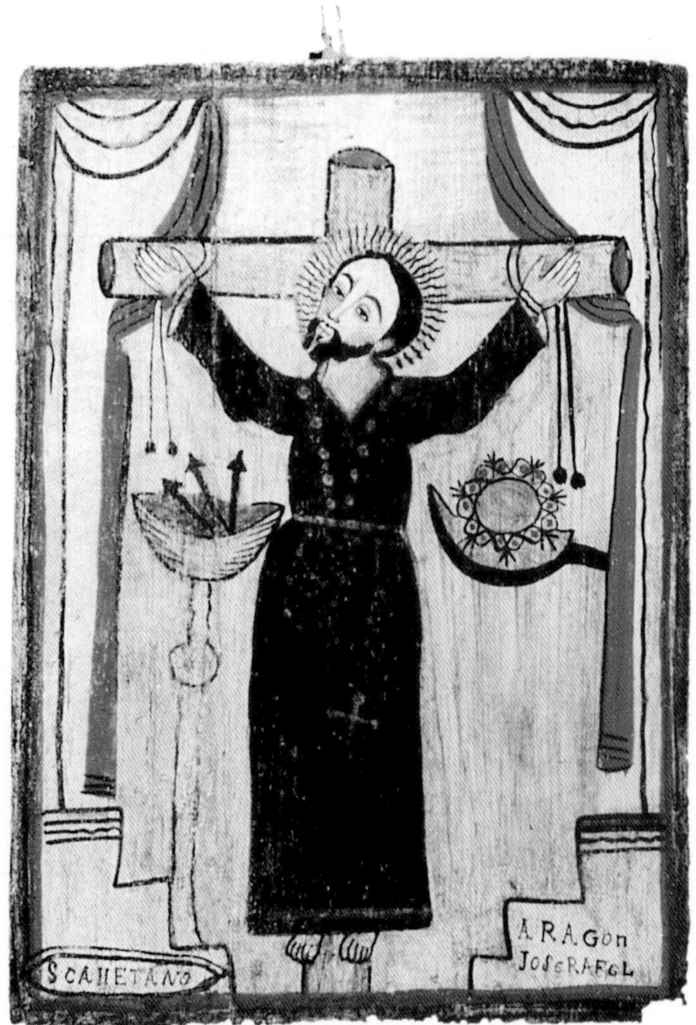

San Caetano retablo by Jose Rafael Aragon.

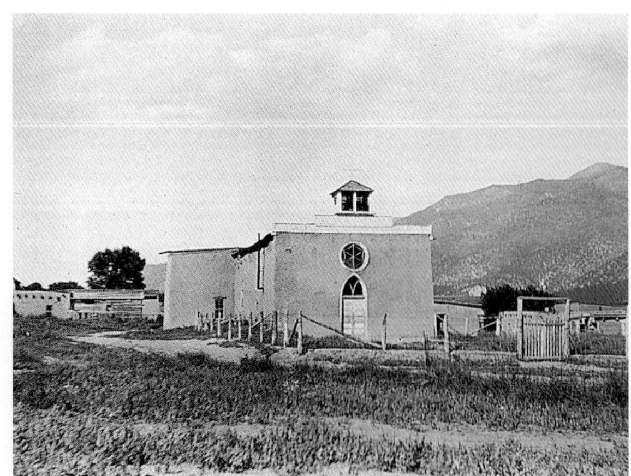
Northern New Mexico church near Taos, 1920s.

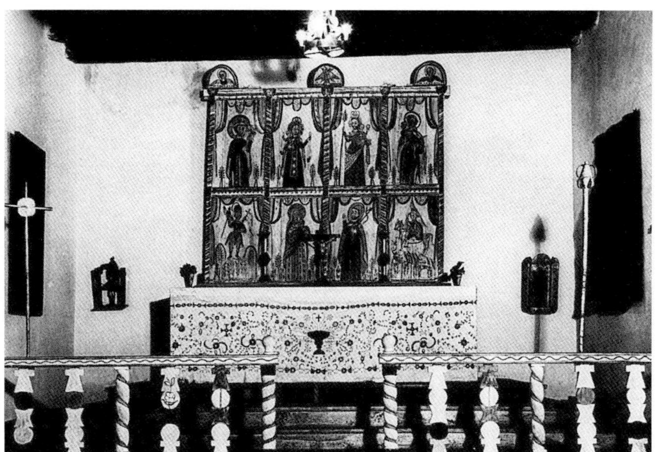

Old Spanish reredos, Palace of the Governors, Santa Fe, New Mexico.

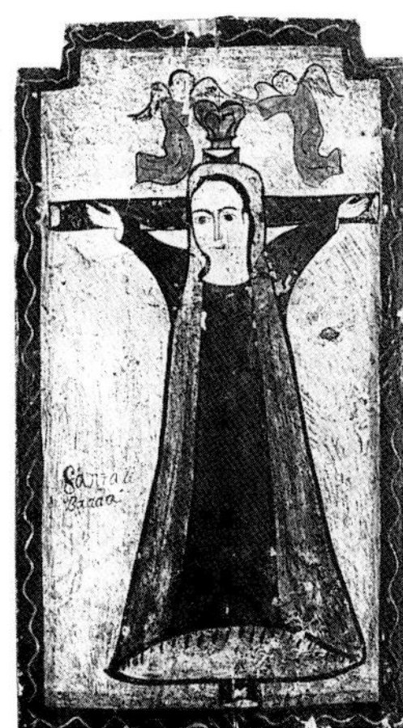

Santa Librada, retablo.

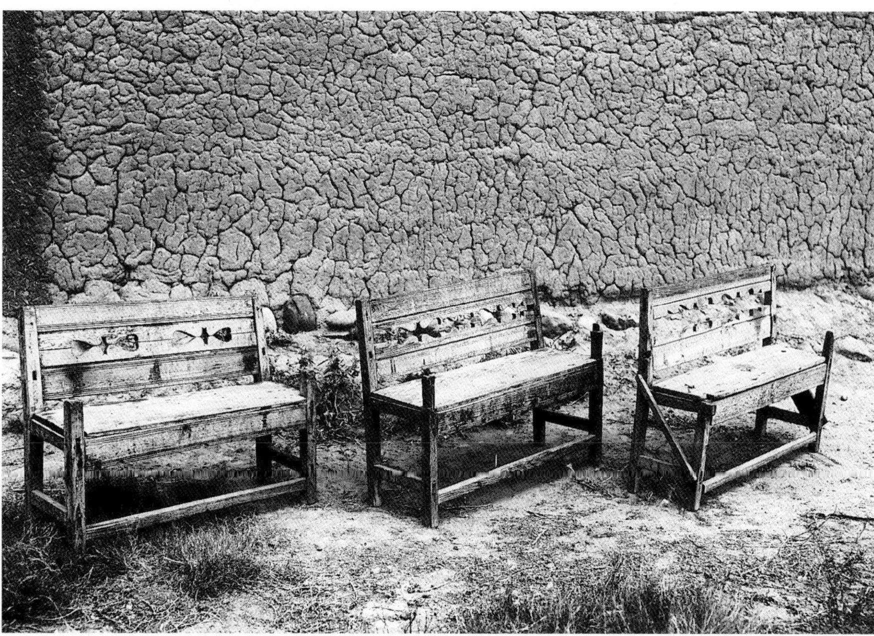

Spanish Colonial benches, northern New Mexico (between Trampas and Peñasco), circa 1912.

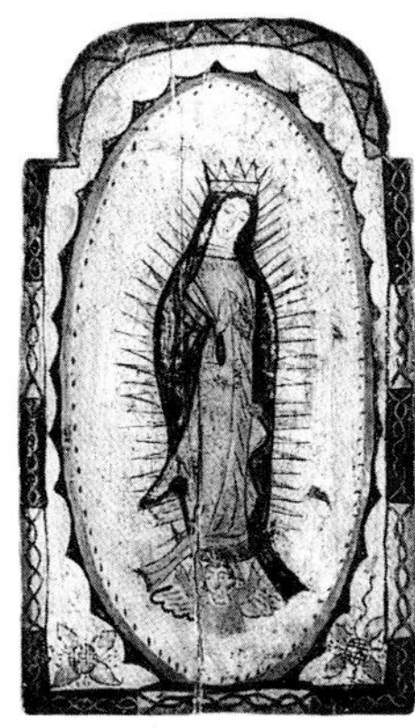

Virgin of Guadalupe, retablo.

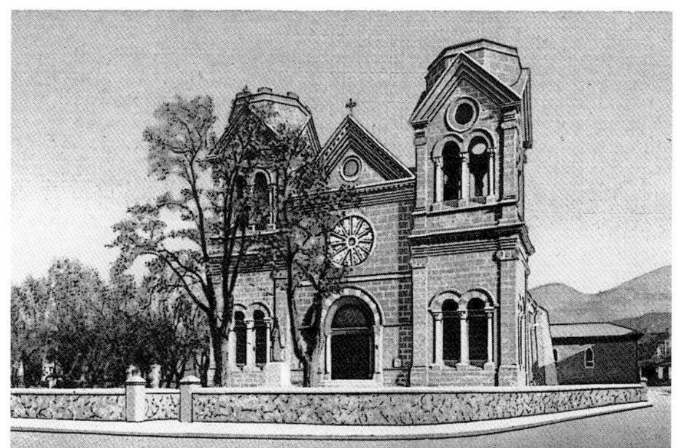

Santa Fe's Romanesque Cathedral of St. Francis remains the crowning achievement of Archbishop Jean Baptiste Lamy who was immortalized in Willa Cather's novel Death Comes for the Archbishop.

own religious needs as well as those of their neighbors.

Housed in their small *moradas,* or prayer houses, the brothers prayed devoutly for grace and forgiveness. The penitentes literally observed the passion of Christ's crucifixion each year during Holy Week, as their brothers in Spain (notably in Sevilla) and Mexico had also done for centuries. Physical penance sometimes involved acts of self-flagellation with cactus whips or the enactment of the role of Christ himself being crucified (though stopping short of death). Accompanying these profound acts of penance were the haunting voices of the brothers singing sacred *alabados,* or hymns of praise, with origins in medieval Spain.

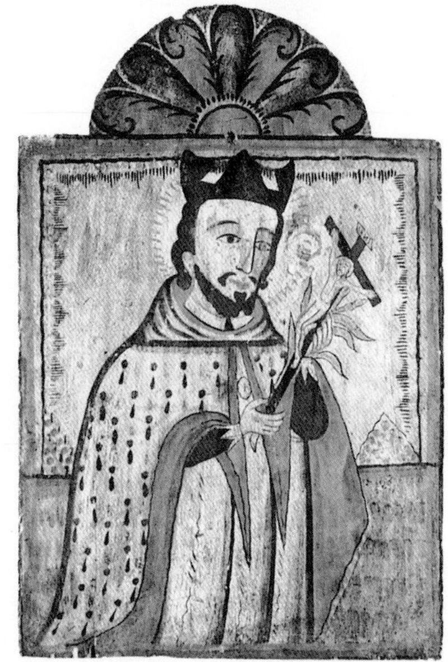

St. John Nepomuceno, retablo.

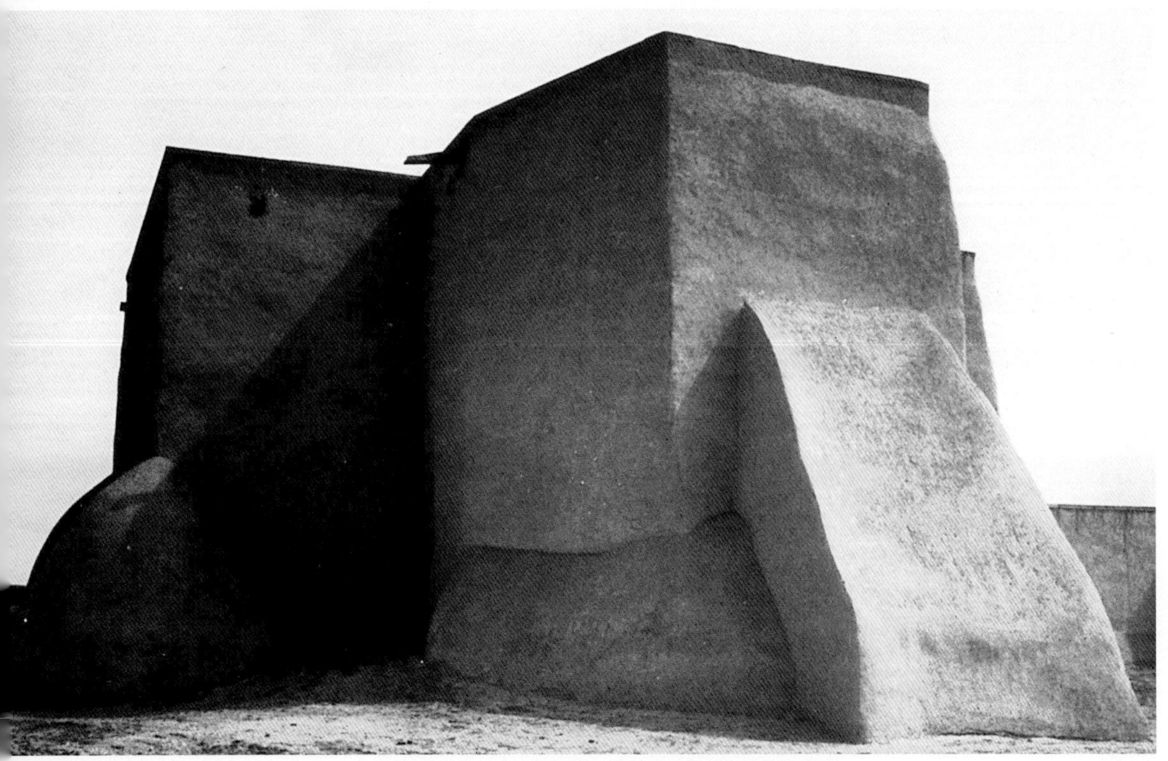

Rear apse, mission church of San Francisco de Asís, Ranchos de Taos, New Mexico.

To many outside observers, including Charles Lummis, who recorded penitente rituals in his 1893 classic *Land of Poco Tiempo,* the practices of the *hermanos* (brothers) seemed bizarre and macabre. But the acts of penance and devotion expressed (if somewhat viscerally) a profound belief in the power of redemption and forgiveness that has also guided the souls of many New Mexicans. Even today, perhaps the most popular spiritual procession in the United States is the annual pilgrimage to the Santuario de Chimayo during Holy Week, which attracts thousands of religious pilgrims of all religious faiths to walk to the old adobe shrine to seek redemption.

What many of the artists and writers who moved to Santa Fe and Taos found in the indigenous cultures of New Mexico was a remarkable integration of spirituality and everyday life. Nature, life, and spirit were celebrated in profound, powerful, and beautiful ways. The richness of spiritual life in New Mexico made mainstream urban life elsewhere seem empty and meaningless. Not only was the picturesqueness of New Mexico staggering, but a sense of the sacred permeated nearly everything.

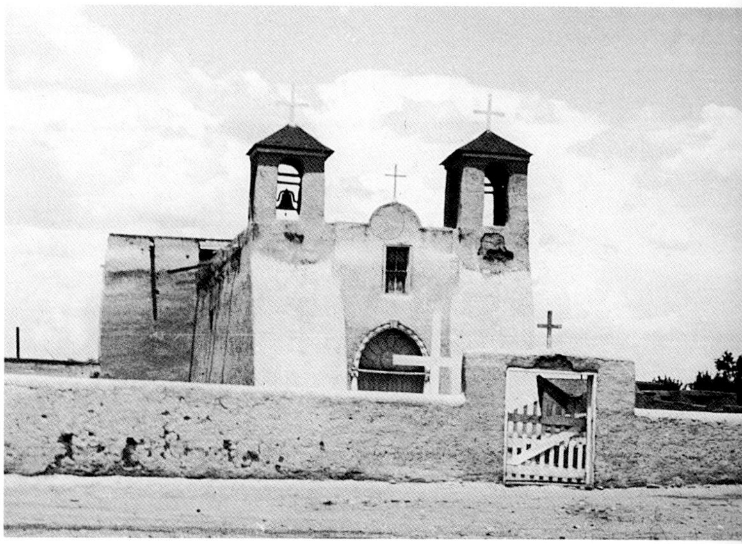

Mission church of San Francisco de Asís, Ranchos de Taos.

"When Trinidad, the Indian boy, and I planted corn at my ranch," D. H. Lawrence wrote after his New Mexican sojourn, "my soul paused to see his brown hands softly moving the earth over the maize in pure ritual." During most of the years he spent at Taos, to which he had come at the request of Mabel Dodge in 1922, the English novelist was obsessed with the "strange blind unanimity" of thought and action he perceived in Indian life—the unconscious poise that seemingly led Indians to plant corn with the same mystical absorption that they performed sacred ritual. Their actions, Lawrence maintained, revealed a spirit that was absolutely lacking in contemporary society, in which men were at odds with nature, and in which he personally felt "dead, dark, and buried."

William H. Truettner, "The Art of Pueblo Life,"
Art in New Mexico 1900–1945, *1986.*

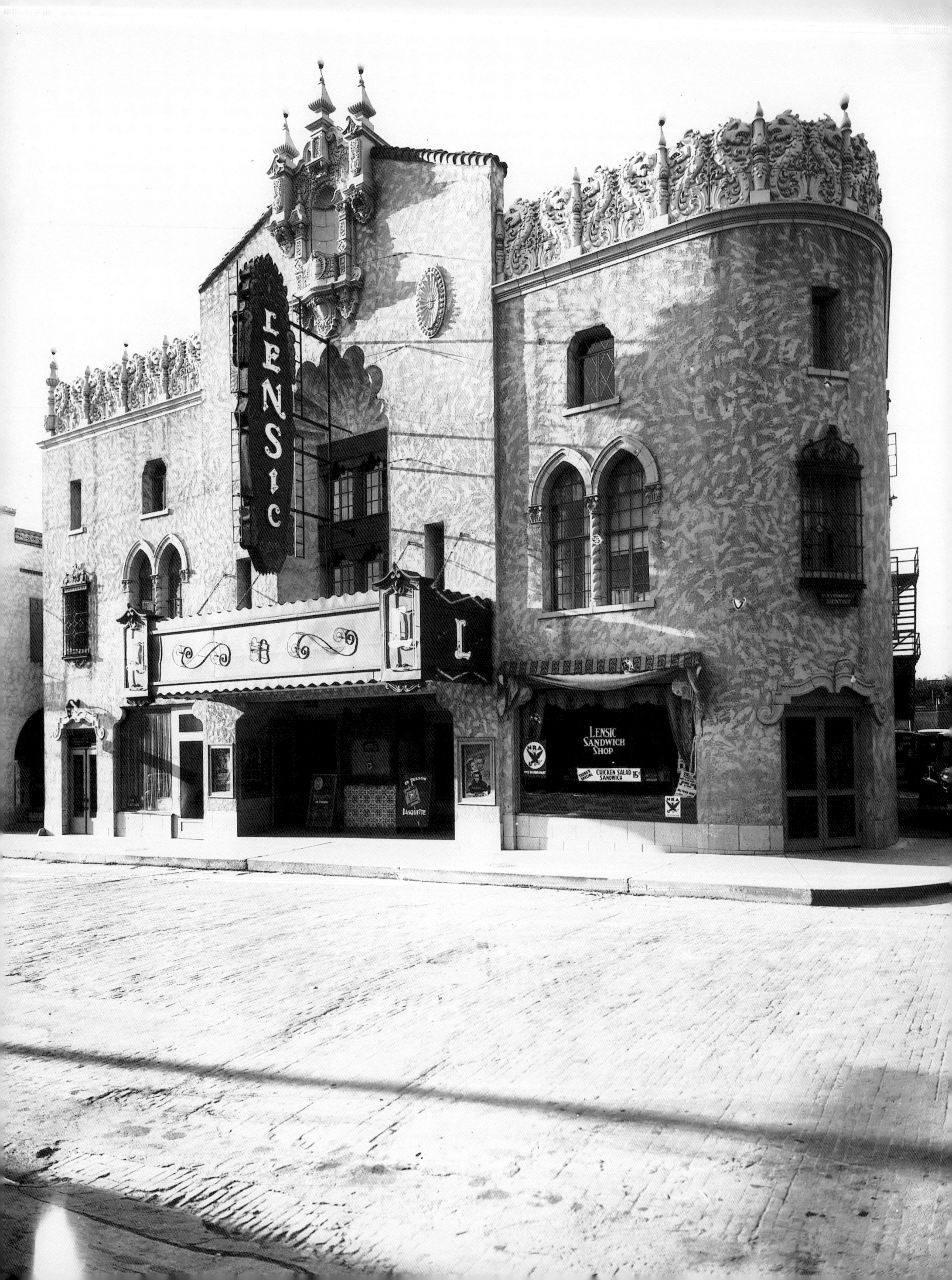

LENSIC
LENSIC SANDWICH SHOP
CHICKEN SALAD SANDWICH 15¢
NRA

Santa Fe Renaissance

Santa Fe struggled to become a modern American city in spite of its ancient *mestizo* (mixed-blood) roots. As the twentieth century unfolded, both Santa Fe and New Mexico seemed desperate for recognition and acceptance from the United States. Rivals Albuquerque and Las Vegas, New Mexico, were booming, both eclipsing the capital city in population and wealth by 1900.

City leaders focused their efforts on business and commercial development and statehood status (finally granted by Congress in 1912) to revitalize their flagging fortunes. A passion for authenticity, especially in architecture, folk traditions, and lifestyle, was being championed by followers of the English Arts and Crafts movement at the same time that Santa Fe boosters were searching for theirs.

During the first decade of the new century, it appeared that the California Mission style could present an appropriate style for New Mexico. The Santa Fe Railroad had built splendid mission-style depots and hotels in Albuquerque and Las Vegas (the Alvarado and Castaneda Hotels respectively) and even in the capital. A New Mexico pavilion at the 1904 St. Louis World's Fair was built in the California Mission style, though it proved far less popular than the stage-set Indian village at the same exposition, "staffed" by Pueblo Indians.

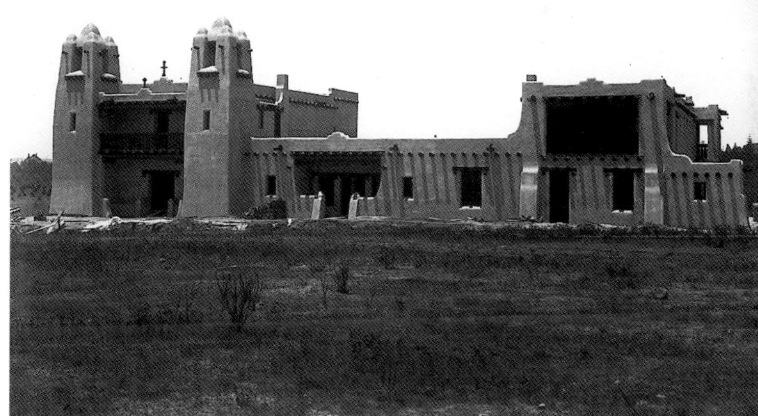

New Mexico Pavilion, Panama-California Exposition, San Diego, 1915. Isaac Hamilton Rapp, architect.

The message soon became clear: Eastern Americans were fascinated by the legacy of the cliff dwellers and their modern descendants who still lived in earthen multistoried villages. The Santa Fe Railroad quickly seized the opportunity and commissioned architect Mary Colter and a crew of Hopi artisans to build the Hopi House at the Grand Canyon in 1905.

A new southwestern architectural expression was struggling to be born. Pueblo building

Lensic Theatre, San Francisco Street, 1932. A Spanish Colonial Revival masterpiece, the Lensic still operates and reigns as one of New Mexico's finest historic theaters.

experiments at the University of New Mexico and along the Santa Fe Railroad's depots (the El Ortiz Hotel in Lamy, New Mexico, of 1909) hinted at the new aesthetic. A pink Moorish monument for the Scottish Rite Temple in Santa Fe of 1910 further piqued interest and intensified the debate. Though overt references to the Alhambra, Spain's great landmark, were celebrated in the Scottish Rite Temple, the building seemed a bit out of place.

The City Beautiful movement of grand Parisian city planning, public art, and classical beaux-arts monuments had remained popular after its great triumph at the 1893 Chicago Columbian Exposition. Santa Fe civic leaders contemplated straightening and widening crooked streets and building great parks. For the Santa Fe City Plan of 1912, Edgar Lee Hewitt and his Museum of New Mexico staff exercised great influence, eventually persuading the community to protect traditional architecture and urban design patterns. Street names became romantic Spanish notions such as Paseo de Peralta and Calle Analco instead of memorials to such dead presidents as Garfield and Grant. The "City Beautiful" became the "City Different."

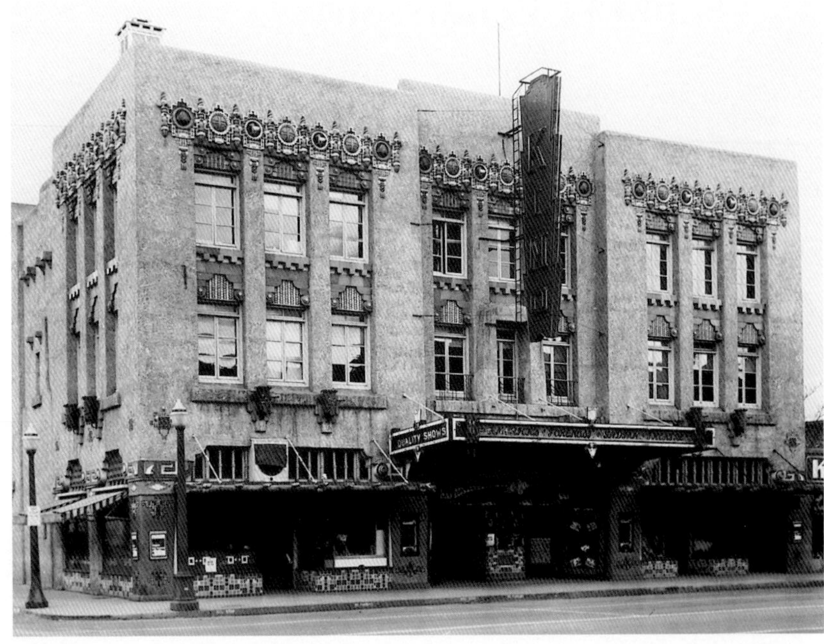

KiMo Theatre, Central Avenue, Albuquerque, circa 1930. The KiMo, carefully preserved today, is one of the country's finest examples of Pueblo Deco architecture. Carl Boller, architect.

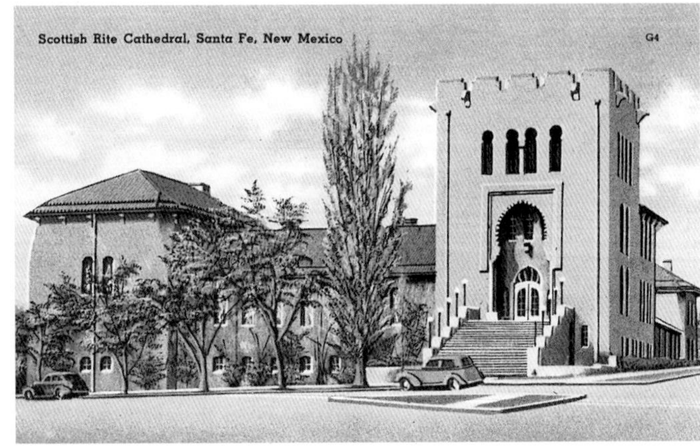

The Santa Fe Scottish Rite Temple of 1910 evokes the Moorish ambiance and monumentality of the Alhambra.

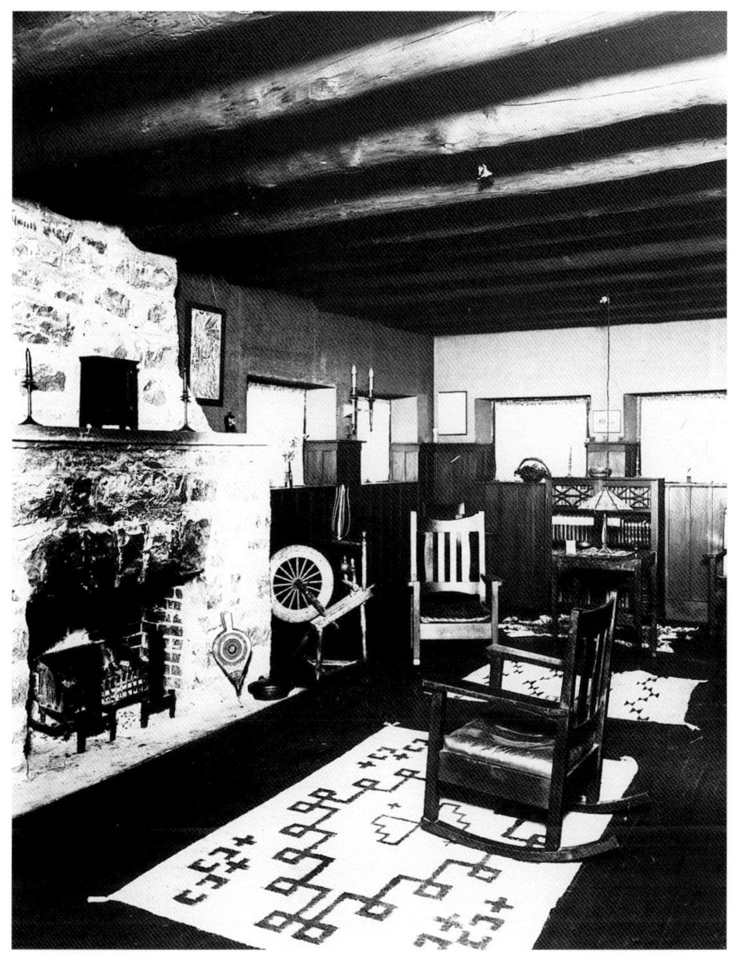

Living room, Sylvanus G. Morley residence, Santa Fe, circa 1912. Morley's design sensibilities included Mission furniture, New England antiques, and Navajo rugs.

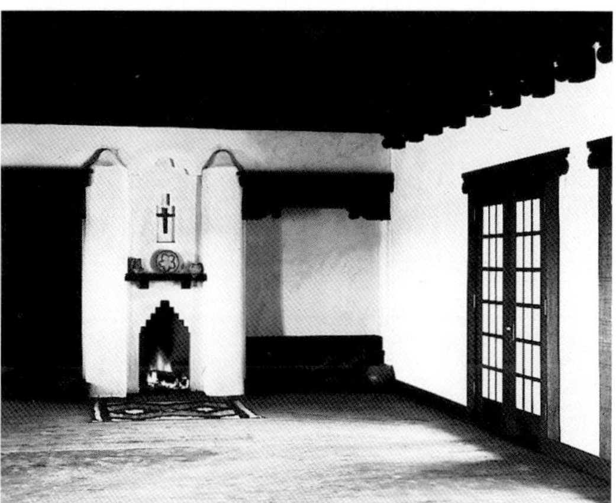

Interior, New Mexico Pavilion, Panama-California Exposition, San Diego, 1915. Still in its experimental phase in 1915, the early Pueblo Revival style featured elements from Mission architecture and the Arts and Crafts movement.

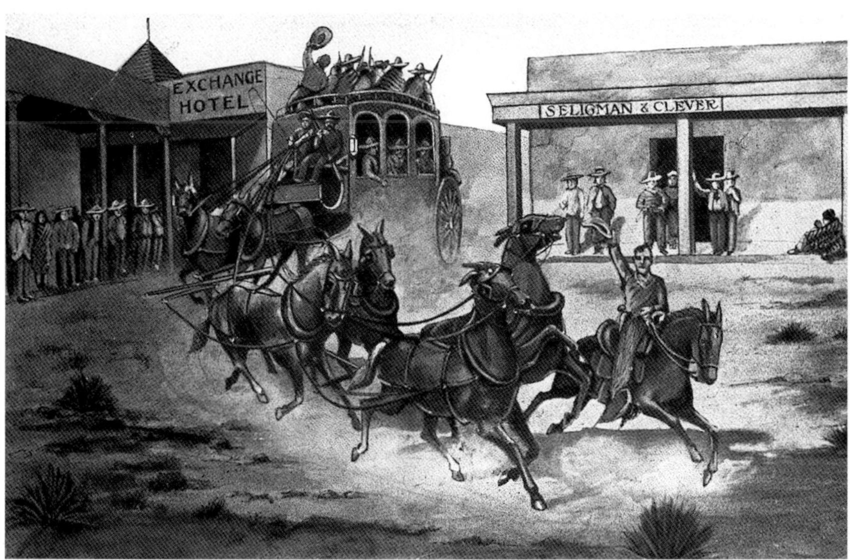

A romanticized illustration recalls the Santa Fe Trail era of Santa Fe's plaza. The former Exchange Hotel occupied the site of the present-day La Fonda.

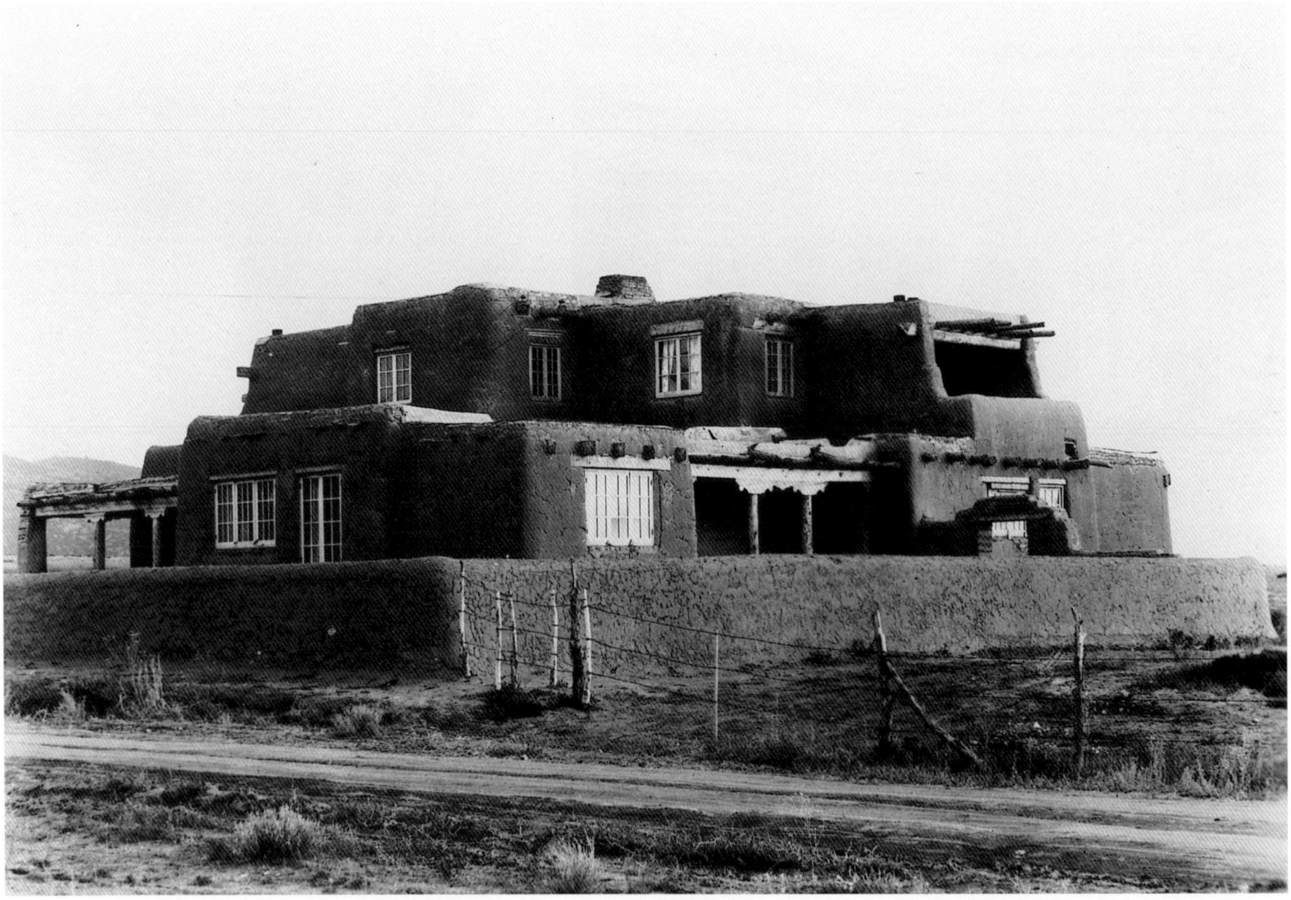

Artist Carlos Vierra married the romance and picturesque quality of Pueblo architecture to his "suburban" residence, seen here about 1920.

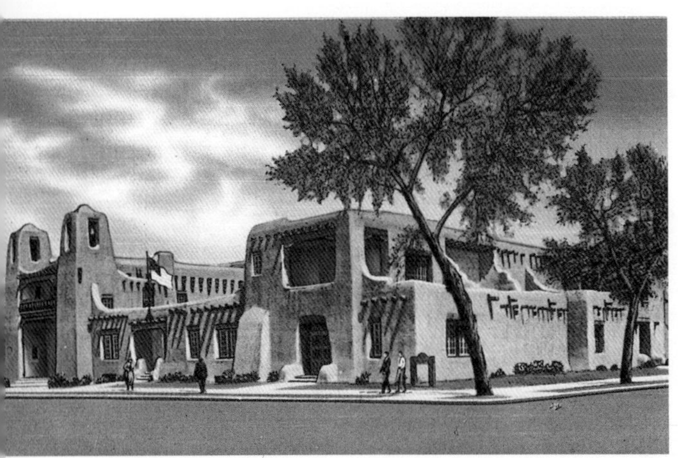

The Museum of Fine Arts (1916–17) was Santa Fe's first public monument of the new Pueblo Revival style. Rapp and Rapp Architects.

The New Mexico Pavilion at San Diego's Panama-California Exposition of 1915 finally provided the picturesque prototype—a lively fusion of Pueblo Mission profiles, asymmetrical facades, and flowing, exuberant details. The collaboration of Hewett's archaeologists and Isaac Hamilton Rapp's architects had produced a masterpiece. The creation of an adobe Pueblo Indian village at the fair's *Painted Desert* exhibit was also a resounding success.

In 1916, after the San Diego pavilion was re-created with some modifications on the Museum of Fine Arts Santa Fe plaza, the new architecture became irresistible. Within a few years, the capital would boast impressive new Pueblo Revival landmarks: the Oñate Theatre of 1920, La Fonda Hotel of 1921, and the Federal Building of 1921 (now the Museum of the Institute of American Indian Arts).

With the arrival of urban refugees, artists, and writers in the 1920s, the Pueblo Revival style gained added vitality as it moved into residential examples. Pioneering the effort was painter Carlos Vierra, who built himself a modern pueblo home on the Old Pecos Trail. Many bohemians instead bought traditional adobe fixer-uppers of several rooms, rehabilitated them in the spirit of the new style, and, in most cases, greatly expanded them.

The 1920s in Santa Fe sparked a dynamic transformation of architecture and lifestyle, in some ways evocative of the great cultural transformation heralded by the arrival of the Santa Fe Trail a century earlier. This time, eastern intellectuals and not Missouri traders were the harbingers of change. They would open wide the floodgates of tourism and picturesque fantasy in a remote outpost of the former Spanish empire.

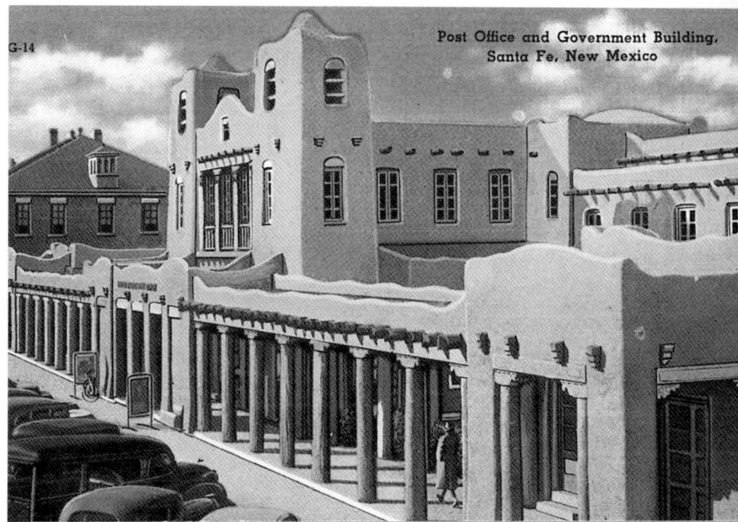

Santa Fe's 1921 Federal Building has been transformed into the Museum of the Institute of American Indian Arts.

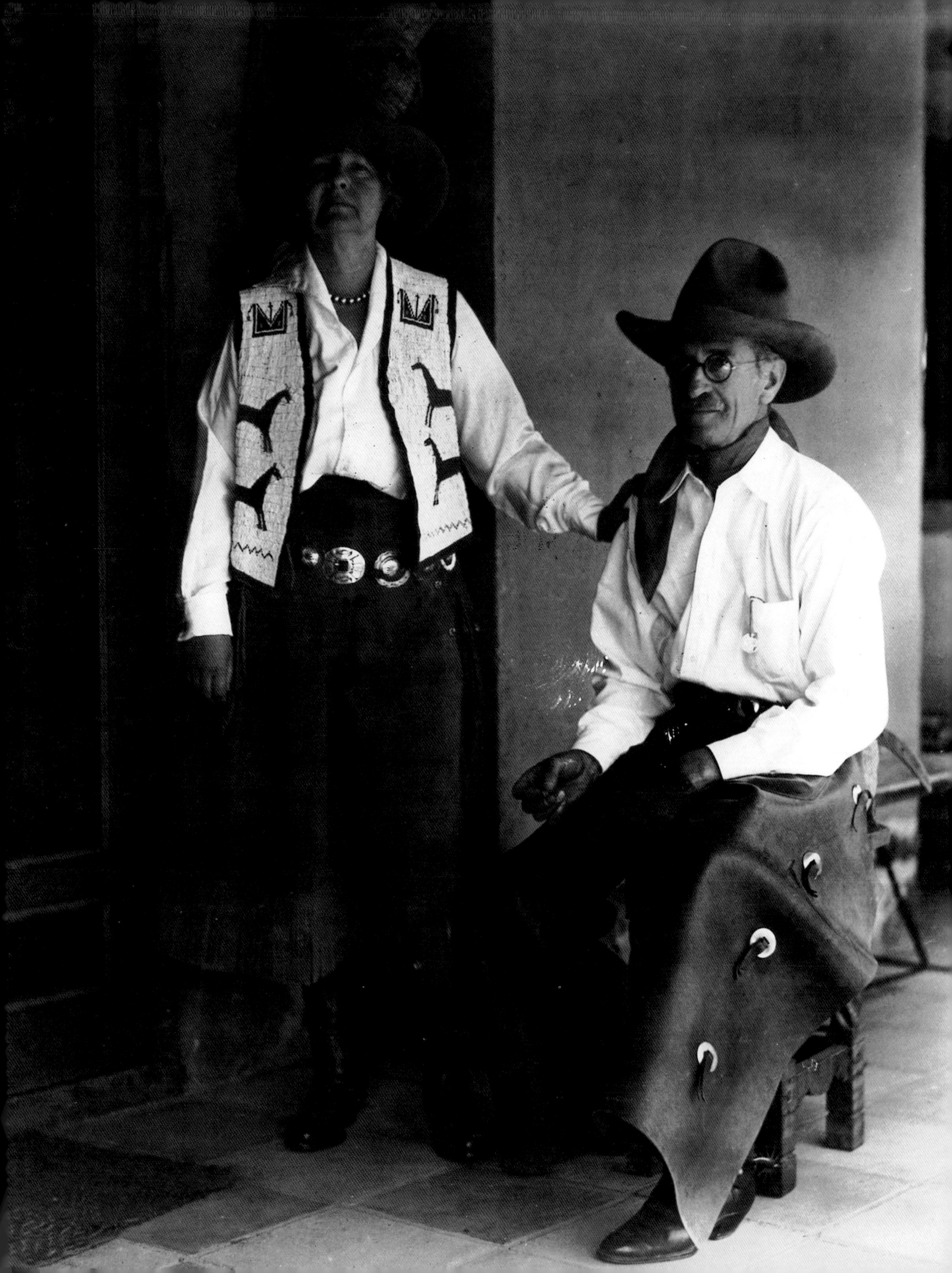

Santa Fe Writers' Colony

Some of them are forgotten now, and some are not. The modest homes they owned in Santa Fe became sanctuaries, grew into fascinating and compelling living spaces, soon into city landmarks, and now into tourist attractions. The Santa Fe Writers' Colony, which flourished between the world wars, changed the city and Southwest forever, yet their work and legacy seems as elusive as an aspen breeze.

From the big cities they came mostly seeking respite from tuberculosis, a cheap place to live, an exotic adventure, or merely the company of other writers. During their heydays, the Santa Fe Writers' Colony grew as impressively as the Taos Society of Artists, gaining national and international acclaim and attracting visits by some of America's greatest literary talents. Among the great authors of the twentieth century who enjoyed visiting friends in Santa Fe and Taos were Sinclair Lewis, Carl Sandburg, Theodore Dreiser, Thornton Wilder, and W. H. Auden.

New Mexico had fostered a long and varied literary tradition, but much of it lay within the realm of the oral tradition of Native Americans. While much of this legacy had been inaccessible, it still inspired contemporary twentieth-century writers by its mere existence. In Alice Corbin's estimation:

> *. . . this great fund of primitive Indian poetry, orally transmitted for untold generations, and now in large measure recorded, is not, however, merely a dead letter contribution, but a vital, contemporary expression of the soil. On the common ground of poetry, indeed, the living Indian poets and the Anglo American poets of New Mexico now meet in friendly contact; and the influence of this primitive verse and thought on the later poets is obvious.* (Turquoise Trail, *1928*)

With the publication of Captain Gaspar Perez de Villagra's great epic poem *Historia de Nuevo México* in 1610, Spanish literary tradition was introduced into the Southwest. For three centuries thereafter, New Mexico boasted a true multicultural literary flowering that included Spanish songs, ballads, poems, stories, and prayers; several well-known travel accounts of the incredible overland adventures of Santa Fe Trail pioneers; and a more recent tradition of cowboy songs and poetry.

With the 1916 arrival of poet Alice Corbin and her artist husband, William Penhallow Henderson, in Santa Fe, a new era began. Fleeing Chicago for the beneficial weather of Santa

Poet Alice Corbin Henderson and her husband, artist/architect William Penhallow Henderson.

Fe, Alice sought to ease her tuberculosis. As an editor of *Poetry Magazine,* Alice knew and befriended America's greatest poets, including Carl Sandburg, Vachel Lindsay, John Gould Fletcher, and Witter Bynner. Within a few years, these men would visit the Hendersons frequently in Santa Fe, offering poetry readings for the public and at parties and social gatherings. Witter Bynner would make his permanent home in Santa Fe after 1922. Among Bynner's first houseguests were D. H. and Frieda Lawrence, newly recruited to Taos by Mabel Dodge.

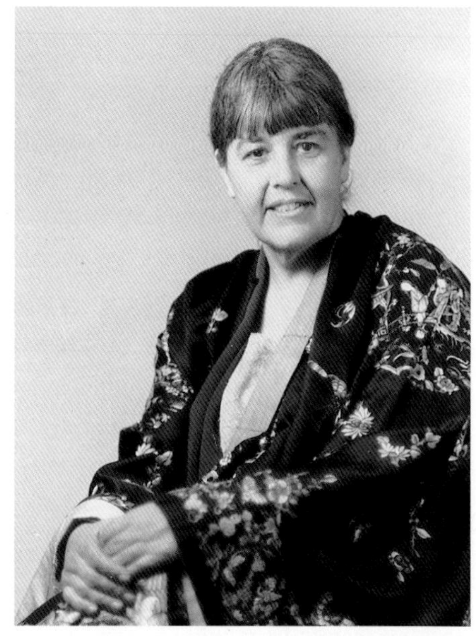

Mary Austin.

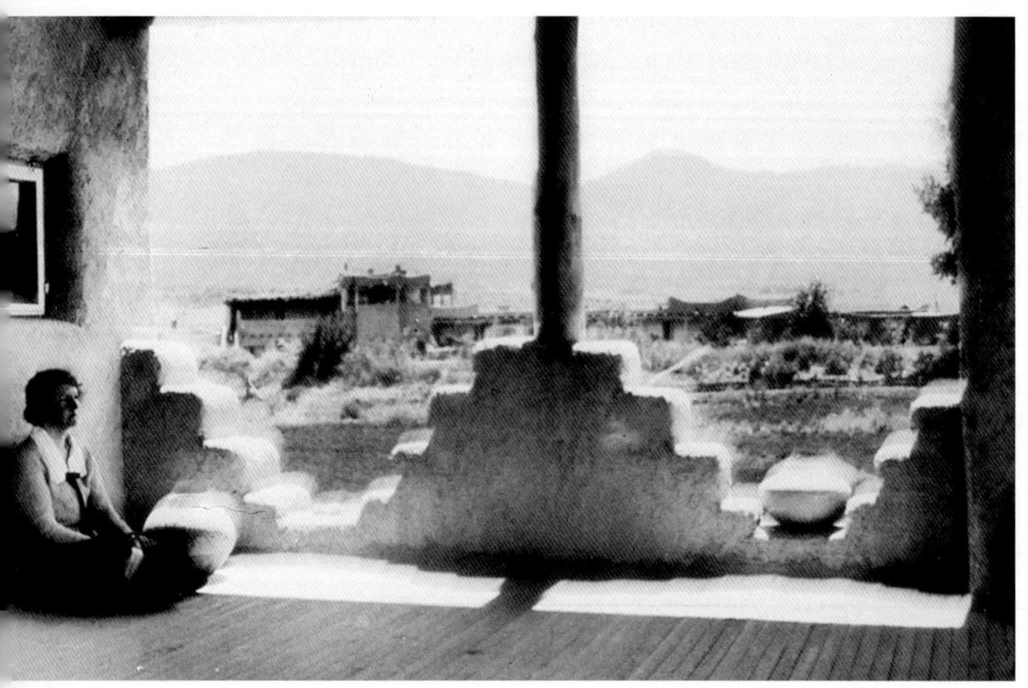

Alice Corbin Henderson in reflection at the two-story guest house of Mabel Dodge Luhan's Taos estate, circa 1925.

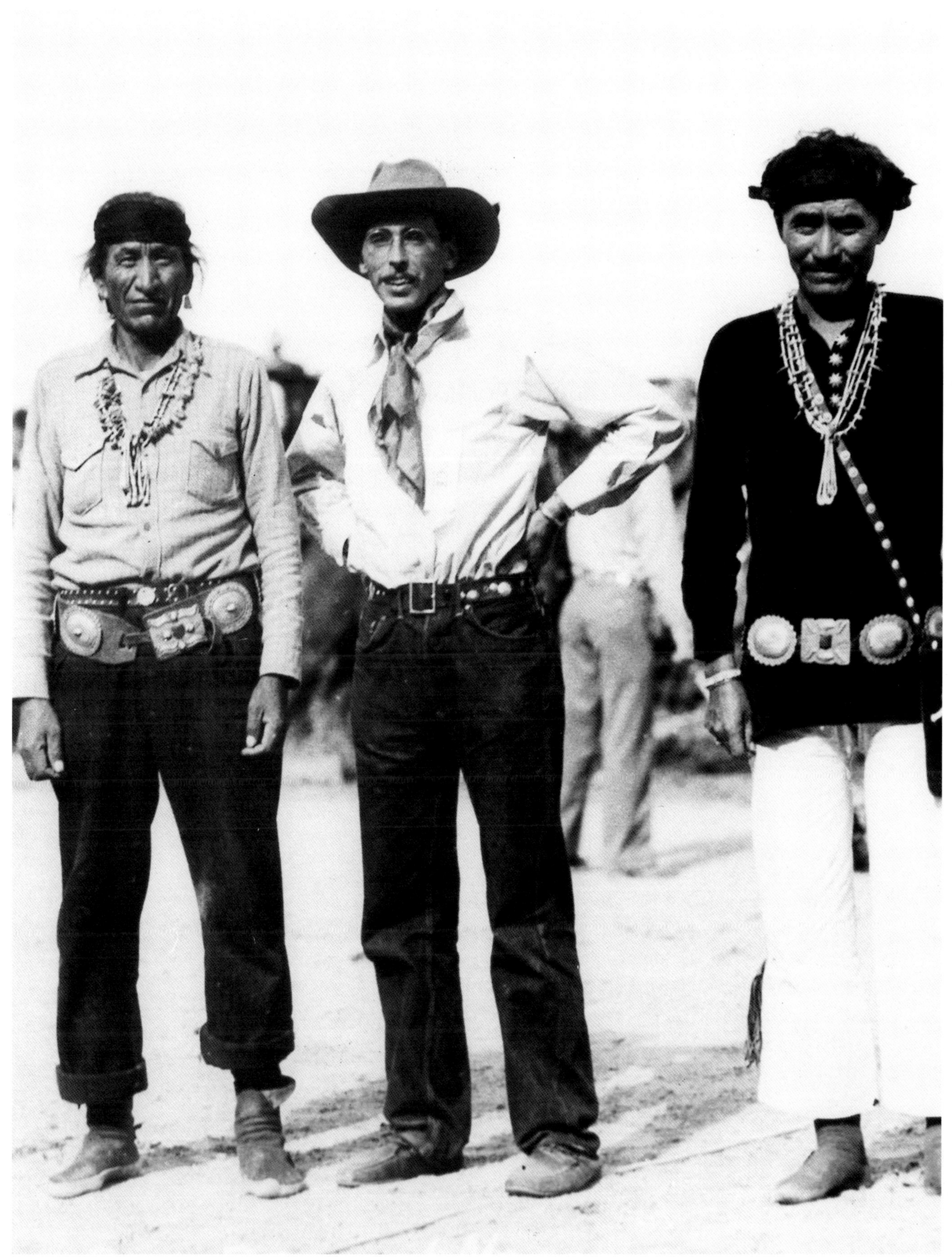

Oliver LaFarge and "best dressed" Navajos at Inter-Tribal Indian Ceremonial, Gallup, 1934.

By 1923, with the arrival of the Hendersons, Bynner, and Lawrence, the colony quickly attracted other notables, including Frank Applegate, Ruth Laughlin Barker, and Pulitzer Prize–winner Oliver La Farge. By most accounts, Witter Bynner served as the social epicenter for the colony, hosting large and frequent parties. His good friend novelist Harvey Fergusson remembered that "I have never seen a host work so hard and yet so joyfully to entertain guests who had nothing in common except that they were fascinated by Bynner. He sat down and played [the piano] and sang out of an enormous repertoire . . . which brought youth back to life in all kinds of people and brought them together."

Bynner, Harvard-educated and an editor of the popular *McClure's Magazine* before World War I, had enjoyed a rather interesting path to Santa Fe and also to the first rank of American poetry. Engaged to Edna St. Vincent Millay (though he was homosexual), Bynner and his close associate Arthur Davison Ficke caused a sensation in literary circles for staging a hoax called "Spectrism," publishing poetry that satirized contemporary poetry styles. It was brilliant and biting; Bynner gained notoriety but maybe lost the respect and goodwill of those poets he lampooned.

During his life, Bynner produced some twenty books, including poetry, plays, and translations of Greek tragedies and Chinese classics. His translation of Lao-tzu's spiritual classic *Tao Te Ching*, which Bynner dubbed *The Way of Life*, rendered the ancient Chinese verses in lively contemporary phrasing.

Bynner's social rival was Mabel Dodge Luhan. During Mabel's early years in Taos, the two powerhouses coexisted on friendly terms, paying each other visits to show off celebrity guests. With the arrival of D. H. Lawrence and his wife Frieda, however, their rivalry quickly turned intense, tinged with overtones of power, jealousy, and sexual innuendo. His acid 1929 play, *Cake*, is a thinly masked satire of Mabel's queenly wiles and arrogance.

Thus, between the two legendary hosts of northern New Mexico paraded a galaxy of America's creative talent between 1920 and 1950. The names include novas and supernovas, comets and constellations: Frost, Garbo, Stokowski, Sandburg, Cather, Flynn, Hayworth, O'Keeffe, Stravinsky, Auden, and many others.

Another powerful personality who mediated between Mabel and Witter (in fact, she mediated between just about everyone and everything she cared for) was Mary Austin. Prodigious of literary output and powerful in her will and force of personality, Mary Austin had earned a national reputation as a writer and public speaker. Her interests ranged from environmental issues to ethnic cultures of Native Americans and Hispanic Americans to a personal mysticism and worship of the pristine landscape of northern New Mexico.

Truly an independent force, Austin had spent years in Carmel's art colony, becoming friends with the likes of John Muir, Ambrose Bierce, and Jack London. In 1907, she embarked for Europe, where she spent three years. While Mabel Dodge Luhan was hosting sumptuous dinner parties at her Villa Corunia, Mary Austin was infiltrating the literary circles of H. G. Wells and George Bernard Shaw.

After her European stint, Austin returned to America and settled in New York City, continuing her intense activity and publishing *A Woman of Genius,* among six other books. During Woodrow Wilson's presidency, Mary became a frequent guest of Mabel Dodge's infamous salons in Greenwich Village, where progressive and avant-garde people and ideas held forth. Among the celebrated guests at Mabel's salons, Mary Austin befriended Bill Haywood, Emma Goldman, John Reed, Lincoln Steffens, and Margaret Sanger. Mabel and Mary would become lifelong friends and allies, especially later in New Mexico when they fought to defeat the Holm-Bursum Bill, which would have deprived the Pueblos of huge tracts of grazing land.

After World War I, America had settled into a conservative mood of getting back to the nation's business. Much of the radical zeal of the prewar years was gone.

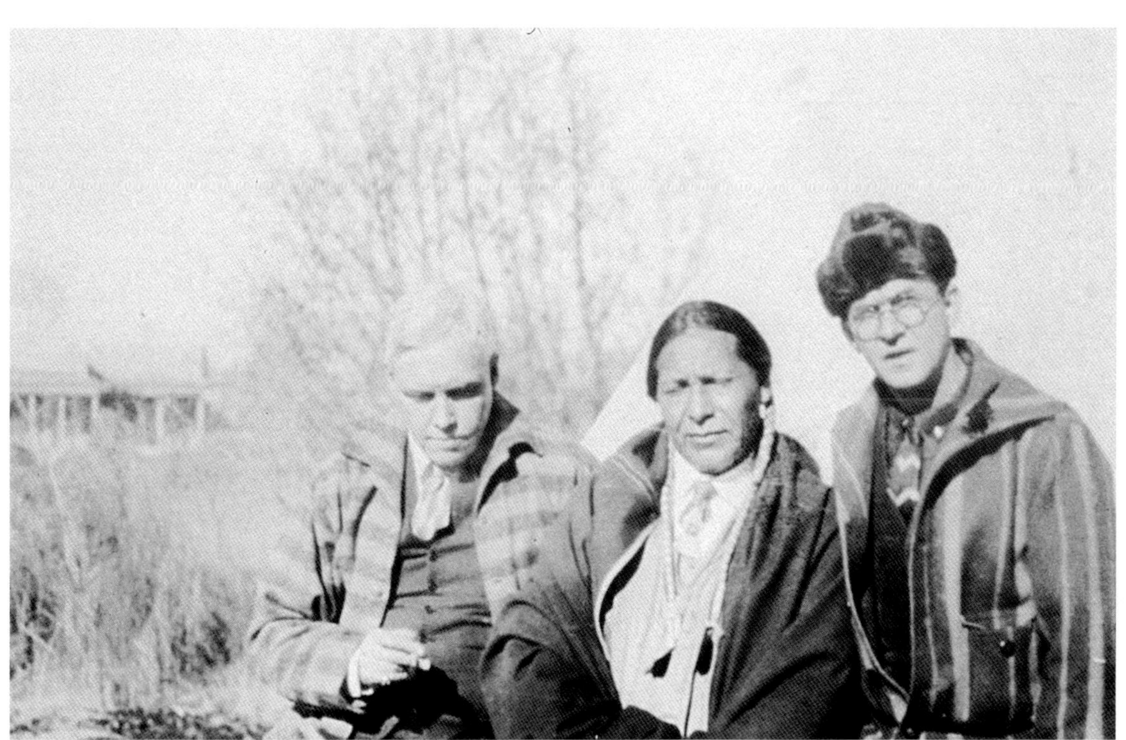

Carl Van Vechten, Tony Luhan, and Witter Bynner.

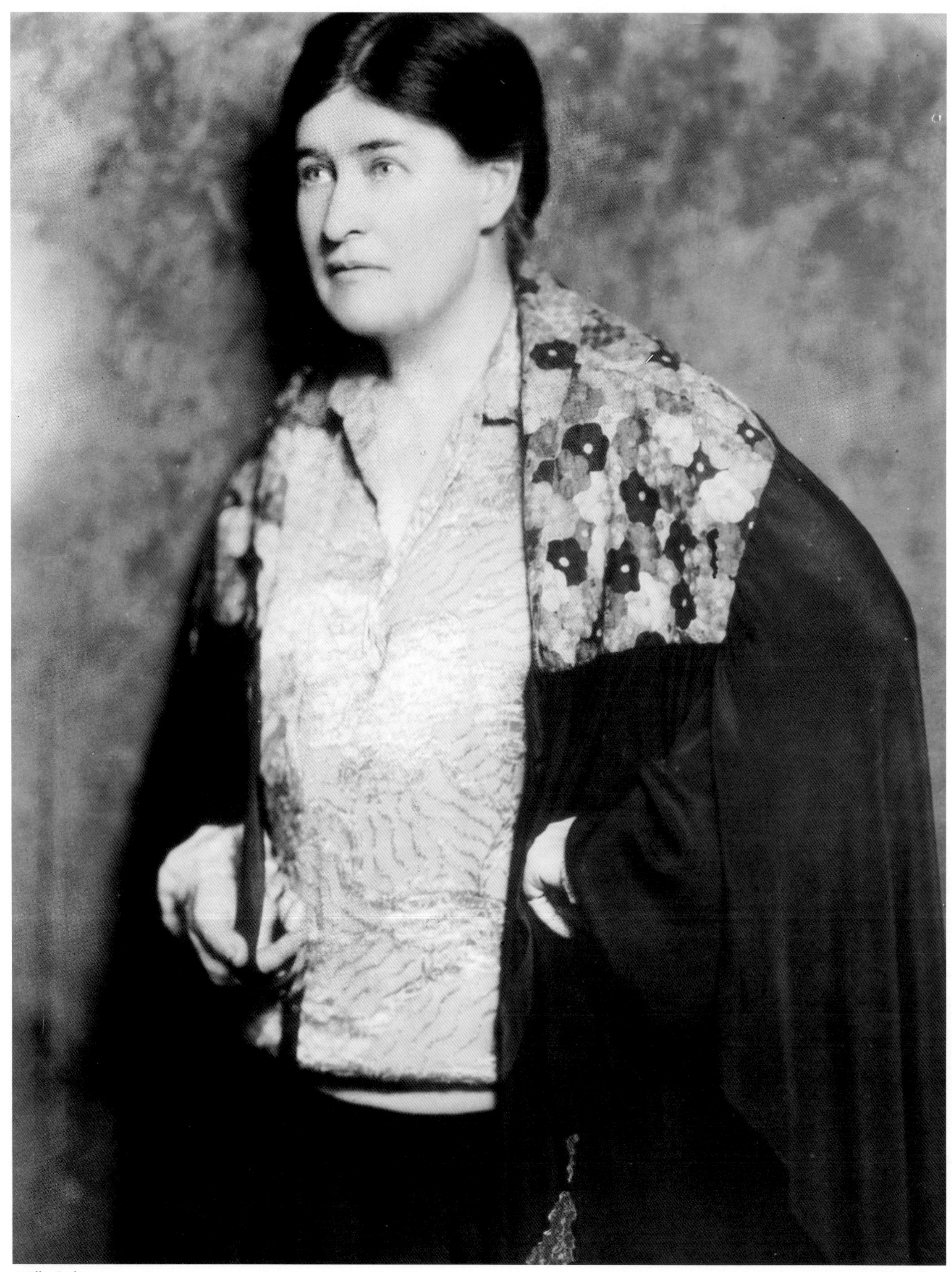

Willa Cather.

Mabel Dodge herself had married artist Maurice Sterne in 1916 and discovered a remote sanctuary in New Mexico, abandoning forever the cosmopolitan charms of Gotham. For Mary Austin, the calls from Taos and Carmel were irresistible. Still, Austin would not settle in Santa Fe until 1924. For twelve years, from Bynner's arrival in 1922 until Mary Austin's death in 1934, the Santa Fe Writers' Colony enjoyed its sunniest days before the Great Depression darkened all horizons.

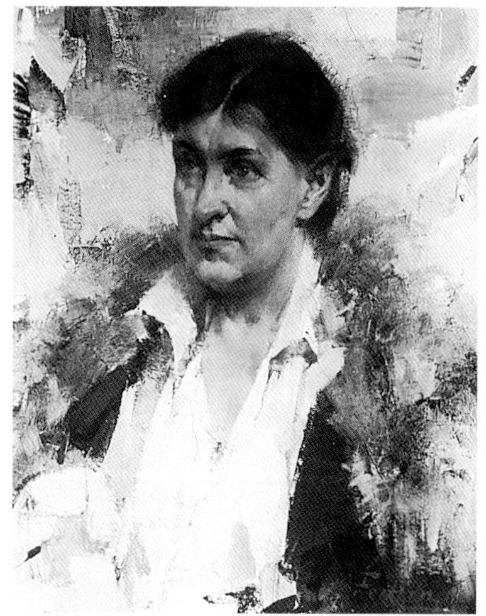

Willa Cather, portrait by Nicolai Fechin.

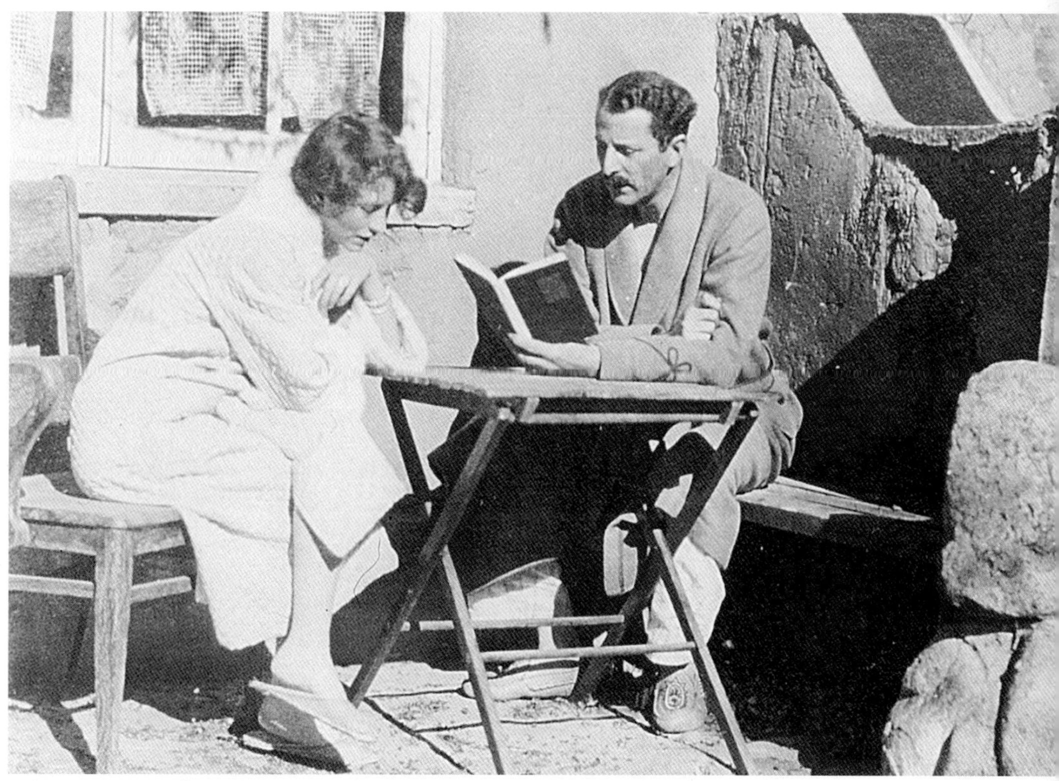

Edna St. Vincent Millay and Arthur Davison Ficke enjoy a morning poetry reading outside Witter Bynner's home in Santa Fe, 1926.

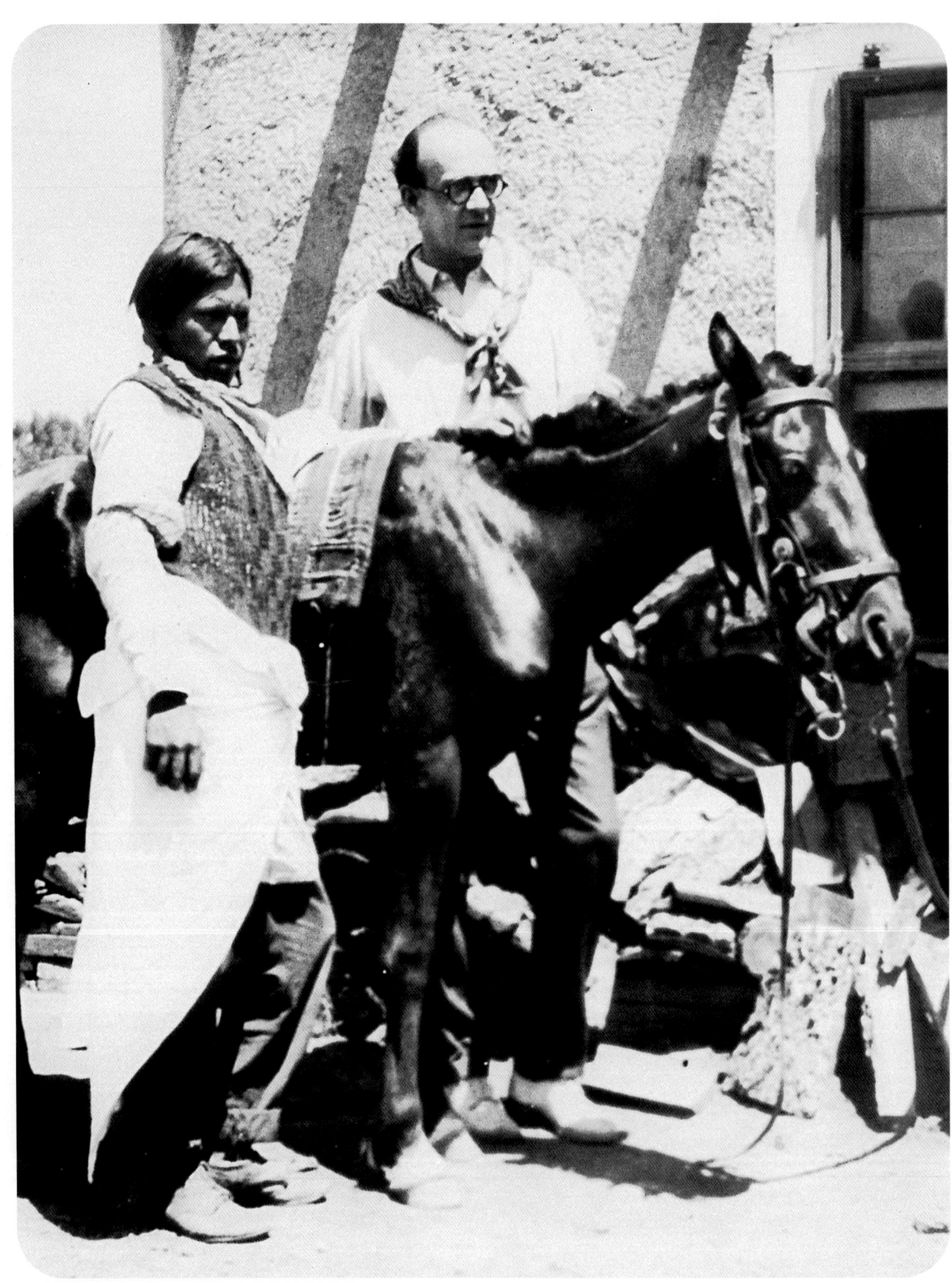

Witter Bynner and Taos Pueblo Indian, circa 1925.

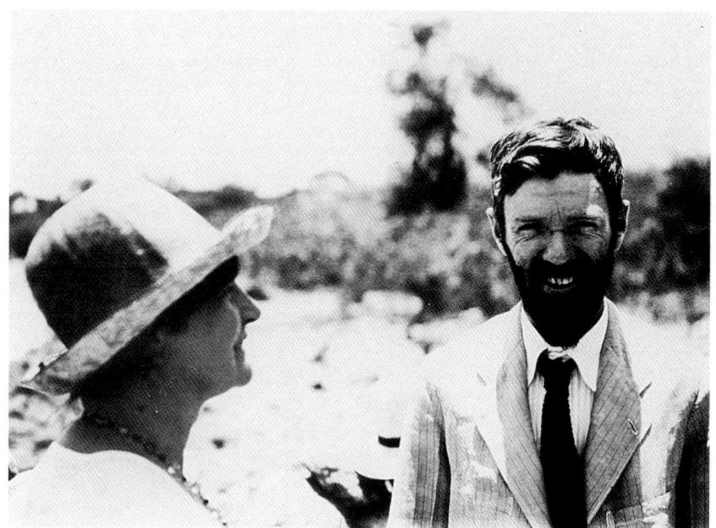

Frieda and D. H. Lawrence spent their first night in New Mexico at Witter Bynner's house, September 1922.

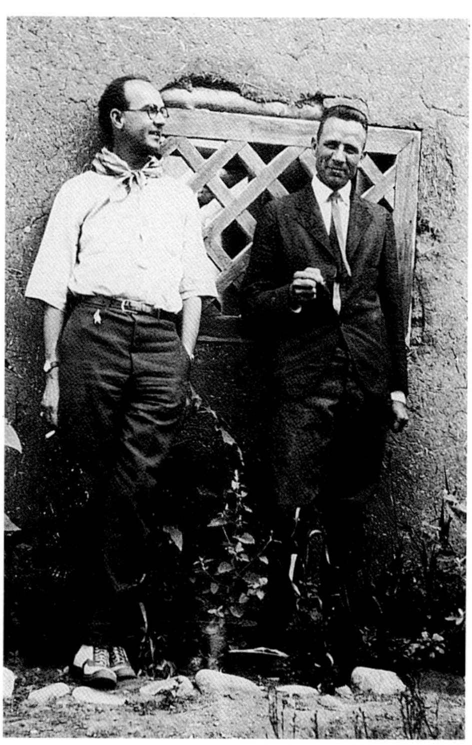

Witter Bynner and Harvey Fergusson, circa 1925.

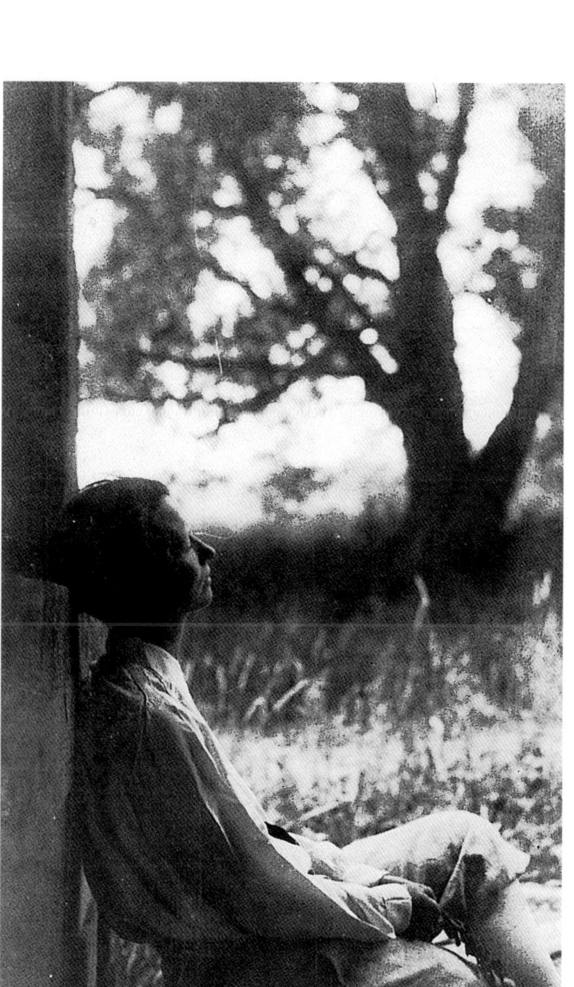

Edna St. Vincent Millay enjoys a thoughtful moment.

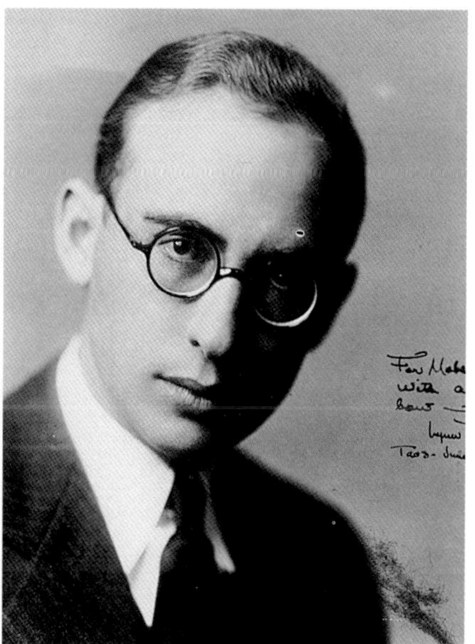

One of America's foremost playwrights, Lynn Riggs enjoyed giving public readings in Santa Fe during the 1930s.

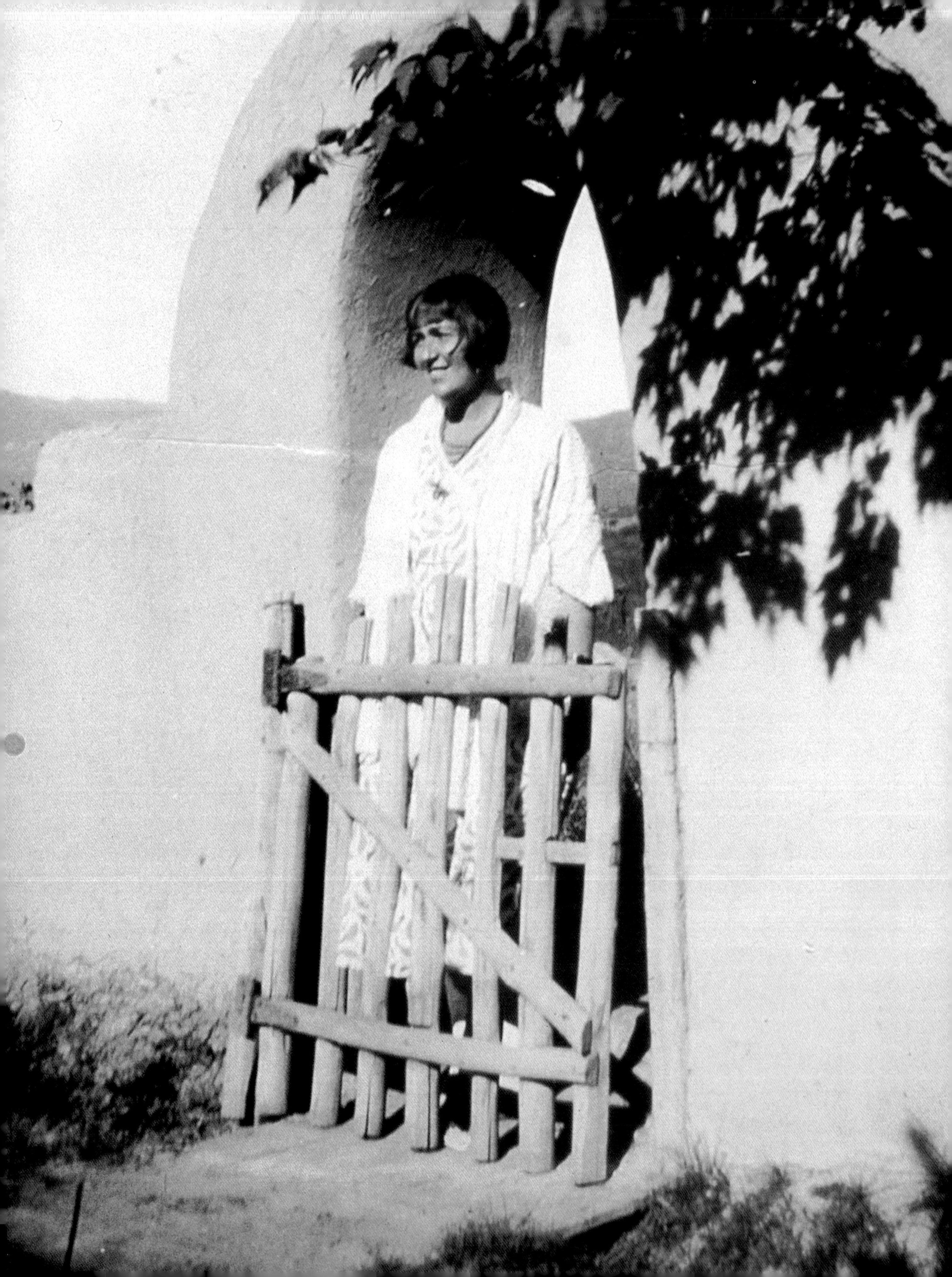

Talons for Talent: Portrait of Mabel Dodge Luhan

The years of carefree decadence at the Villa Corunia near Florence ended for Mabel Dodge and her husband Edwin and their young son, John, in 1912 when Mabel decided it was time to go home. The family settled into an apartment at 23 Fifth Avenue in New York City, and Edwin took a job as an architect at 101 Fifth Avenue.

During these early years in New York, Mabel began to meet and acquire the friends who would become part of her social galaxy for the rest of her life, many becoming frequent guests at the Taos estate in later years. Journalist and photographer Carl Van Vechten met Mabel at a party soon after her arrival and quickly became a lifelong confidante. Another important friend Mabel met soon after her arrival in New York was journalist Hutchins Hapgood, who was heavily involved in labor politics.

It appears through Hapgood's observation that Mabel was beginning to formulate her spiritual being and personality at this time; describing Mabel as "God-drunk," Hapgood noted:

If at any time she became aware of something lying just out of reach, she was intensely restless until she had drawn it into her web. She was always talking about "It"; and this was why Mabel and I understood one another. I have been conscious since my childhood of the unseen cause of all seen things, which gives to all seen things their superlative beauty; and have been engaged in the hopeless quest of the cause.

Perceptively, Hapgood also described the peculiar attraction that emanated from Mabel—one that could equally repel and inspire loathing. Hapgood once asked fellow radical journalist Lincoln Steffens if Mabel was not like a cut flower, rootless and voraciously seeking nourishment from other people.

Hapgood quickly assessed Mabel's flaws, and they were many, among them her

. . . eager, sometimes graceless searchings, her terrific but formless needs, her occasional sharp unkindness, her extraordinary and otherwise incomprehensible jealousy, her inability to let go of anything even for a moment within her domain.

Like many others, Hutchins Hapgood chose to ignore or endure her shortcomings because he was charmed and fascinated by Mabel (and probably in love with her). She had an inscrutable sphinxlike presence that filled a room; in close quarters it could suffocate.

Through Hapgood and Steffans, Mabel soon met many of the leading radicals in New York, including Bill Haywood, Emma Goldman, Max Eastman, and Margaret Sanger. At the famous Armory Show of 1913, which introduced Europe's leading avant-garde artists such as Matisse and Duchamp to America, Mabel met many of New York's emerging modernists.

Mabel Dodge Luhan in the gateway of Tony Luhan's Taos house, circa 1925.

The Armory Show marked a turning point for Mabel. Dazzled by her new acquaintances, she became disenchanted with her bourgeois lifestyle and husband. Edwin Dodge left their Fifth Avenue apartment and never returned. Mabel produced an article for *Arts and Decoration* magazine called "Speculations, or Post-Impressions in Prose," describing the Paris atelier of Gertrude and Leo Stein, praising Gertrude's literary inventions and their art collection, which included many of the Armory Show artists. Mabel had become a sensation, gaining the approval of New York's art elite and starting a literary career at the same time. Her notoriety gained her favor with photographer Alfred Steiglitz, who operated the progressive Gallery 291, and a flock of young modernist artists, including Andrew Dasburg, John Marin, and Marsden Hartley. All of them except Steiglitz would later do important work in New Mexico.

Flush with her newfound fame, Mabel was highly suggestible to Hutch Hapgood's idea that she host "evenings" where intellectuals could freely discuss progressive ideas. Lincoln Steffens asserted that Mabel had a gift, similar to a hetaera in Greek mythology. She attracted people like moths to a flame. Men were inspired by her; their minds, hearts, and souls revealed their secrets to her. She would be a perfect salon hostess.

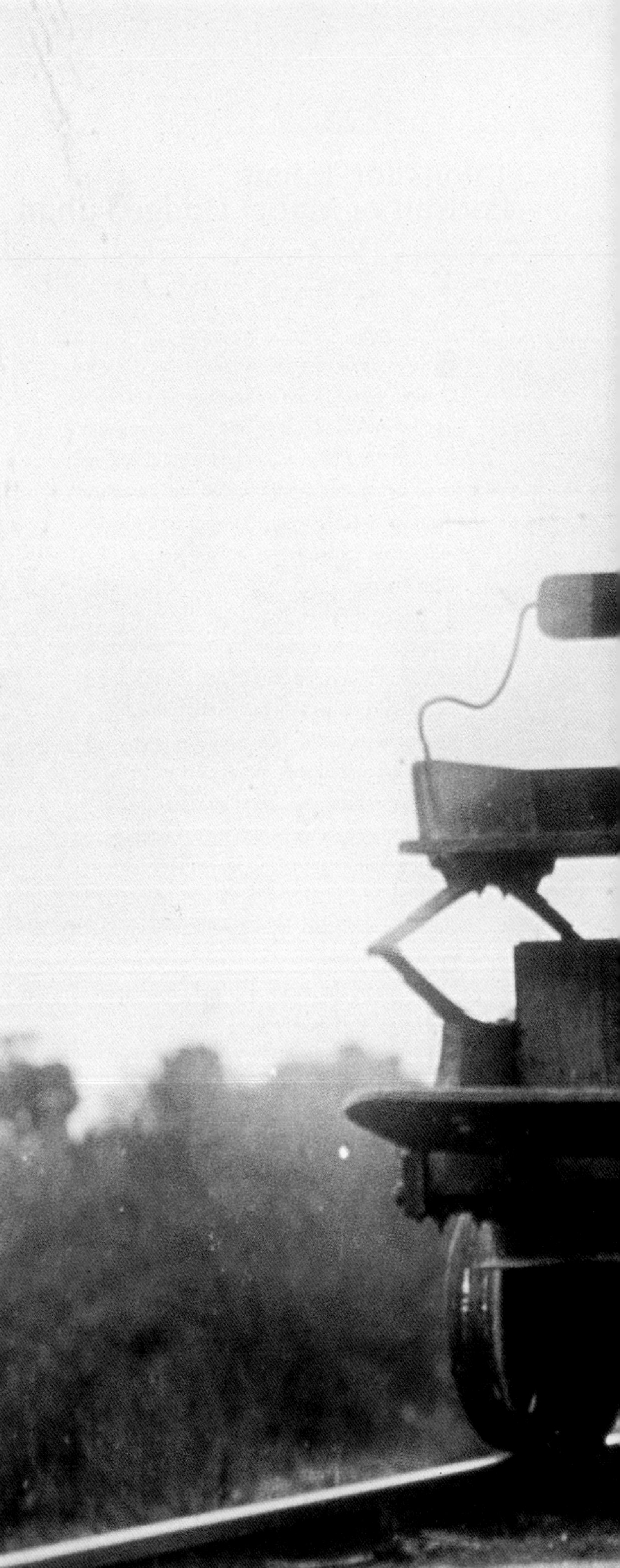

John Reed (center) and unidentified companions on railroad car, circa 1915.

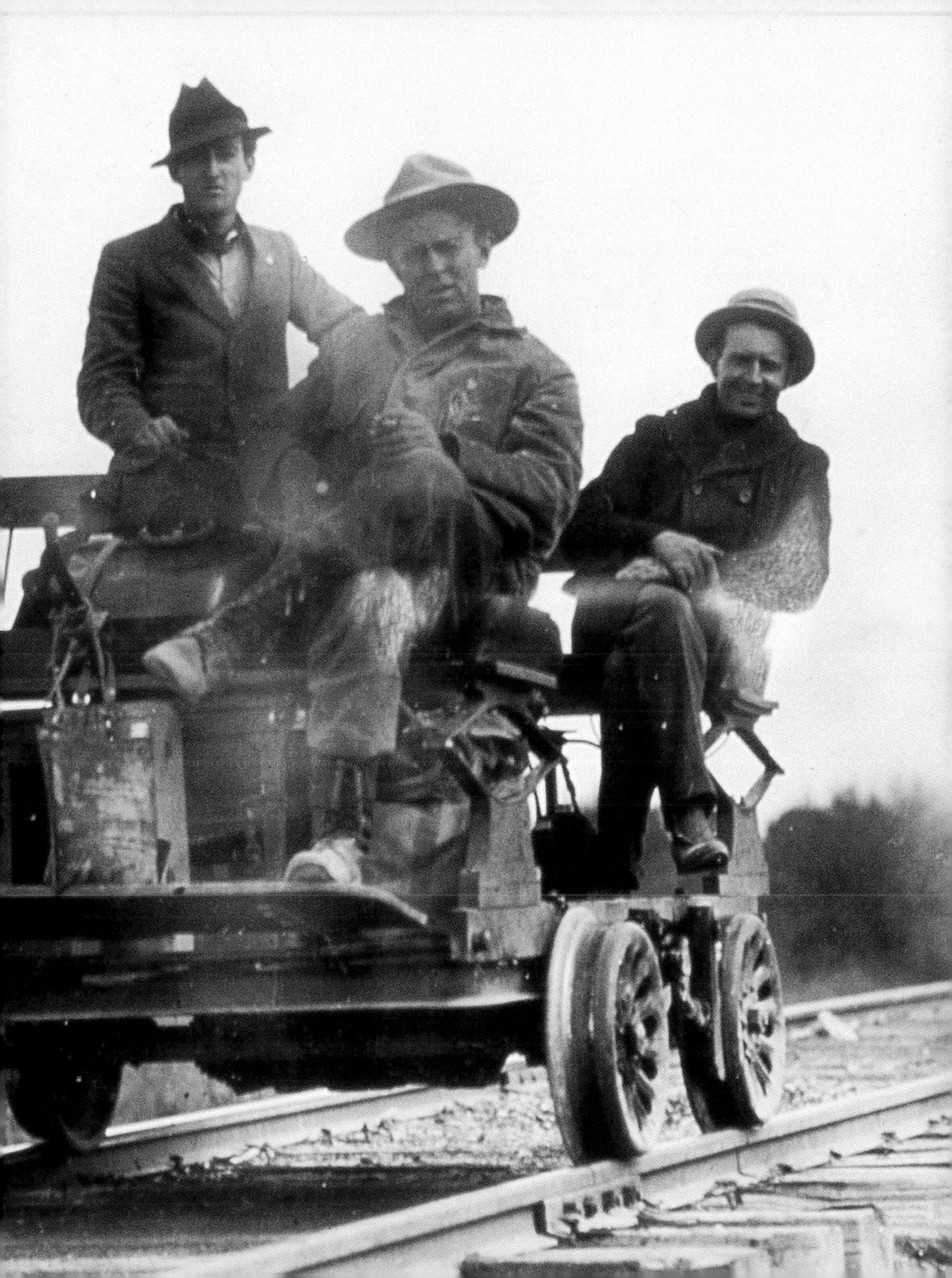

Many recall Mabel answering her door at 23 Fifth Avenue on Sunday evenings dressed in a long white gown accentuated by a vivid scarf. Flowing wine, spirited conversations and debates, and cold-cut suppers at midnight proved to be an exhilarating combination. Mabel's salons became all the rage for leftist intellectuals and aesthetes. Often Mabel would introduce a controversial topic such as birth control or even modern poetry, retire to the back of the room, and silently watch her guests rhetorically devour each other.

During those highly charged radical years before World War I, Greenwich Village was too small for John Reed and Mabel Dodge to miss each other. Just graduated from Harvard (1910), Reed was brilliant, burly, curly-haired, and full of energy, especially for socialist causes. After hearing him speak at a labor rally in 1913, Mabel was smitten. Of her many conquests, lovers, and husbands, perhaps Reed was the crazy love of her life, causing such passion that she pursued him on his journalistic assignments across Europe and even to El Paso en route to finding and interviewing Pancho Villa.

For nearly two years until World War I broke out, John Reed and Mabel played cat-and-mouse, and occasionally house, together, causing a minor scandal among their friends and New York's bohemian circles. Mabel's salons continued sporadically, sometimes with her, sometimes without her, and her friends took notice. Handsome young Andrew Dasburg (who probably had a crush on Mabel) went so far as to paint a dramatic new painting called *The Absence of Mabel Dodge,* which was a catharsis for Dasburg but was hailed as a breakthrough by his friends.

In the end, Mabel committed the mistake of which all obsessed lovers are guilty: she smothered Reed, and he left her in Paris for another woman. As the war in Europe was darkening, Mabel, crestfallen, fled back to New York but resolved to restart her salon life. Reed's adventures in Bolshevik Russia would be romanticized many years later in the 1981 film *Reds,* in which Warren Beatty portrayed Mabel's long-lost lover.

Back in Manhattan, Mabel's attention was drawn to the dreams of dancer Isadora Duncan. The two women had become acquainted during childhood, and now Isadora was hoping to provide dance instruction for poor children, perhaps driven by the ghastly memory of seeing her own children drown on the Seine River. A disastrous encounter with New York mayor John P. Mitchell dashed Isadora's dreams and Mabel's ardor. But a Duncan recital proved to be the segue for the next chapter of Mabel's life.

She noticed an attractive man with a "dark brown look," who turned out to be artist Maurice Sterne. Sterne was becoming well known in New York art circles, especially for a series of neo-Primitive paintings he had just completed in Bali. Sterne was looking for a patroness, and Mabel was in need of someone who could fill the emotional void left by Jack Reed. They were drawn to each

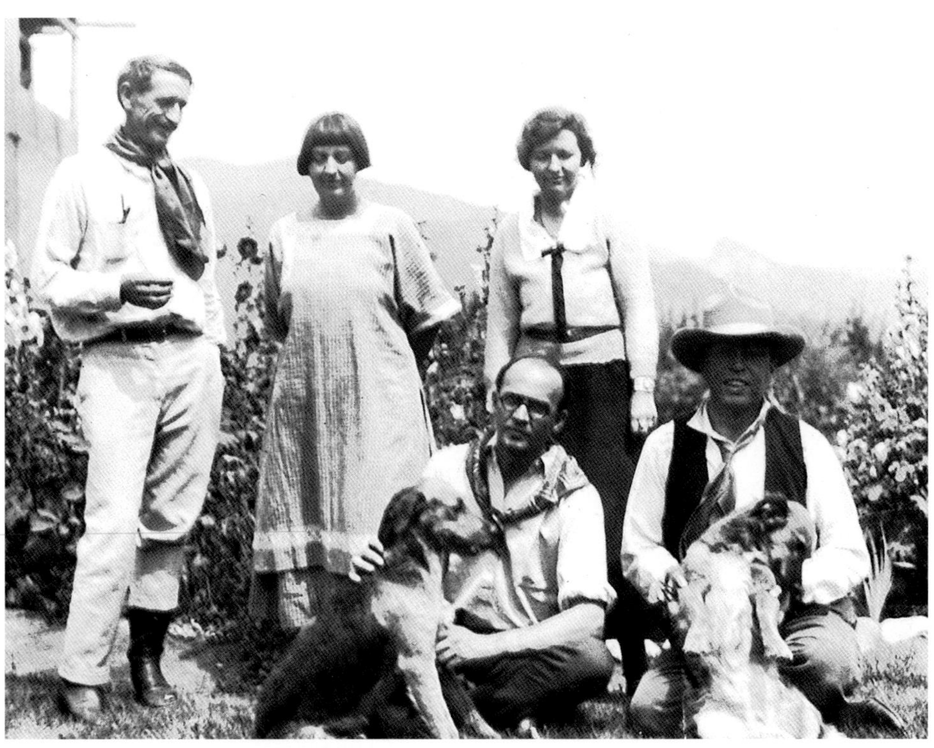

Left to right: William Penhallow Henderson, Mabel Dodge Luhan, Alice Corbin; seated: Witter Bynner and Ralph Myers.

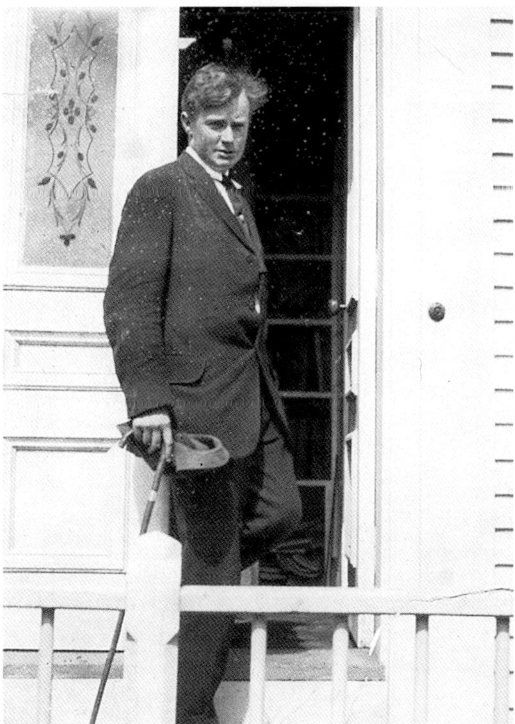

Andrew Dasburg, circa 1914.

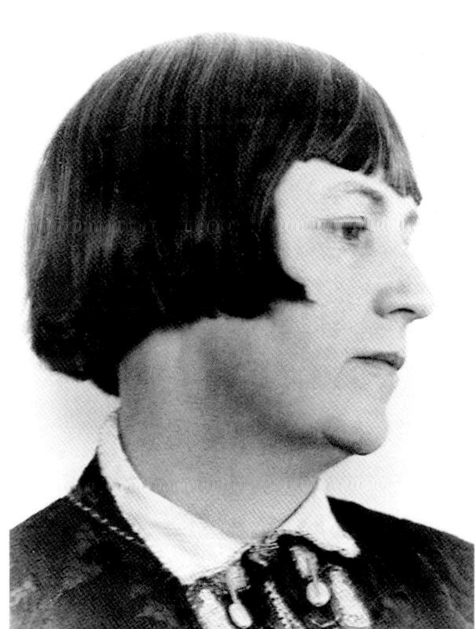

Mabel Dodge Luhan, circa 1930.

other in a curious way, often vindictive. Mabel enjoyed Sterne's sexual charms but secretly despised what she considered the parasitic nature of artists, including Maurice.

Maurice found himself drawn into Mabel's vortex, not fully comprehending the attraction even years later. In contrast to the fine-featured beauties he favored, Mabel's physical charms seemed matronly. Her dark bobbed hair and eyes were intense. To Maurice, they were "cool, dark grey pools shaded with long, black lashes." These were offset by her voice, which soothed "like a viola, soft, caressing, mellow, with confidential overtones."

The couple enjoyed retreats at Provincetown, Massachusetts, and Croton-on-Hudson, north of New York City, while their friends observed the couple's cycle of fighting, reconciliation, and discussions of marriage. Seemingly, they decided to marry on a whim in August 1917. Maurice wanted a wife to accompany him on a trip to Wyoming. Mabel impulsively accepted his proposal in the morning, and in the afternoon they were married. All who knew them could see the mismatch but to no avail.

Mabel and Maurice always had sparked teapot tempests during their days of cohabitation. Just about anything could trigger an argument—a cat's sexuality, a move on the Ouija board, or the stink of Maurice's after-dinner cigars. Only sex seemed to keep them together. Finally, after just a few weeks of a stormy marriage, Maurice sought advice.

His doctor suggested Santa Fe. He'd heard it was a great place. Why not go and paint Indians? For Maurice, it was the right idea at the right time. For Mabel, it proved to be the opening of a Pandora's box, or perhaps (as former New Mexico governor Bruce King liked to say) a box of Pandoras. By November 1917, Mabel grew restless and lonely. Maurice's simple telegram inviting her to come visit and save the Indians was all she needed. A cold delayed her exit, but on December 17 she said goodbye to Manhattan.

In typical Mabel fashion, she arrived in New Mexico with an arrogant and condescending attitude. Among the first persons she met in Santa Fe was Alice Corbin Henderson, who tried to draw Mabel out on the subject of poetry. Mabel, irritable and disoriented, wanted to get away from the social niceties. She conjured up a place from deep within her subconscious memory. She wanted to go to Taos.

In the dead of winter, on a dirt road through the awesome canyons of the Rio Grande, this was a full day's journey. Alice Corbin and her Santa Fe friends (and Maurice) were stunned at Mabel's impulsiveness. But she was delighted with her own paradoxical self-control and lack of control of the situation. Her own first impressions of the tiny village were Zen-like. How could this haphazard, dusty little town coexist with the majestic grandeur of its towering mountain crown?

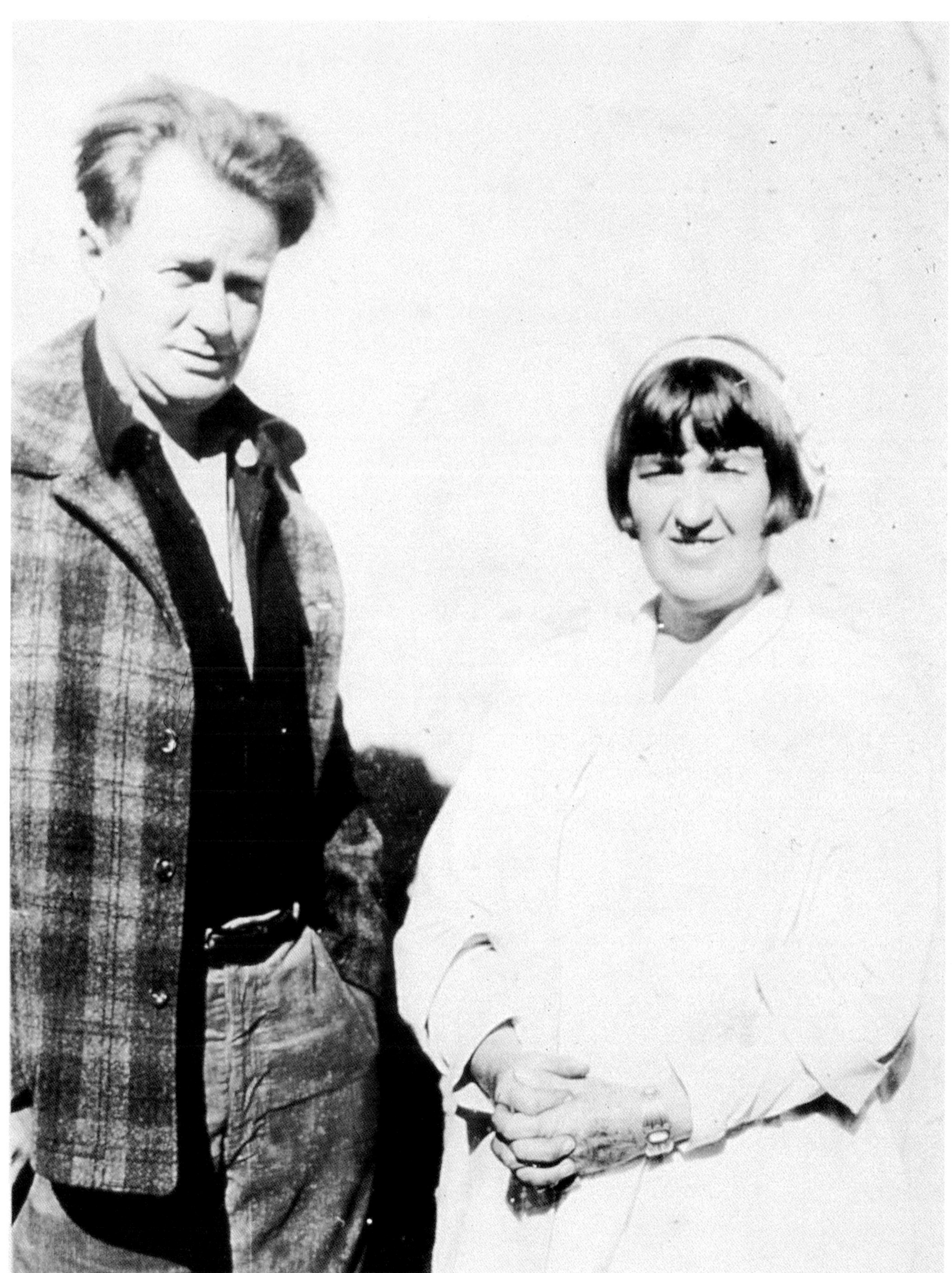

Andrew Dasburg and Mabel, circa 1920.

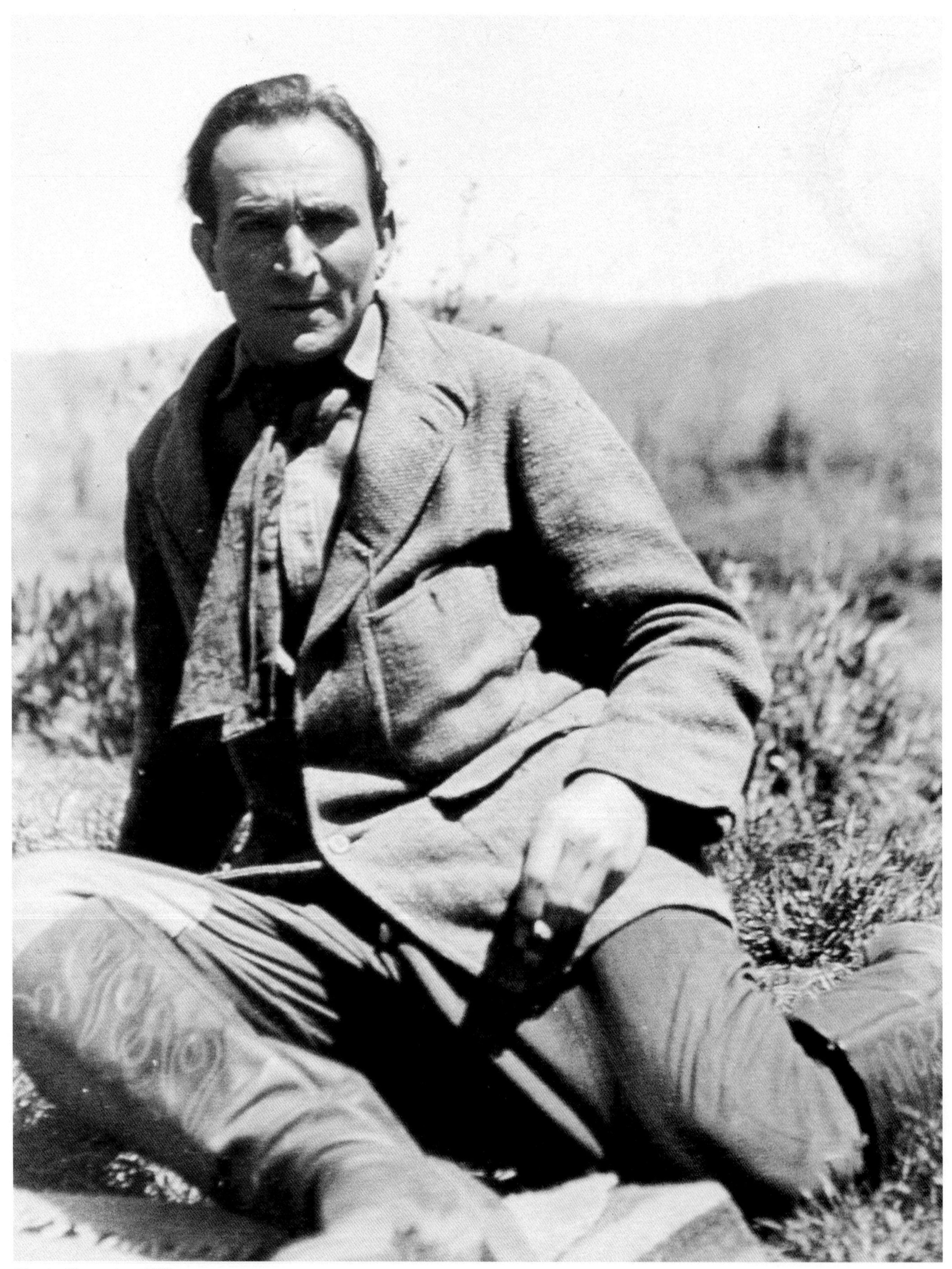

Maurice Sterne, circa 1917.

Perspectives on Mabel by Her Contemporaries

The following is a fictional portrait of Mabel as Mary Kittredge:

Mary Kittredge was an extravagant person. She was almost as extravagant as the God who made her, and he so loaded her with whims and vigor and talent and money and a thirst after the true meaning of life, that she acquired the renown and popularity of a circus. She was always just entering upon some new spiritual experiment that involved a complete break with everything that had gone before. Either she was getting married, or she was getting divorced, or she was testing out unmarried love, . . . or snake-charming, or Hindu philosophy, or Hindu turbans, or female farming, or opium-eating, or flute playing. There was nothing in the world that Mary could not want to do, and there was very little that she could not, in a surprisingly short space of time, do. She waged a perpetual war on habit, a war in which she had already routed and driven from the field three husbands, nine lovers, and a half-dozen religions, although she was only thirty-five years old, and as she possessed an enormous fortune, and by right of "heredity" a certain position in American society, her career and character were well known. She was a public institution.

—Max Eastman, Venture *(1927).*

Mabel was born bored. She had an appetite for tasting life in all its aspects. She tasted and spat it out. She was unsentimental: she sized up a situation between two people and proceeded to break it to pieces as soon as possible. Whatever was wilting, she aided and abetted to wilt. In that way she was dangerous and cruel.

—Dorothy Brett, "Autobiography," South Dakota Review.

Mabel has already decided that the rebels are part of the great world-movement, whatever that may be. . . . I think she expects to find General Villa a sort of male Gertrude Stein, or at least a Mexican Steiglitz. . . . With me in my bright yellow corduroy suit and Mabel in her orange hat and satin-lined tiger-skin hunting jacket with . . . an expense account and a roll of blankets and 14 kinds of pills and bandages, we shall descend upon El Paso.

—John Reed, December 1913, as quoted in New Woman: New Worlds *by Lois Palken.*

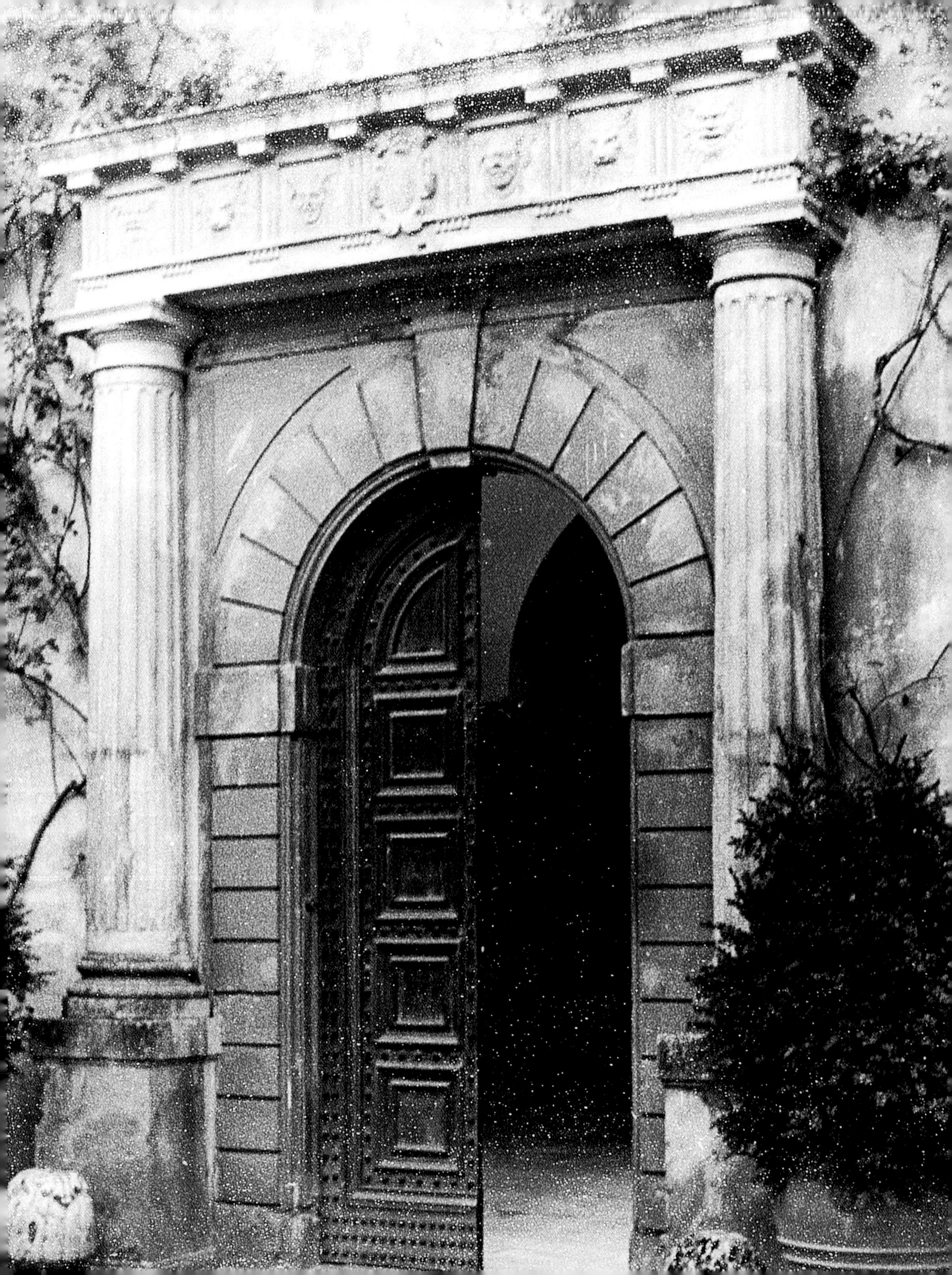

Mabel's Houses: Architecture of Passion

For many of the creative spirits who discovered New Mexico during the Mabel Dodge Luhan era, the opportunity to live in an adobe home was compelling. The humble building material embodied everything held sacred by the artists: it was ancient and traditional, durable yet malleable, handcrafted and organic, and it weathered beautifully. The sun-dried earthen bricks implied a connection to both Pueblo and Hispanic cultures, and best of all, it was affordable.

Nearly every artist consummated a love affair with adobe in highly personal ways. Mabel and Hal (Witter) Bynner shaped the bricks into sprawling *salas* (living rooms) and dining rooms where they could stage their lavish parties and human dramas. Photographers Edward Weston, Paul Strand, and Ansel Adams luxuriated in the subtle textural effects of light on the walls, aged like an *anciano's* (elder's) skin. Visual artists rose to the challenge of animating the large expanses of neutral earthen wall colors with flashes of brilliant flowers or sky. Poets interpreted the old adobe buildings as a metaphor for people, time, life itself.

Few of the artists in the 1920s, however, had the generous resources of Mabel Dodge or Hal Bynner to fully realize their architectural fantasies. Most were able to locate and purchase interesting properties to rehabilitate and redecorate in the new Pueblo Revival style. Thus, members of the Taos Society of Artists, such as Blumenschein and Couse, found great studio homes near the Taos Plaza. Others, by pure genius (notably Nicolai Fechin and William Penhallow Henderson), were able to build distinctive adobe houses.

For Mabel Dodge, architecture and interior design became an intuitive means of creative and personal expression. Symbolically, her residences in Italy, New York, and Taos embodied her transformation from an intellectual dilettante and pleasure hostess in

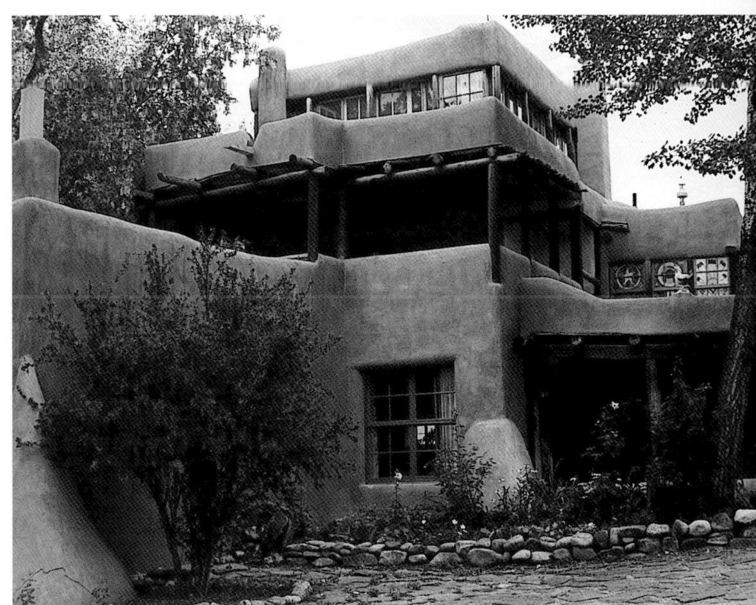

Mabel's Big House in Taos was crowned with a solarium on the third floor and a glazed bathroom on the second.

The main entrance to Mabel Dodge's Villa Corunia in Tuscany articulates Renaissance ideals of classical order and reason.

Florence to a sophisticated salon hostess in New York City and a romantic spiritual adventurer in Taos.

The exquisite Villa Corunia near Florence was a shell of a palace when Edwin and Mabel Dodge found it in 1905. Crowning a small hill that rose within a bowl-like valley, the villa had been built in the late fifteenth century for a physician of the Medici family, the powerful rulers of Florence. It had everything Edwin and Mabel Dodge were looking for: generous grounds, southern exposure, rooms with a view (of Florence), and distinguished architecture. For Edwin, just graduated from the Beaux-Arts Academy in Paris, the villa provided a splendid project in restoration. For Mabel, the villa became a stage for her manifestation as an American princess in the heart of Renaissance Italy.

The Dodges delighted in restoring the villa. Edwin devoted himself to rehabilitating its architectural grandeur and formal gardens, and Mabel supervised the interior decor and furnishings. Edwin discovered a buried *cinquecento cortile,* or columned fifteenth-century courtyard, within the entrance to the villa that was transformed into a formal entrance hall.

Mabel had free rein to decorate the villa's interior to suit her whims, both sexual and psychological. The formal Renaissance dining room, furnished with heavy carved Italian antiques, was the scene of

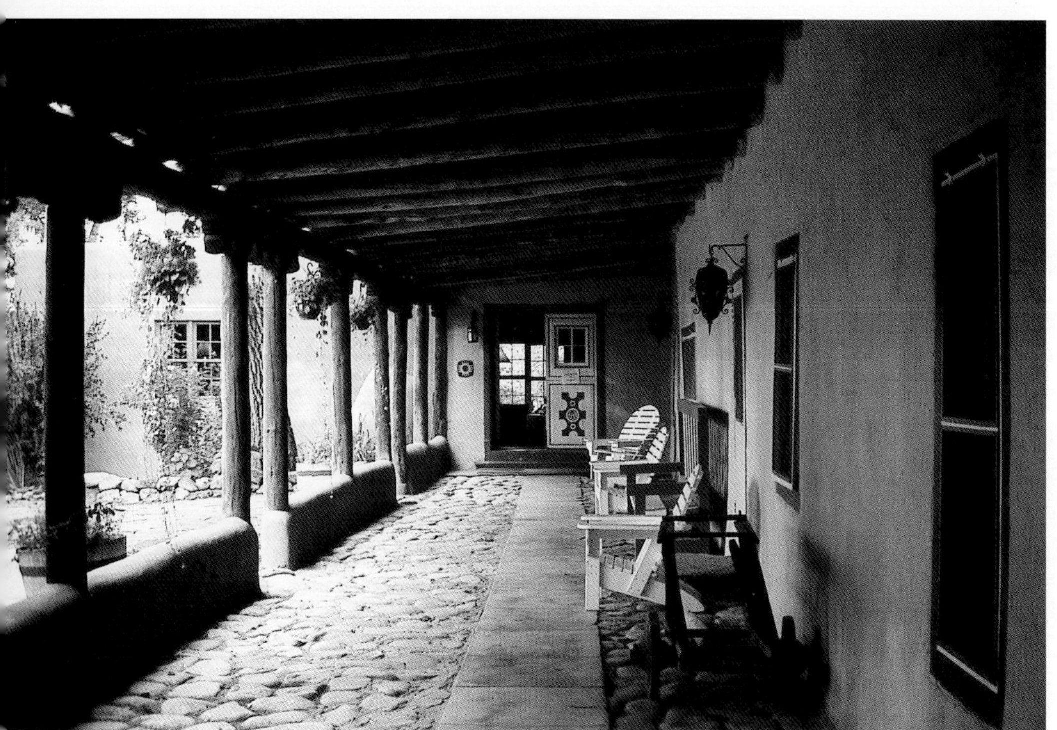

A deep and generous portal links together the long and rambling elements of Mabel's Los Gallos estate.

much sumptuous dining and revelry. The yellow salon was designed in a sober and sophisticated French neoclassical style, conducive to reflection. Mabel's bedroom, on the other hand, featured a hidden trapdoor in the ceiling for a lover to descend into the midnight-blue realm of her desire.

Lois Palken Rudnick has reflected on Mabel's unorthodox transfiguration of the villa's architecture for highly personal ends:

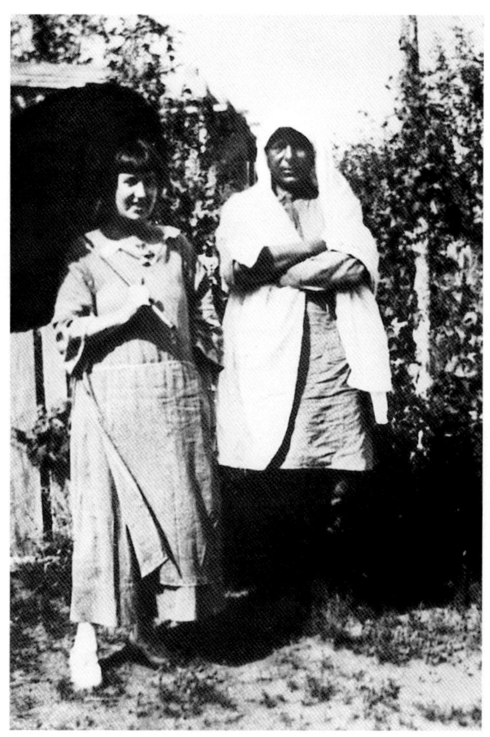

Mabel Dodge Sterne and Tony Luhan, about 1920.

The non-sequitur style [of Gertrude Stein] was appropriate for expressing Mabel's mode of existence at this time. . . . In the villa, one walked from a room inspired by the nineteenth-century English arts-and-crafts movement to the grandeur of a cinquecento salon, rooms that were juxtaposed for no other reason than they pleased Mabel's taste. The roles she played were, as we have seen, even more illogically juxtaposed than the villa's rooms. Depending on the day or mood, Mabel projected the mental habits of a fin de siecle femme fatale, the hauteur of a Renaissance princess, the lust after status of the arriviste, the innocent coquetry of a Daisy Miller, and a cautious sense of marital propriety.

Mabel's bridge between the old-world villa and the new-world Taos estate was appropriately her Washington Square salon in New York's Greenwich Village. The salon's restrained and mostly neutral interior served as a psychological cleansing for Mabel from the excesses of Florence and also as a subdued stage for the Sunday-evening gatherings.

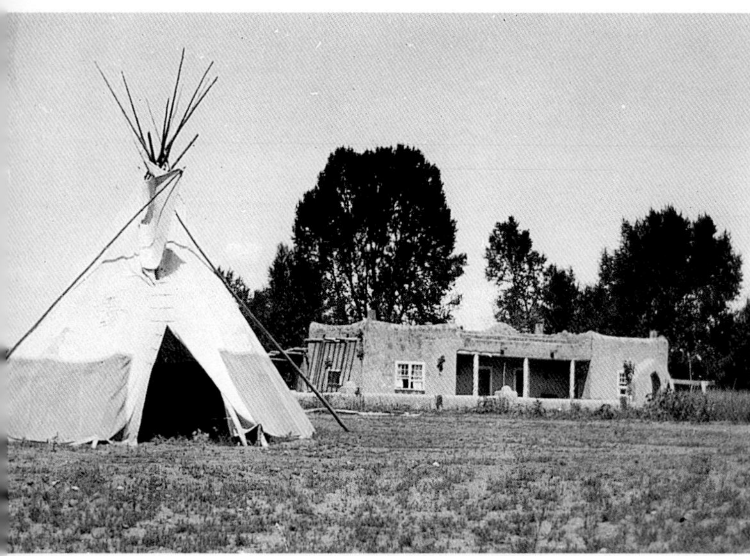

A tipi adds a picturesque counterpoint to one of Mabel's guest houses, about 1925.

Dreams Fulfilled

Upon arriving in Taos, however, Mabel encountered a new style of architectural and human expression far removed from the serene aesthetics of Florence and the vigor of New York. The dialogue of buildings and people in New Mexico was subconscious and silent. It communicated on wavelengths Mabel had not known, stirring her innermost curiosity.

Almost immediately upon arriving in Taos during the Christmas season of 1917, Mabel met Tony Luhan, a Taos Pueblo Indian. Much to husband Maurice Sterne's consternation, Mabel and Tony seemed drawn to each other by powerful and inexplicable forces.

Tony's appearance and presence were unlike anything Mabel had experienced before. In personality, he was her antithesis. Tony's face was noble—a strong nose, full lips, and high cheekbones gave him the profile of a chieftain. His barrel chest and braided pigtails shrouded within the classic Taos men's white shawl lent him the air of an exotic nomad.

Tony had learned how to capitalize on his unique and impressive looks. In his youth he had been a "show Indian," traveling with a Wild West company to Coney Island. He knew how to pose for the cameras and for an audience. In 1905 he appeared in a portrait by famed photographer and anthropologist Edward Curtis as Red Willow, his Pueblo name. Later Tony would become a favorite portrait subject for Ansel Adams, Edward Weston, and Carl Van Vechten.

Mabel and Tony confessed to each other that each had appeared in the other's dreams before their auspicious meeting. During the winter months of 1917–18, Tony appeared sometimes unpredictably and sometimes at Mabel's invitation to have dinner and meet her guests. Though he said little or nothing at all, he occasionally would sing while pounding his tom-tom drum. Tony's hypnotic chanting broke through the veils of Mabel's heart.

Many friends who knew Mabel were amazed and intrigued by her relationship and subsequent marriage to Tony Luhan. How he had managed to "tame" this proud, imperious woman was the topic of much speculation. Mabel admitted that "Tony developed my latent feeling, and made me learn to love for the first time in my life, but he had no need to talk to me or have me talk to him."

Perhaps in bitterness, Maurice Sterne reflected upon Mabel's transformation in Taos:

Part of the problem was that Mabel had always been enthralled by the mystical. She thought that she had finally found what she had been searching for in Tony and in the Indian mystique. As soon as she discovered the Pueblo Indians, she was like someone under hypnosis. She sat entranced when they beat their tom-toms and chanted their weird music. Most of all, their silence fascinated her . . . Mabel found the perfect rainbow . . . Tony was what she needed. Mabel had no vitality or creative power of her own. She was a dead battery who needed constantly to recharge with the juice of some man, though she might leave him dead in the process.

Others guessed that Tony was the first man to satisfy Mabel sexually, but Mabel would not say so explicitly.

By the summer of 1918, as their romance was becoming obvious, Tony suggested a homesite for Mabel on the edge of

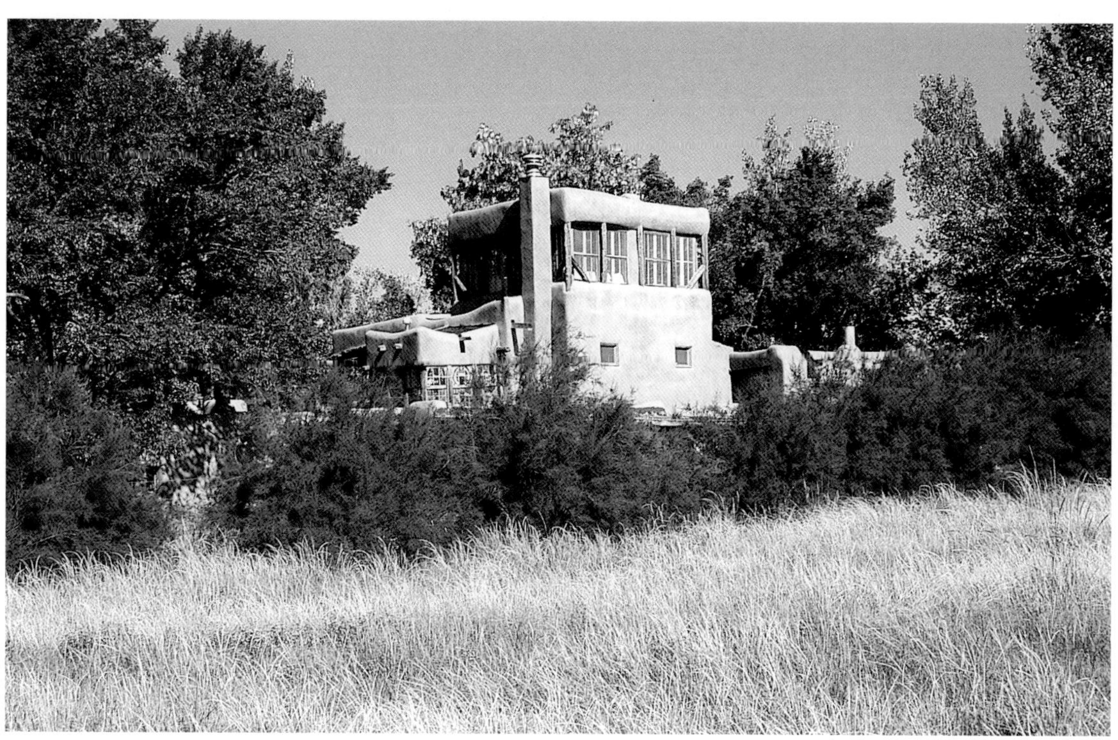

Rear view of the Big House, Mabel's Los Gallos estate.

Taos Pueblo lands. The twelve-acre site included a small adobe homestead dating back to the eighteenth century, orchards, and a traditional *acequia* (irrigation ditch) that ran through the property. It was (and still is) a magnificent estate with unrestricted and uncluttered views of the Taos mountains. In June 1918, Mabel purchased the property and quickly proceeded to hire Tony to organize a Pueblo work crew to build what was to become a sprawling Pueblo Revival villa. The construction of the big house was as much an act of courtship as it was a process of construction. Mabel and Tony communicated daily as if they were building their dream house together. The architectural drawings for the project were scratched in the ground with a stick. It was truly an organic process, and Mabel reveled in it.

In sharp contrast to the Villa Corunia, which was a formal, precisely proportioned block, the Taos estate flowed sinuously across the land, long and low except for the three-story main house. It was eclectic and rambling, even incorporating a log cabin for Mabel's son John.

The work began on the big room and on the small three-room original house. Arched doors were cut in the old house

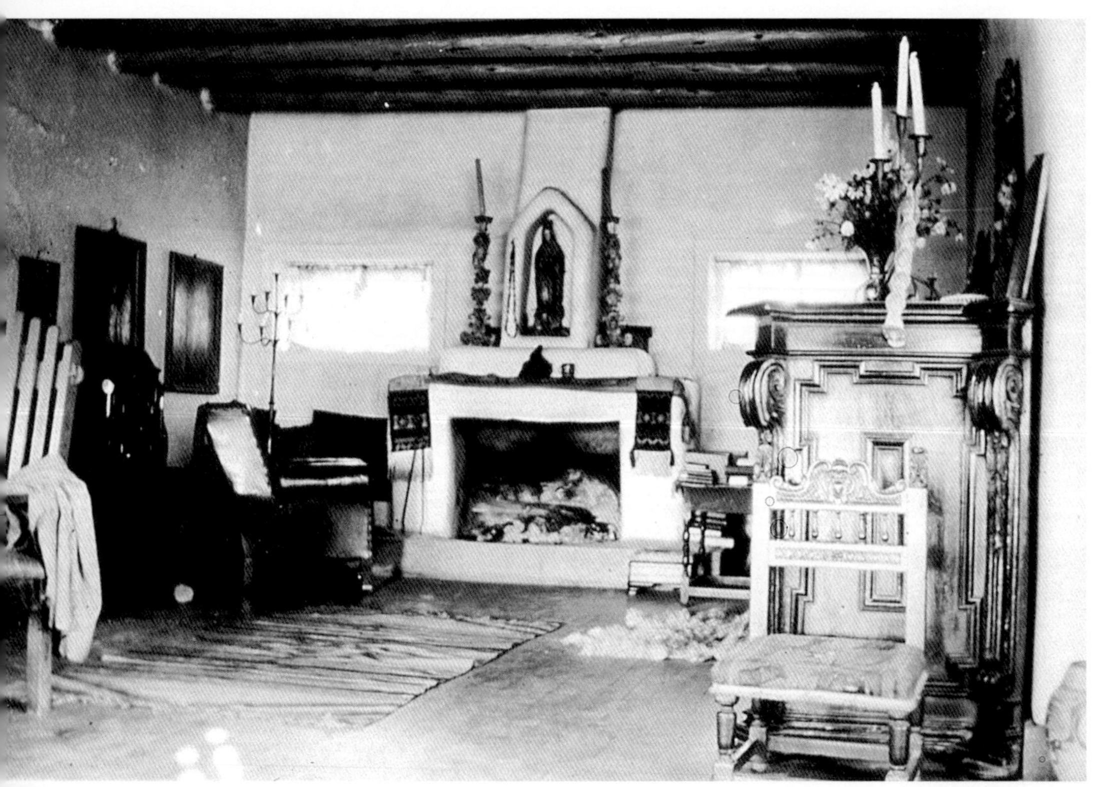

The sala, or living room, of Mabel's home, 1920.

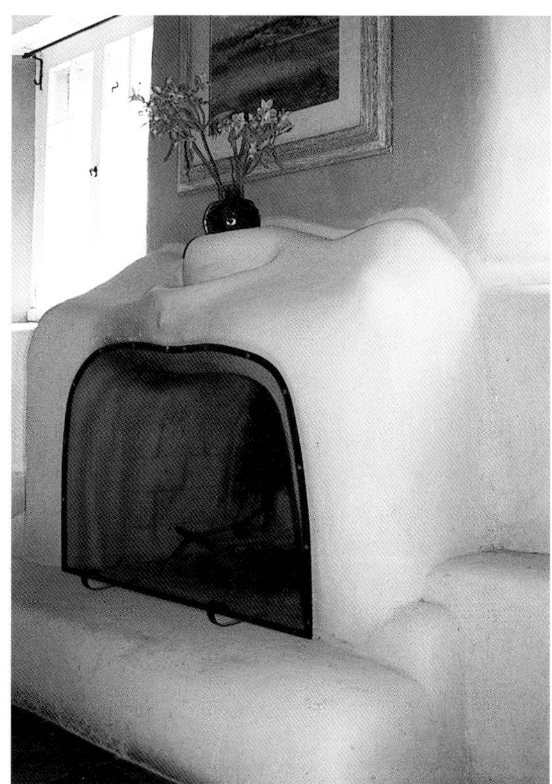

An adobe fireplace in the dining room of the Mabel Dodge Luhan house.

and a long grand portal was added to connect with the Big House. A large generous *sala*, or living room, featured a splendid massive fireplace at one end flanked by large windows offering views of the mountain. Above the big room on the second floor was Mabel's bedroom and bath, which caused a sensation in Taos. It was the first indoor bathroom in the small village to house plumbing.

The bathroom was generously glazed on all sides with awesome views of the mountains. Local legend has embellished Mabel's bathroom with stories of the unabashed Mabel proudly displaying her nudity as gawkers hid in the bushes below. Perhaps this is the reason D. H. Lawrence and Dorothy Brett felt compelled to paint charming designs on the "public" side of the bathroom, which have been lovingly preserved for nearly eight decades.

Mabel's house became known as Los Gallos, named for a row of Mexican ceramic roosters that were installed on the roof. In a few years, a grand dining room and master bedroom were added. The dining room was a celebration of pattern and form. William Penhallow Henderson crafted burnt sienna and black floor tiles, and the ceiling's beam structure of *latillas* (smoothed branches) was painted to look like a Navajo rug. At one end of the room, Tony sculpted another magnificent hearth. The Big House boasted an open-air solarium on the third floor that was later glazed in.

Within ten years, Mabel had manifested an impressive estate of six houses, stables, corrals, barns, walls, gates, and even a large pigeon coop. The Big House eventually spread to seventeen rooms, more than 8,000 square feet, 450 feet in length.

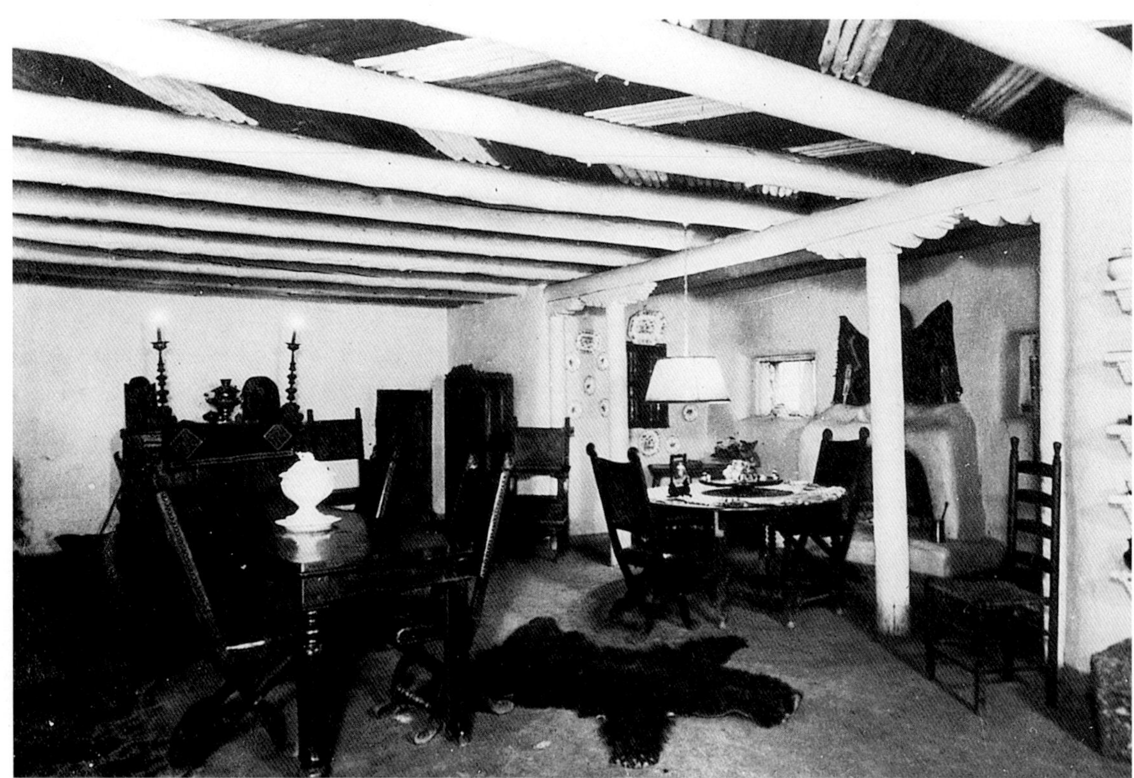

The dining room of Mabel's house, about 1920. Note the "Navajo rug" painted on the latilla *ceiling; also, Tony Luhan designed and sculpted the adobe fireplace seen at the right.*

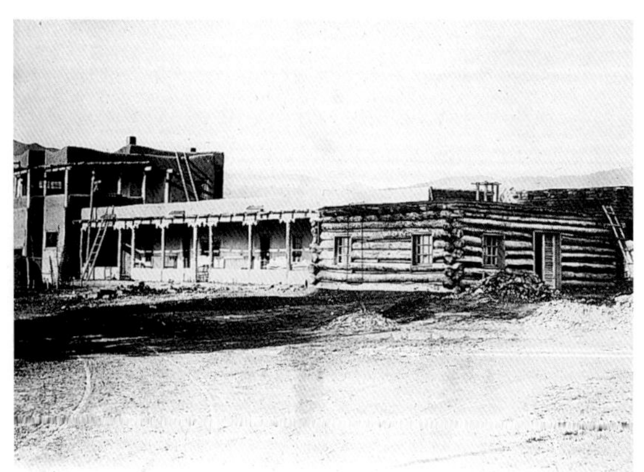

Mabel's Big House in the process of construction, around 1920. The log cabin built for Mabel's son, John Evans, is at the right.

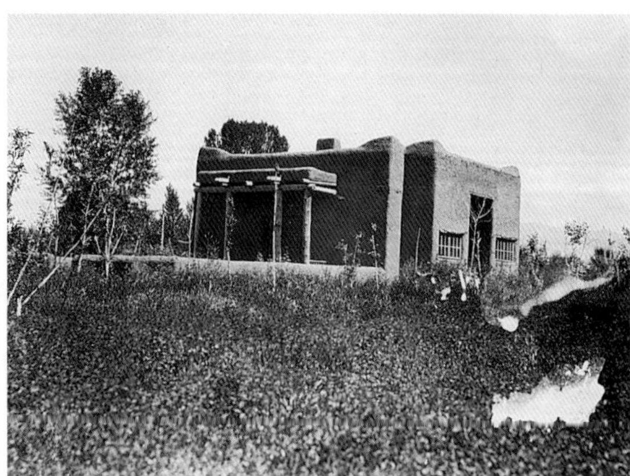

Studio, Mabel Dodge Luhan estate, 1925.

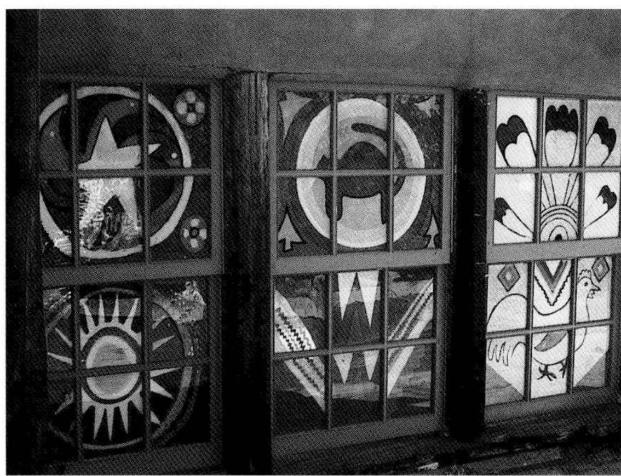

Bathroom windows at Mabel's Big House, with designs painted by D. H. Lawrence and Dorothy Brett.

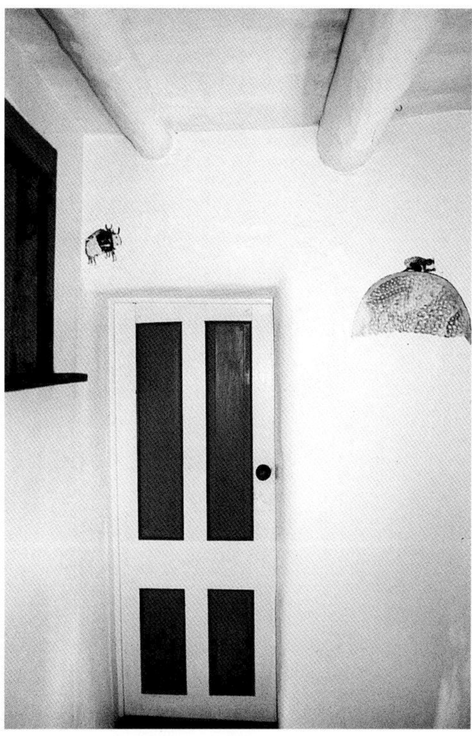

Door to Mabel's bedroom, adorned with painted Taos Pueblo designs.

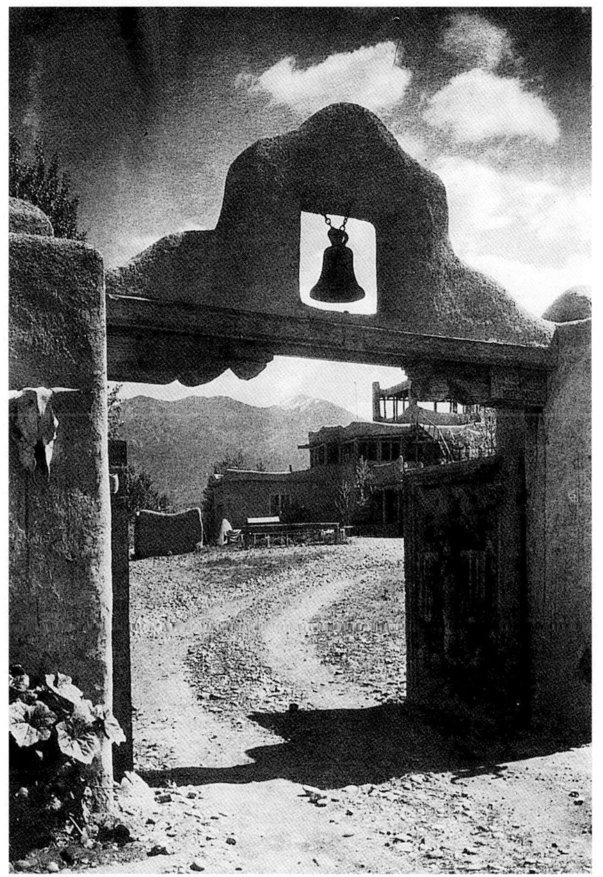

The front gate of the Los Gallos estate.

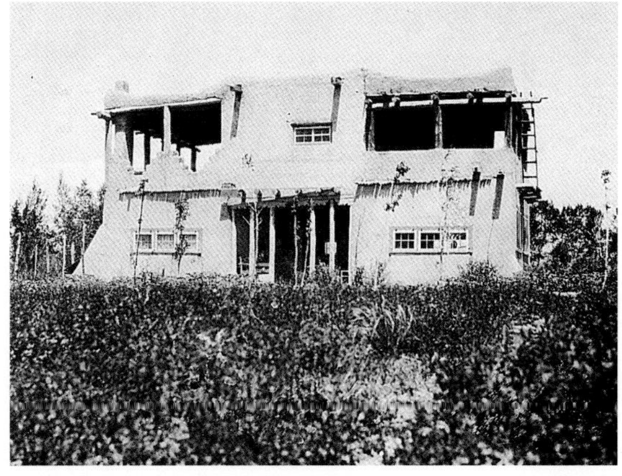

Two-story guest house, Mabel Dodge Luhan estate, about 1920.

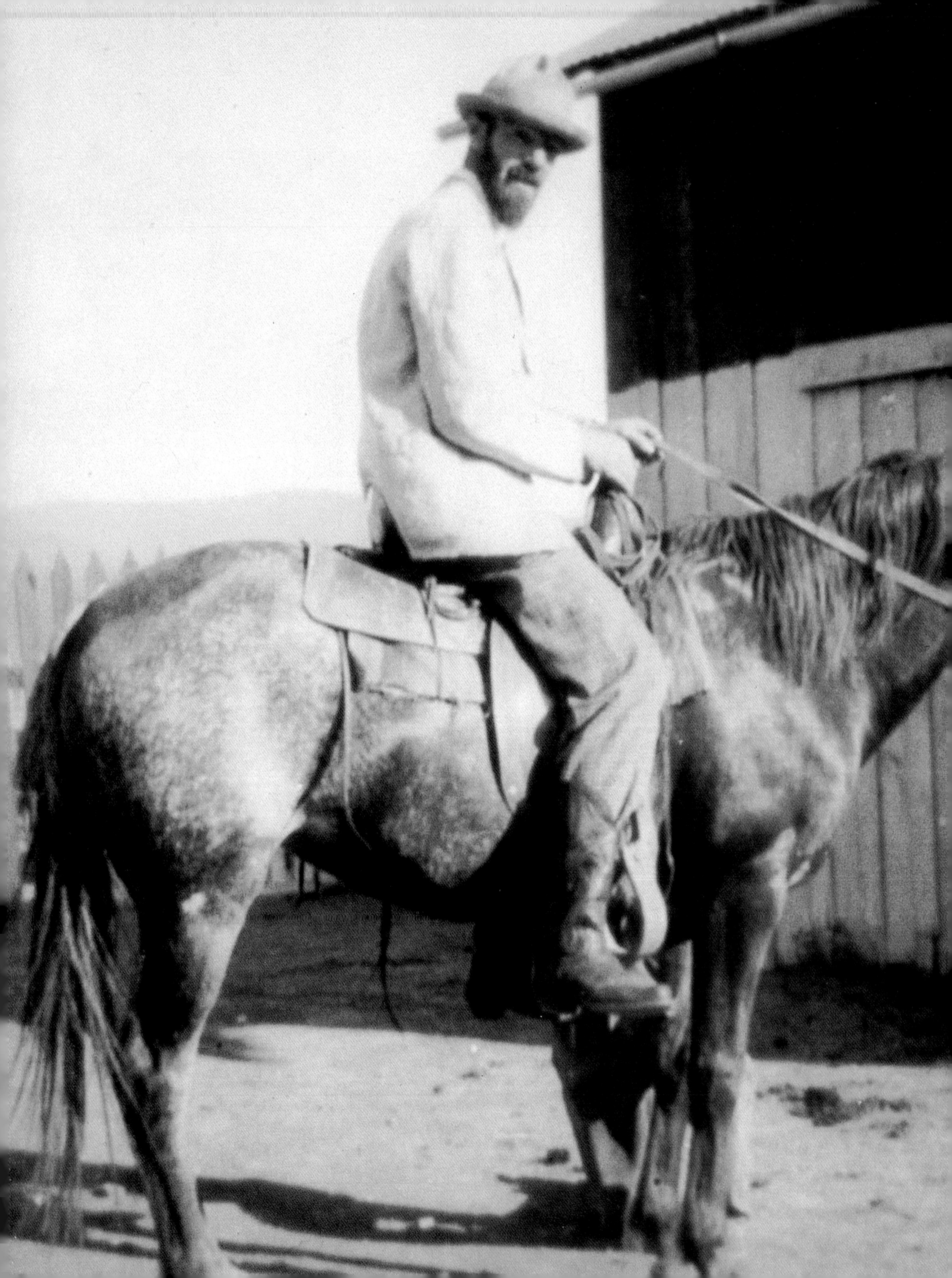

D. H. Lawrence: The Red Wolf Trail to Taos

The Taos Pueblo Indians called him the "Red Wolf," and in retrospect it seems appropriate. He was proud of it. Like his totem animal, D. H. Lawrence was cunning, lean and handsome, mysterious, and roamed over vast distances. Witty, insightful, and entertaining as the great novelist he was, Lawrence could inspire enthralled and adoring friends. But his wit was biting and judgmental—an offhand remark from Lorenzo could wound deeply. Sometimes his brilliance got the better of him; he was prone to violent outbursts and rages, especially terrific arguments with his wife, Frieda, which were often public.

During the 1920s, Lawrence's travels were many and legendary. Among his ports of call were Italy, Ceylon, Australia, New Mexico, Mexico, New York, and Los Angeles. He was always in search of new material for his novels, poems, and short stories, and exotic cultures fascinated him. The pale, lanky coal miner's son had barely tolerated a gray climate and dreary lifestyle in his youth, and as an adult he sought the radiance of sun and vibrant cultures.

The last decade of Lawrence's life (he died of tuberculosis in March 1930 at the age of forty-four) was his most productive. Streams of great prose flowed out of him, and he had the amazing ability to write in the midst of company and carry on a conversation at the same time, which of course unnerved other writers, such as Witter Bynner.

Once, artist Dorothy Brett asked him if he knew what he would say when he started writing.

No, I never know, when I sit down, just what I am going to write. I make no plan; it just comes, and I don't know where it comes from. Of course I have a general sort of outline of what I want to write about, but when I go out in the mornings I have no idea what I will write.

Before the publication of *Sons and Lovers* in 1913, Lawrence had resigned his teaching position at Davidson Road School in Croydon, England, and began writing full-time. He met Frieda Weekley, wife of a former professor, in 1912. A daughter of Baron Von Richthofen, the famous World War I ace pilot of Germany, Frieda was thirty-two years old and mother of three small children when she met the young English writer (then twenty-six years old).

Frieda radiated a lusty and voluptuous sexuality that Lawrence found irresistible. Her green eyes blazed with amber overtones, and her habit of wearing her hair in a pompadour masked her lethal charms with innocence. Young friend David Garnett described "her head and the whole carriage of her body were noble. Her eyes were green with a lot of tawny

D. H. Lawrence on horseback, Kiowa Ranch, Taos, 1924.

yellow in them, the nose straight. She looked one dead in the eyes, fearlessly judging one."

The improbable lovers were drawn to each other by potent psychological needs as well as erotic ones. Frieda's quiet and predictable bourgeois life withered away beneath the blast of Lawrence's ardent love poetry. He promised her a life with him, brilliantly painted with the artistry of his pen:

You call and I am the answer,
....
What else? it is perfect enough.
It is perfectly complete,
You and I,
What more ——?
Strange, how we suffer in spite of this!

The bright spot in young David Herbert's life (as a child he hated David and preferred Bert) was his intelligent and kind mother, who fought fiercely to save her sons from a life in the mines. When she died in December 1910, Lawrence was devastated. Frieda would provide the surrogate emotional anchor of an "earth mother" for Lorenzo's unconventional psycho-sexual imagination.

In May 1912, Frieda left her husband and young children and cast her lot with Lorenzo. The couple began their lifestyle pattern of wanderings that would last until his death, in spite of Frieda's pleas for a home and settled life. Two years later, after Frieda's bitter husband finally granted a divorce, the Lawrences were married on June 13 in Kensington.

Lawrence's path to Taos and his subsequent arrival and residence there after 1922 was convoluted and difficult. During the war years in England, Lorenzo and Frieda's antiwar sentiments and German ties were closely watched by authorities who suspected them of spying for Germany. They were ordered out of Cornwall in 1917 and instructed not to live on the coast. With the publication of his novels—*Sons and Lovers* in 1913, *The Rainbow* in 1915, and *Women in Love* in 1920—Lawrence had created a unique place for himself in English literature. He had dared to write openly about sexual relations between men and women, both heterosexual and homosexual. But his courage and daring carried a heavy price.

Censorship of his books, controversial and critical reviews, poor sales, and the gloom of war finally forced Lorenzo and Frieda to leave England for Italy in 1919. The balmy coasts of the Mediterranean were to nurture Lawrence before and after his forays to New Mexico and Mexico in the early 1920s. Invigorated by the warm air of Capri, Sicily and Sardinia, Lawrence enjoyed a prolonged period of prodigious writing, including the vivid travelogue *Sea and Sardinia* of 1921 and a collection of poetry later published as *Birds, Beasts and Flowers.*

In November 1921, Mabel Dodge wrote to Lawrence in Ceylon, praising *Sea and Sardinia.* Along with her effusive letter, Mabel sent Frieda an Indian necklace and an open invitation to the Lawrences to come and visit in Taos. Mabel would provide them a house for as long as they wished to stay. She boldly suggested to Lawrence that the Pueblo Indians would provide him excellent

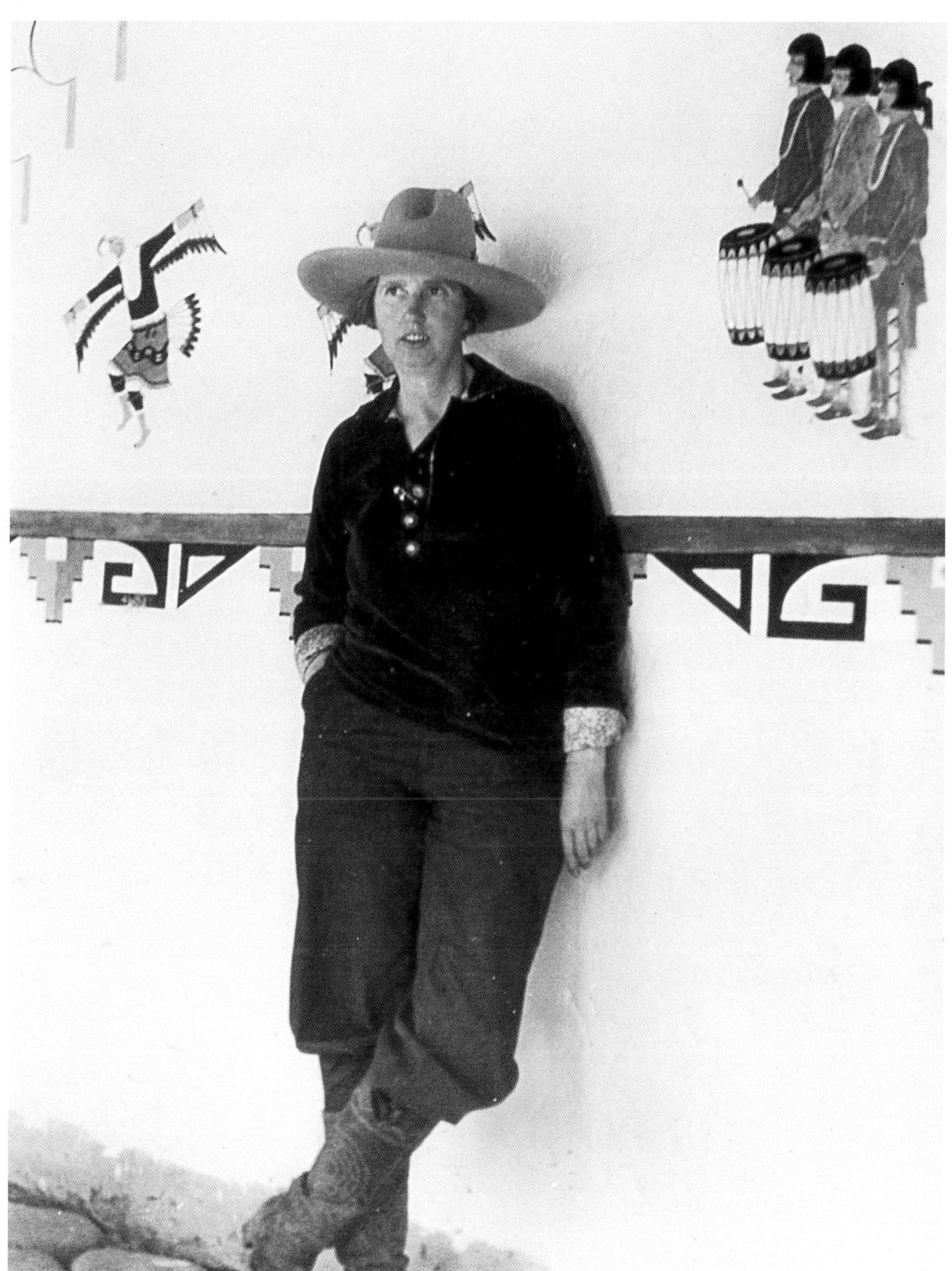

Dorothy Brett, framed by Taos Pueblo artist Awa Tsireh's mural at Mabel's house, 1930.

subjects for his literature.

Both Frieda and Lorenzo were intrigued by Mabel's offer to visit Taos. For Lawrence, the power of America was enticing and intimidating, and he was eager to encounter it for himself:

You have cajoled the souls of millions of us,
America
Why won't you cajole my soul?
I wish you would.
I confess I am afraid of you.

But he was also wary of Mabel's intentions. Typically, he put off his decision in favor of another adventure—to Australia. There, the Lawrences enjoyed inexpensive and bountiful living ("a huge piece of beef enough for twelve people, forty cents") before sailing for San Francisco in August 1922.

Lorenzo and Mabel

At first frustrated by Lawrence's delays, Mabel later claimed that she and Tony "willed" the English couple to come. She advised Tony that Lawrence could help the Indians with his perceptive writing. Each night she imagined herself joining "the central core" of Lawrence in Ceylon and Australia and moving his spirit across the Pacific. She poured resources into completing an adobe guest house, later known as the Pink House, so that it would be ready when the Lawrences arrived.

After a long train ride from San Francisco to the depot at Lamy (about twenty miles from Santa Fe), Frieda and D. H. descended from the ramp to find Mabel and Tony waiting for them. Mabel was dressed for the occasion in a turquoise blue dress and flaunted her silver Indian

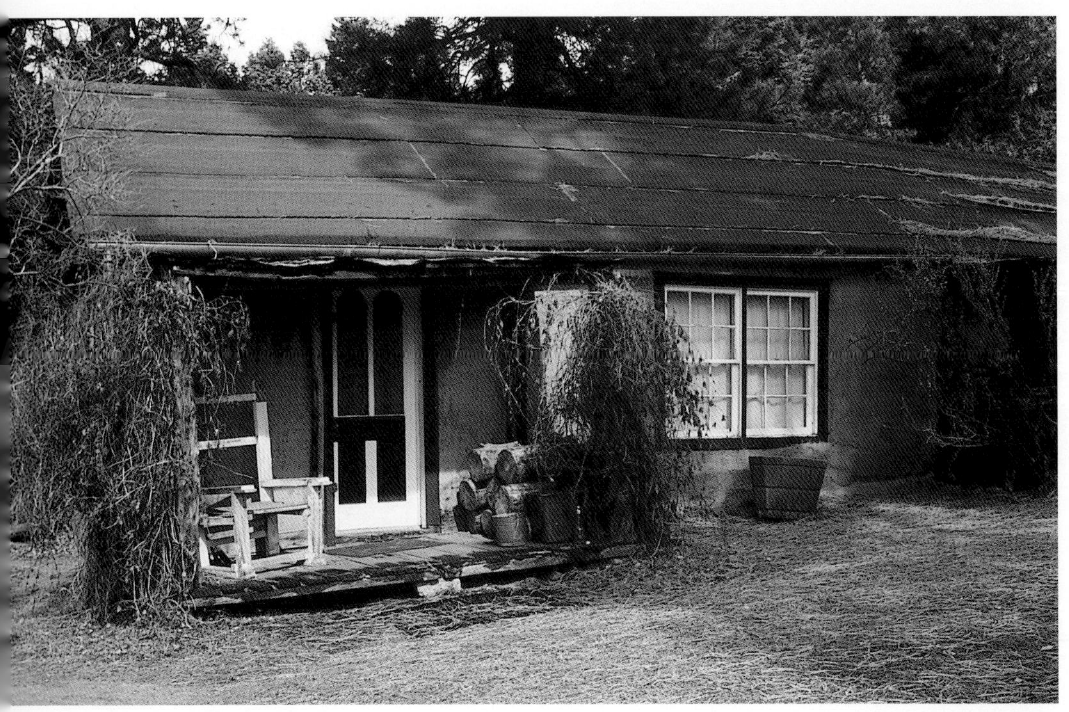

D. H. Lawrence's ranch house, Kiowa Ranch, New Mexico.

jewelry. Tony wore an Indian blanket and silver concho belt. "She has eyes one can trust," was Frieda's first impression.

Finding the hotels in Santa Fe booked, Mabel cajoled her friend (and future nemesis) Witter Bynner to house the Lawrences for the night. She and Tony would stay elsewhere, since Bynner's house (just acquired) only consisted of three rooms. The Lawrences were joined at dinner by Tony and Mabel (not yet divorced from Maurice Sterne), Bynner and his companion, Willard "Spud" Johnson, William Penhallow Henderson and his wife, poet Alice Corbin, and their daughter, "little Alice." It was a fateful gathering. The following spring Bynner and Spud would accompany the Lawrences on a trip to Mexico and eventually Mabel would hire Spud as her secretary and publicist. Thirty years later, in his memoir, *Journey with Genius,* Bynner would recall the evening clearly. Upon first sight, Lawrence struck Bynner as a "bad baby masquerading as a good Mephistopheles," and Frieda as a "household Brunhilde," blessed with a booming figure and booming voice, peppered with "Ja! Ja! Jas!" and a hearty laugh.

Bynner failed to appreciate the physical attraction and magnetism many women responded to in Lawrence. He ventured that, in fact, Lawrence could change the color and intensity of his deep turquoise-blue eyes, perhaps described by Lawrence himself in a passage from *The Rainbow,* "one could watch the change . . . from laughter to anger, blue lit-up laughter, to a hard-blue staring anger."

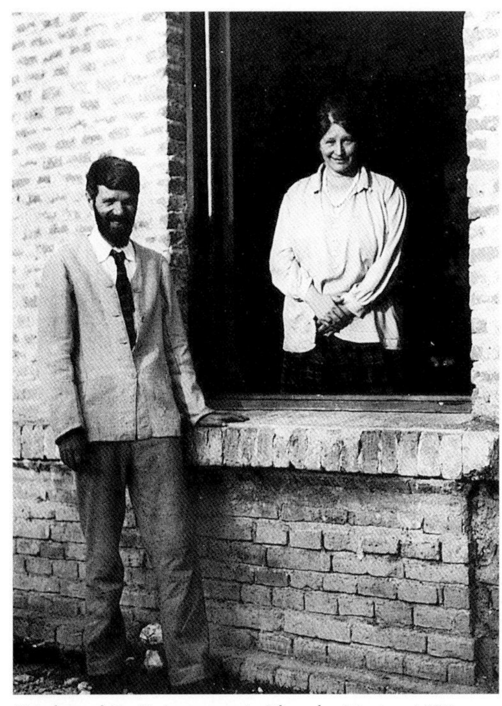

Frieda and D. H. Lawrence in Chapala, Mexico, 1923.

Everyone who met Lawrence remembered his red beard, which Catherine Carswell (a friend and biographer) described as "deep glowing red in the sun and in the shade the color of strong tea." Many responded to a mercurial flame-like quality in Lawrence—the volatility of his emotions but also a touching tenderness in the man. Mr. Earl Brewster, an American expatriate who lived on the isle of Capri when he met the Lawrences, recalled in his book *Reminisces of D. H. Lawrence* that "he brought with him some quality of the outside world, from the shrubs and flowers. The sweetness of sun-dried leaves and grass never seemed to leave him." And his wife Acsah Brewster added in the same book that "he moved with lithe precision, his feet alive in his shoes. . . . The nose was blunted; and from certain angles, together with his great brow, suggested the statues of Socrates."

If Lawrence had a visible shortcoming, it was his voice—shrill and high-pitched. It was a voice that could weigh heavy with sarcasm or punctuate with amused jeer. Lawrence could indulge in silly English "tee-hees" and "too-hoos," which fellow-writer Norman Douglas describes as "that squeaky suburban chuckle." Nonetheless, men and women both found D. H. Lawrence riveting but for entirely different reasons.

Lawrence caught Bynner by surprise when, the following morning, the Englishman awoke early and cooked everyone a full breakfast. Lorenzo never forgot the tough lessons of his poverty-stricken childhood, and throughout his life he proved resourceful and handy around the house, learning how to cook, sew, make furniture, and milk his black-eyed cow Susan. Hard honest work was something D. H. admired. In her memoirs about Lawrence, Mabel recalls how she scrubbed floors and baked bread "for Lorenzo."

Tony drove them away from Santa Fe in Mabel's Cadillac and on to Taos. Both Lawrences were greatly impressed by the landscape, especially the rise of the road out of the canyon and up to the vast high plain of Taos where the mountains asserted themselves most dramatically. This

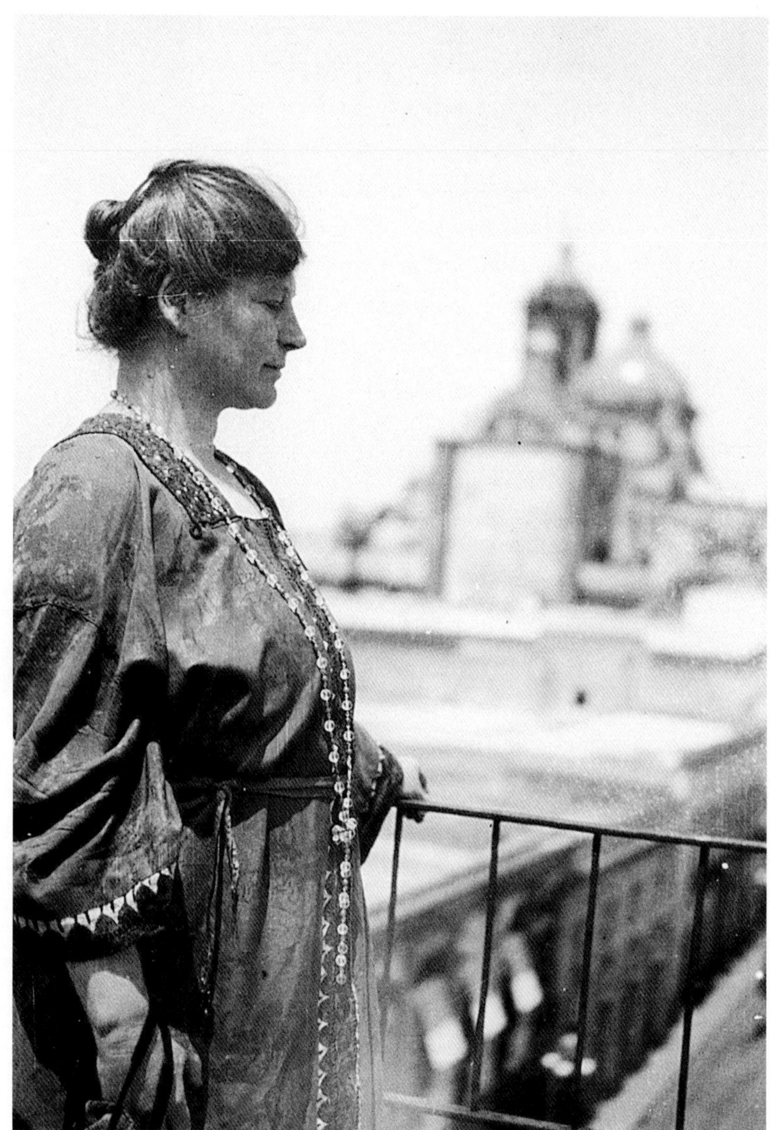

Frieda Lawrence in Mexico City, 1923.

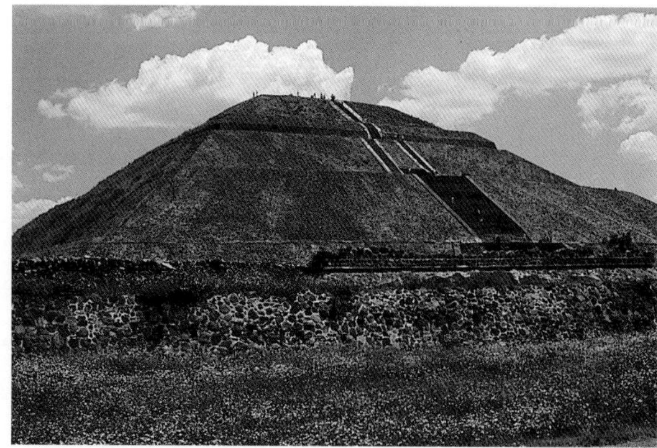

Pyramid of the Sun, Teotihuacan, near Mexico City.

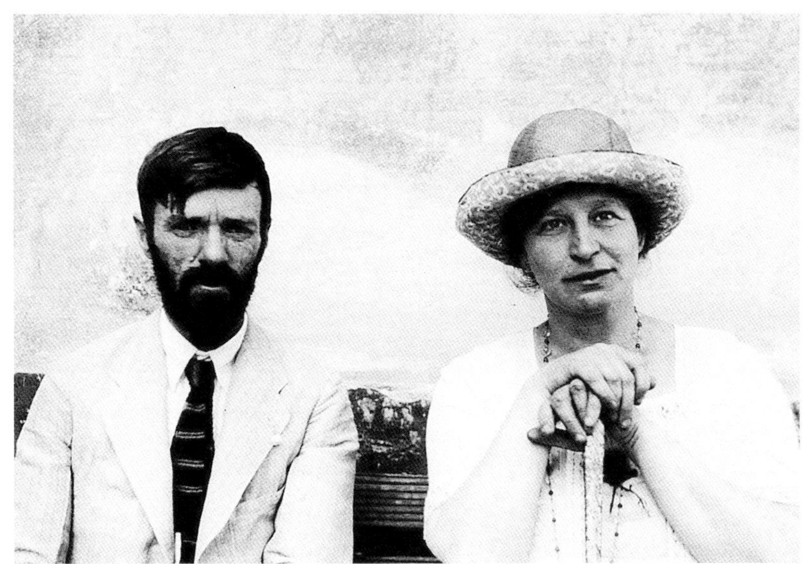

D. H. and Frieda Lawrence in Mexico, 1923.

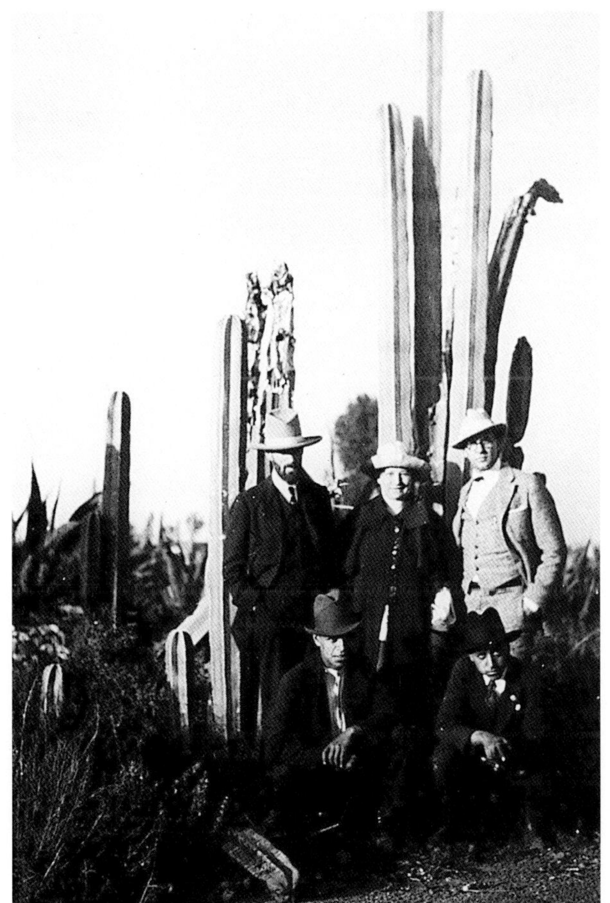

D. H. Lawrence, Frieda Lawrence, Witter Bynner, and two unidentified Mexican guides, 1923.

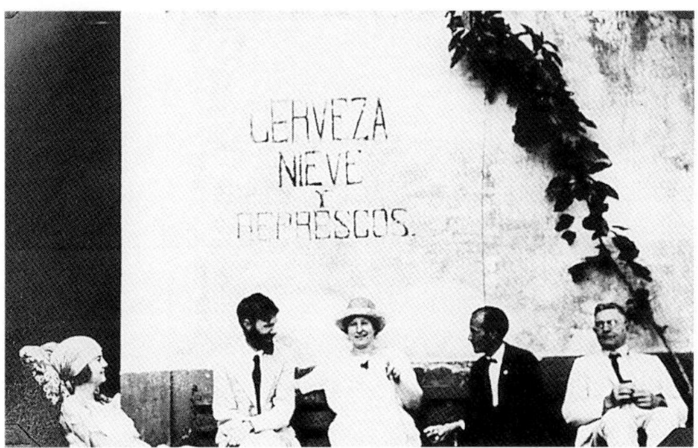

D. H. Lawrence, Frieda Lawrence, Spud Johnson, Idella Purnell, and an unidentified friend in Guadalajara, 1923.

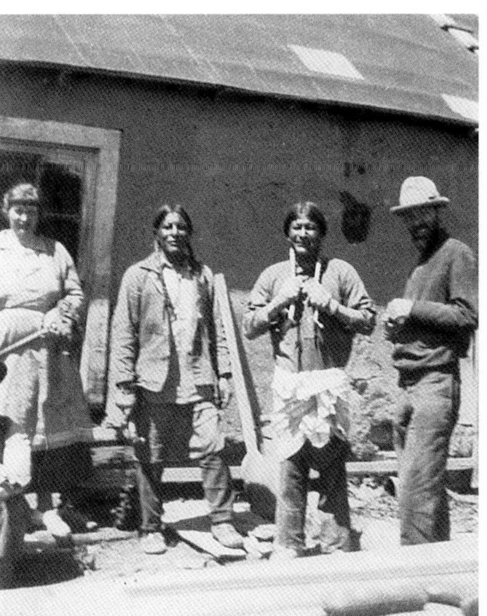

Frieda and D. H. Lawrence with a Taos Pueblo Indian work crew, Kiowa Ranch, New Mexico. 1924.

day, the sky brooded low and gray on the sage and a horrific lightning bolt and thunder clap startled the motor party. Tony would never forget the omen of Lawrence's arrival in Taos.

Settled in at Mabel's new guest house, the Lawrences were sensitive to the "feel of the Indians" emanating from nearby Taos Pueblo, which was different than anything they had known. Mabel quickly arranged for Tony to chauffeur Lorenzo to a Navajo ceremonial for three days; she wanted to size up Frieda, woman-to-woman.

Mabel harbored personal and selfish designs on Lawrence. "I wanted to seduce his spirit so I could make him carry out certain things. . . . I did not want particularly, to touch him. He was somehow too dry, not sensuous enough, and not attractive to me physically." Later she admitted that her behavior was highly suggestive and could have been interpreted by both Lorenzo and Frieda as seductive overtures. Nevertheless, Mabel didn't hesitate to tell Frieda that she wasn't the right woman for Lawrence. Frieda shot back: "Try it then yourself, living with a genius, see what it is like and how it is, take him if you can."

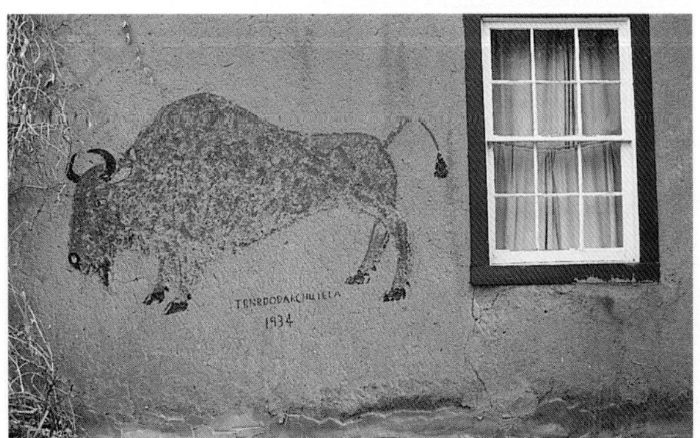

Wall drawing of a buffalo at D. H. Lawrence's ranch house, Kiowa Ranch, New Mexico.

Lorenzo quickly saw through Mabel and her intentions. He would learn to play cat and mouse, and their friendship was stormy. He sketched an unflattering portrait of Mabel in a letter to Frieda's mother:

Mabel Dodge: American—rich—only child—from Buffalo, on Lake Erie—bankers—42 years old—looks young—Has now an Indian, Tony, a fat fellow. Has lived much in Europe—Paris, Nice, Florence—is rather famous in New York, and little loved—very clever for a female—another culture-bearer—likes to play the "patroness"—hates the white world, and loves the Indians out of hate—is very "noble," wants to be very "good," and is very wicked—has a terrible will to power.

Lawrence observed that Mabel destroyed (or tried to destroy) every man she met, but in her heart of hearts wanted to be dominated by a strong male will. He would satirize her in later writings, especially in the short story "The Woman Who Rode Away" and in *St. Mawr,* a short novel.

Lorenzo did respond to New Mexico, and to Taos, and to the Indians. Mabel was determined to keep her remarkable guests entertained, and soon the Lawrences began to appreciate the splendor of autumn in the Taos high country. The climax of the golden season was the awesome Feast Day of San Geronimo at Taos Pueblo on the last day of September. The spectacle of men clad in fox skins followed by women shaking gourd rattles and chanting prayer songs touched Lorenzo's primal convictions. Here was real religion!

The days were filled with magic. Mabel and Tony regularly took D. H. and Frieda bathing in one of the natural hot "radium" springs, where the contrast between Tony's robust deeply tanned body and the pale and thin Lorenzo was almost comical. Tony taught them how to ride horseback, and frequently they would enjoy Indian dances at Mabel's house with the backdrop of a roaring fire in one of the great hearths. Several times the Lawrences joined in the dancing and chanting. Lorenzo even indulged in the romantic western fantasy of shopping for cowboy clothing. "You should see me," he wrote in a letter to his agent, "cowboy hat, good one $5; sheepskin coat—$12.50—corduroy riding breeches, very nice, $5." He bragged about his $20 pair of Justin cowboy boots.

As the shimmering luminous yellow cottonwood leaves carpeted the ground, the test of wills at Mabel's intensified. Mabel relentlessly demanded the writer's attentions, and the writer challenged Mabel's shallow preoccupation with "money, motorcars and the wild west." Frieda was caught in the middle. Finally, Lorenzo had to escape his hostess. In December, the Lawrences relocated to the Del Monte Ranch, a sanctuary of small cabins some seventeen miles from Taos that they rented from Bill Hawk.

At 9,000 feet in elevation, the ranch would present a formidable challenge to the intrepid Lawrences. Walter Ufer (of the Taos Society Artists) recommended that two young Danish artists, Knud Merrild and Kai Goetzsche, accompany the Lawrences. Frieda and Lorenzo occupied a five-room cabin and the Danes a smaller one nearby. The men quickly felled dead trees and stockpiled wood. Lawrence seemed to delight in the tough conditions, enjoying simple pleasures like playing chess and singing English Christmas carols and talking into the fading hours of the night with the Danes.

Because of the distance and the deep snows that winter, they had few visitors. Lawrence maintained his correspondences and finished his books *Kangaroo, Birds, Beasts and Flowers,* and revised others. He rekindled his dream of a special place, "a community of those who had given up the world to go into a place apart, to live life as Lawrence thought it should be lived," a place where creative men and women could live in harmony off the land, with little need of money or other extravagances, a place he called "Rananim." He wondered if Taos was that place.

By March he longed for the warm sun once again. Mexico, an enigma of cultures and confrontation, preoccupied Lawrence's imagination through the short days of January and February, and he prepared for the journey by reading voraciously about it. They invited Witter Bynner and Spud Johnson to come along, and by late March, Frieda and Lorenzo had left "Mabeltown" far behind.

Land of Quetzalcóatl

Mabel, of course, was stung by Lawrence's invitation to Bynner and Spud,

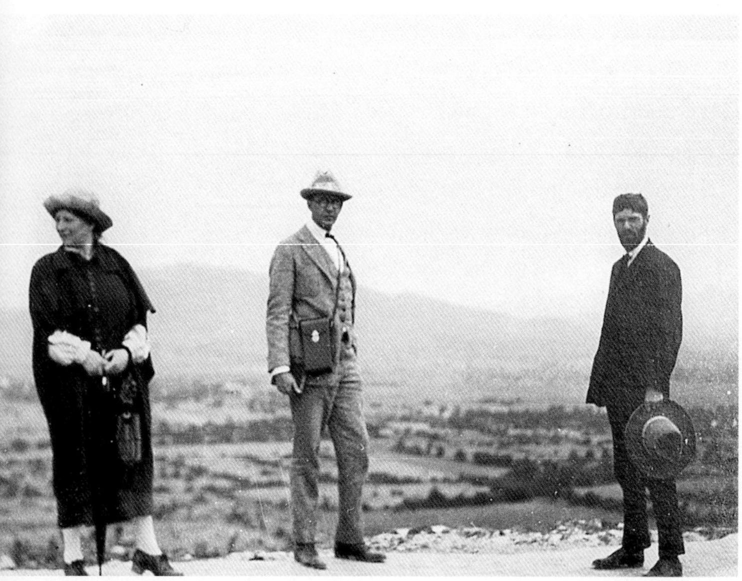

D. H. Lawrence, Witter Bynner, and Frieda Lawrence atop the Pyramid of the Sun, near Mexico City, 1923.

which was likely one of Lorenzo's motives. In time she would be anxious to forgive. In spite of his devastating personal attacks and "portraits" of friends (delivered personally and in his writings), Lorenzo's genius often won them back. He loved having an audience for his verbal entertainments of mimicry, charades, and highbrow conversation. During their Mexican adventure, Lorenzo relished arguing heatedly with Bynner, and Spud didn't mind typing and editing Lawrence's daily scribblings.

In Santa Fe and Mexico the openly homosexual literary couple could live relatively unmolested. Frieda secretly called Bynner (at forty-two years old) the "old woman," and Johnson (at twenty-six) "the young woman."

Bynner favored the genial Frieda, advising her during their Mexican trip to "strike first" when Lawrence was about to fly off the handle. When Bynner privately asked Frieda why she continued to put up with her husband's abuse, she shrugged and admitted that she had no money and no way to make a living. She had learned to tolerate the fighting and humiliations, knowing that they were temporary.

Lorenzo's closest friends had noted that his rages were surfacing more frequently and violently. In fact, he was suffering from the ravages of tuberculosis, although he had refused to admit it. Later that year, he coughed up blood in the winter cabin at Taos, and "Doc" Martin dismissed the cause as a bronchial infection. Nevertheless, Lorenzo probably knew that he only had a few more years to live.

In Mexico City, the small group of writers settled into the Hotel Monte Carlo, which Lawrence liked because of its air of European hospitality and Italian menu. Prohibition was in force in the United States, but in Mexico the group savored the opportunity to have wine with dinner.

Mexico both fascinated and repelled Lorenzo. Though he hated big cities, Mexico City's Spanish Colonial architecture seemed grand and tragic at the same time, having been superimposed by force on the Aztecs. Mexico was a savage and raw land ruled by passion visible to the naked eye, not falsely sublimated like those in England where proper appearances counted more than feelings.

Lawrence's razor-sharp perceptions appreciated the essential existential reality of Mexico: the proximity of death to everyday life. It was celebrated everywhere. One day in a *pulquería* (where tequila is made and sampled), Lawrence was admiring a colorful mural on the wall. Bynner noted in *Journey with Genius* that "it showed a group of erect and busy pigs dealing with human sinners as devils deal with them in theological pictures of hell: piercing them with spits, shoving them into hot cauldrons. Yes, I think it was on a pulque shop, though it might have been on a barbershop." Lawrence emphatically called it "much better than Diego Rivera."

The Mexican landscape was scarred by the recent revolution of 1917, essentially a revolt of the peasants against wealthy and brutal landowners, socialist causes versus capitalist causes, and patriotic nationalism against foreign exploitation (like U.S. industrialists). These were all efforts that the idealistic Lawrence could champion.

Maybe he found the inspiration for his new novel at Teotihuacán, the monumental pre-Columbian ruins near Mexico City. Dominated by the Pyramids of the Sun and Moon, Teotihuacán teemed with stone carvings of a fantastic creature—Quetzalcóatl, a mythical feathered-serpent god. Lawrence adopted the creature as the symbol and muse for his political/religious Mexican novel *The Plumed Serpent.*

Bored with Mexico City, Lorenzo defiantly struck out on his own at the end of April with little notice to his companions. His temper was flaring and he was becoming more irritable. Frieda told Bynner that this was when he would look for a safe haven to settle down and write. A few days later the telegram came: "Chapala paradise. Take evening train." Lake Chapala near Guadalajara is Mexico's largest inland body of water. In late April and May, the climate is balmy and most agreeable. Here on the shores of Chapala beneath a tree, Lorenzo would craft his own Mexico in the story, exacting his revenge on Mabel, European culture, Christianity, even caricaturizing his companions Bynner and Spud.

Bynner became the bon vivant Owen Rhys, and Johnson the bland Bud Villiers in Lorenzo's saga. In *The Plumed Serpent,* Rhys "is so empty, and waiting for circumstance to fill him up. Swept with an American despair of having lived in vain, or of not having really lived . . . having missed something."

Lawrence began the book on May 10 and wanted to finish by the end of June. Bynner knew what the maestro was up to, confiding to a friend in a letter that "he is having his revenge on me in a novel—which Spud is copying and I am not allowed to read. . . . He has been defeated by people all through his life and has consequently lashed their paper images with his poor fury."

Lawrence, indeed, was feverishly developing *The Plumed Serpent,* completing 450 pages of manuscript within a month, even taking time to enjoy a three-day boat ride around the lake on June 3 with Frieda, Bynner, Spud, and a group of American friends. But in mid-June he stopped writing and declared that he couldn't finish. It was time to move once again. Frieda was desperate to see her children in England and her ailing mother in Germany.

The couple left Mexico in July and traveled by train up the east coast via Laredo, New Orleans, and Washington, D.C., to

New York. They stayed for a month in a New Jersey suburban home rented for them by Lawrence's American publisher, Thomas Seltzer. When Frieda boarded a ship bound for England on August 18, Lorenzo stayed behind. He claimed he did not have the stomach to see Frieda reunited with her children. Frieda sailed away, not knowing if and when they would be reunited. It was their first separation in over a decade.

European Interlude and "the Brett"

Lawrence seemed to be aimless without Frieda's grounding influence. He took a long train ride back to Los Angeles (curiously stopping in Buffalo to visit Mabel's mother). In the booming southern California film capital he met up once again with the Danish artists. It took all of his persuasive gifts to enlist Kai Goetzsche to drive him to Mexico and be his companion for three months. Knud Merrild stayed behind, having had enough of the temperamental author's whims and rantings. The odd couple of Goetzsche and Lawrence left Los Angeles on September 25 and arrived in Guadalajara in mid-October. Frieda had not written to Lawrence.

Lawrence dove back into work once in Guadalajara, revising *The Boy in the Bush*, a novel set in western Australia, coauthored with Mollie Skinner. *The Plumed Serpent* languished, as its author had other things on his mind. Goetzsche could readily see how much he missed Frieda.

Free-spirited Frieda was making the most of her European interlude. Her promiscuity had tortured Lawrence since the first fevered days of their courtship. Men were wildly attracted to her aristocratic looks, Rubenesque figure, and jovial charisma. She had seduced several men within hours of their first meeting, including Lawrence, who she had in bed within twenty minutes of their introduction. Lawrence had asked his closest and oldest friend, John Middleton Murry, to look after Frieda, and look after her he did.

Recently widowed by the death of his wife, writer Katherine Mansfield, Murry had begun to cast about. In April of that year (while the Lawrences were in Mexico), he had seduced the shy thirty-nine-year-old virgin Dorothy Brett. The modest and deaf Brett fell easy prey to the suave and handsome Murry.

For Frieda, Murry offered a possible way to extricate herself from what was becoming a trying marriage to a temperamental genius. She offered "body and soul" to Murry, and it's likely that he took the former but hesitated on the latter out of loyalty to his old chum. As literary editor of the new review *Adelphi*, Murry likely had business considerations to weigh if he betrayed Lawrence. In any case, Lawrence probably could sense from afar that it was time to reunite with his wife. When she sent the one-word telegram "Come" in November, he did, arriving in England on December 7. He disembarked frail and sick; Murry noted Lorenzo's "greenish pallor."

D. H. Lawrence had grown to detest his native England. He had toiled feverishly to overcome his working-class childhood, and the critical rejection of his revolutionary novels had fueled his wrath. Almost immediately upon arriving, he wrote to Mabel asking if he and Frieda could come back to Taos.

This time he wanted to take some of his friends back with him. Lawrence still dreamed of an ideal colony, his "Rananim," a place he'd named after an Old Testament Hebrew song. At a famous drunken "last supper," Lawrence appealed for recruits to his Rananim in Taos, but only Dorothy Brett accepted the invitation. In March 1924 the trio of Frieda, Lorenzo, and Brett sailed to New York.

Sexually, Brett posed no threat to the vivacious Frieda. They were both aristocrats: Frieda, born of a baroness, and Brett, bred of Viscount Esher. Because of her serious deafness, Brett wielded an obtrusive and intrusive ear trumpet that she called "Toby." She had grown up shy and sheltered, decided she had some talent as an artist, and studied at the Slade School. Brett worshipped Lawrence and his "humanness" and would have followed him anywhere. Frieda called her "the Brett" with a hint of derision. Lawrence's intimate and incestuous Rananim colony arrived in New Mexico in late March 1924 to the delight of many friends who were genuinely glad to see them again, even Hal Bynner and Mabel.

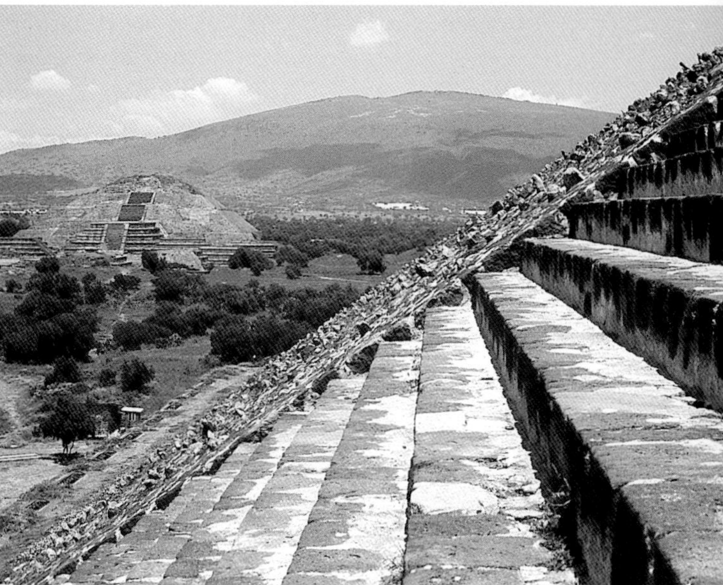

Steps of the Pyramid of the Sun, Teotihuacan, near Mexico City.

Mabeltown Revisited

Mabel didn't quite know what to think of Dorothy Brett. Back at Taos, Mabel gave the Lawrences the two-story guest house and Brett a studio. Instantly Brett adopted her new homeland and created her own costume of ten-gallon hat, culottes, cowboy boots, and dagger (she loved swords and knives), sometimes topped off with buckskin vests or jackets. Mabel sized her up as a "tall, oldish girl with pretty, pink round cheeks and a childish expression. Her long, thin shanks ended in large feet that turned out abruptly. . . ."

Lawrence was not any more generous in his appraisal of Brett, who was "sometimes like a bird, sometimes a squirrel, sometimes a rabbit: never quite like a woman."

Within days of their arrival, Mabel shocked everyone by offering Frieda a gift of the Flying Heart Ranch on Lobo Mountain above the Del Monte Ranch, where the Lawrences had spent their first snowy winter in New Mexico. Why Frieda? Lawrence vowed that he would not own property on this earth (part of his rampant idealism). But, Mabel wanted the Lawrences as part of her permanent colony, and she knew that the wander-weary Frieda would gladly accept.

Frieda, quick to the draw, knew that Lorenzo would not be indebted to Mabel. Her sister Else had recently written from Germany that she had found Lawrence's manuscript for *Sons and Lovers*. Frieda offered it as a goodwill trade, and everyone was appeased. Lorenzo later heard through the Taos grapevine that his manuscript was worth far more than the 160-acre run-down ranch. He immediately instructed his agents in New York and London to secure his manuscripts in vaults. Curiously, up to that point, Lawrence never valued his own personal drafts of prose and poetry; they kept turning up in boxes and drawers after his death.

Lorenzo was secretly delighted with Frieda's ranch and fired off letters to friends and family describing the new homestead. The property included three cabins badly in need of repair. At once, Lawrence hired a work crew of three Indians and a Mexican carpenter and together with Frieda and Brett proceeded

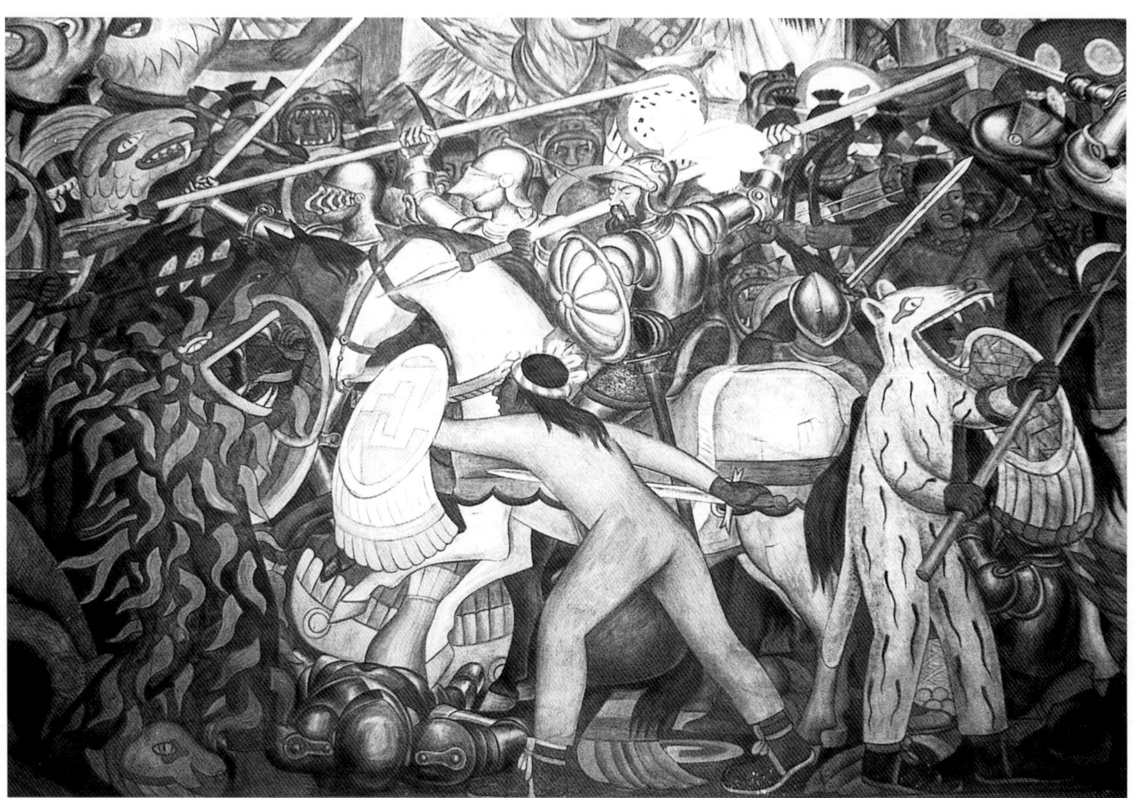

Detail of a mural by Diego Rivera, National Palace, Mexico City.

to begin repairs on the cabins. The Lawrences kept the three-room cabin for themselves, a two-room cabin was reserved for guests, and Brett was consigned to a tiny one-room hovel barely large enough for a bed and a cookstove. The motley crew enthusiastically tackled their chores, which included building chimneys and an adobe *horno* (beehive oven), cleaning out a well, and building fences. Before too long, Lorenzo fired the Mexican carpenter for calling Frieda *chiquita* (dear littl'e one).

At nearly 9,000 feet, the rechristened Lobo Ranch (later renamed the Kiowa Ranch) soared nearly two miles along a road above the Del Monte Ranch. The view out toward the high mesa of Taos was awe-inspiring. The hard work and grandeur of nature tempered Lawrence and even humbled him:

There is something savage, unbreakable in the spirit of the place out here—the Indians drumming and yelling at our camp fire at evening . . . there is the pristine something, unbroken, unbreakable. . . . It is good to be alone and responsible. But it is also very hard living up against these savage Rockies.

Just outside the front door of his cabin, a towering pine tree yearned skyward. Lawrence had always felt an affinity for trees—most of his books were written beneath a tree on schoolboy notebooks in his fast, small, and neat handwriting. The great pine was especially dear to him, and he acknowledged its benevolence in his essay "Pan in America."

Here on this little ranch under the Rocky Mountains, a big pine tree rises like a guardian spirit in front of the cabin where we live. . . .

The tree's life penetrates my life, and my life the tree's. We cannot live near another, as we do, without affecting one another.

Five years later during her summer of discovery, Georgia O'Keeffe would immortalize the lofty pine in her great painting *The Lawrence Tree.*

The "war" for Lorenzo picked up intensity as the summer got hotter. Mabel broke down crying during one of her visits to the ranch, pleading to D. H., "How can you treat me like this?" Frieda was at her wit's end with "the Brett," who followed her husband around like a young puppy. Mabel's new protégé that summer was twenty-two-year-old Clarence Thompson, a movie-star-handsome dropout of Harvard who fancied himself a freelance writer and character actor in Hollywood "B" films. He was flamboyant and homosexual, angling for Lawrence's affections.

In his account of Lawrence in Taos, Joseph Foster described Thompson as an "unpleasant homosexual: gentle, effeminate, weighted down with Indian silver—a delicate face but an inner black ruin He longed for Lawrence in his strange and effeminate way. He was tall and blond and vainly arrogant." Thompson did gain Lorenzo's friendship; they would take long horseback rides together, and Mabel even wondered if they were having an affair. One night at Mabel's, under the influence of smuggled moonshine, a jealous Lorenzo

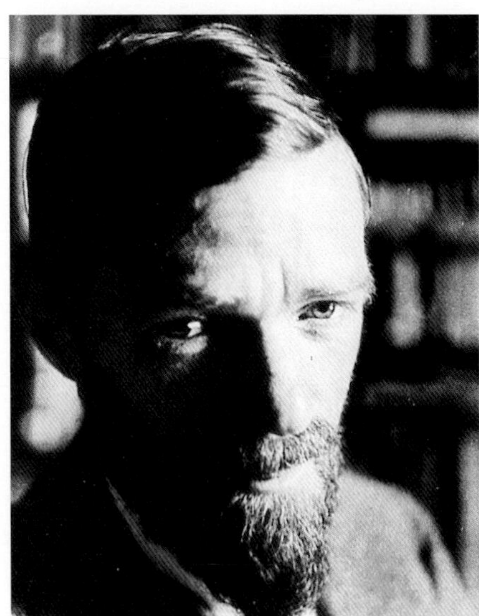

D. H. Lawrence, 1929.

caused a commotion on the dance floor (he never danced, calling it "indecent tail-wagging"). As Clarence and Frieda were gaily and expertly promenading, an aroused Lorenzo grabbed Mabel and aimed to disrupt his wife's fun by bumping into the couple. The party broke up amidst much insinuation and hurt feelings.

The situation was loaded with dynamite for a writer of Lawrence's inclinations and abilities. He couldn't help but psychoanalyze Mabel's chosen male companions: the oversexed but silent Tony, two homosexual men who posed no threat to her—the theatrical Thompson and the modest Spud Johnson.

The three stories he wrote during the summer of 1924 in Taos have been called "masterworks of misogyny" by Brenda Maddox in her recent biography *D. H. Lawrence: The Story of a Marriage*. In "The Woman Who Rode Away," a beautiful blond woman is ritually sacrificed during the winter solstice by an Indian tribe. As the woman dies under the knife in sacrifice for the tribe's well-being, the story confirms "the mastery that man must hold, and that passes from race to race." Many critics agree that the sacrificed woman is Mabel Dodge Luhan. Feminist critics are united in their disgust of Lawrence's male chauvinism.

In the short novel *St. Mawr,* Lawrence re-creates himself as the magnificent stallion "St. Mawr," an impressive symbol of male force. Mabel is again satirized as a rich woman who wants to buy St. Mawr. The horse recoils at the sight of a snake and suffers a ghastly fall. The woman and her money are powerless to save him. Animosity had been simmering between Lorenzo and Tony for months, and in

St. Mawr, Lawrence diminishes an arrogant Indian who

was ready to trade his sex, which in his opinion, every white woman was secretly pining for, for the white woman's money and social privileges. In the daytime all the thrill and excitement of the white man's motor cars and moving-pictures and ice-cream sodas. . . . In the night, the soft, watery-soft warmth of an Indian or half-Indian woman.

"The Princess" is the tale of an aristocratic thirty-eight year old English virgin (guess who?), the victim of an eccentric father. Escaping her traditions by fleeing to the American Southwest, she is seduced and repeatedly raped by a dark Mexican guide while on a horseback ride in the high forest timberland. In spite of the harsh sexual attacks on women, many critics rate the three New Mexico stories of 1924 among D. H. Lawrence's best work. The violence of the pieces led others to believe Lawrence was nearing the edge, frustrated at his own sexual impotence and the waning of his vital forces due to his advancing illness.

The death of his father on September 10 cast a pall of gloom on Lorenzo and the ranch as cooler air settled in. With autumn's crisp air advancing, Lawrence's chest ached. It was time to go south once again. Frieda was reluctant. She had come to love Lobo Ranch. She hadn't owned much of anything since she said good-bye to her dearest possesions—her children—a dozen years before. Besides, Lawrence had invited Brett to come along. Frieda left New Mexico in early October with a lump in her stomach and a heavy heart.

The Serpent Strikes Back—Mexican Sequel

The trio arrived in Mexico City on October 20, 1924, and checked into the familiar Hotel Monte Carlo. Lawrence was eager to reach Oaxaca farther south—a lovely colonial capital still embroiled in the aftermath of the revolution of 1917. It was a risky venture. Foreigners were eyed suspiciously as a cause of Mexico's troubles. But Lorenzo decided the risk was worth it. Oaxaca's warm climate would soothe his burning lungs.

At last he could resume his opus, *The Plumed Serpent.* It became a curious and powerful symbiosis of Taos imagery and experiences and Mexican philosophy and politics. Here was the great work Mabel had dreamed of, only set in the wrong place! Brett dutifully and devotedly typed the manuscript each day as it flowed off of Lorenzo's pen. His was a vision of a modern Mexico, free of the twin demons that had plagued the country for centuries—Catholicism and capitalism. The people

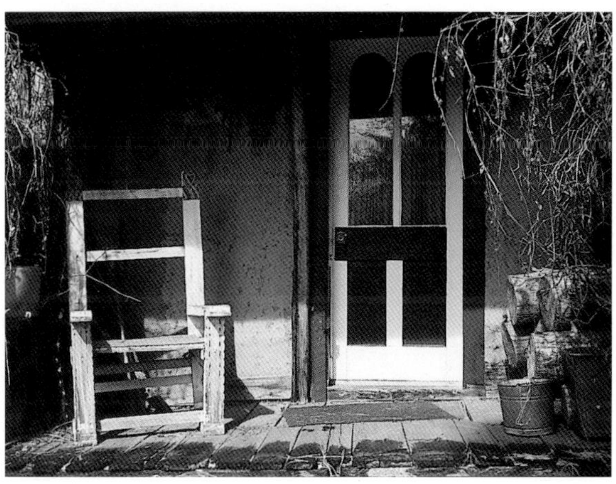

Porch chair made by D. H. Lawrence, Kiowa Ranch.

could find their salvation in the ancient pre-Columbian traditions.

By January, Frieda could tolerate Brett no longer. She ordered Lorenzo to send her packing, back to Taos. Lorenzo obeyed by slipping Brett a note at her hotel:

You, Frieda and I don't make a happy combination now. The best is that we should prepare to separate: that you should go your own way. I am not angry; except that I hate "situations" and feel humiliated by them. . . . I am grateful for the things you have done for me. But we must stand apart.

Frieda was more direct. She blew into Brett's room and exploded. She could understand better if Brett and her husband were having sex, but to pursue him blindly like she did—it was pathetic!

Shortly after Brett departed, the Mexican serpent struck at Lawrence in the form of malaria and dysentery. Lorenzo said it felt like he had been shot in the intestines. Bedridden with a high fever and stomach cramps, Lawrence believed he was dying. He confessed to Frieda that "if I die, nothing has mattered but you, nothing at all." She prayed over him nightly and nursed him back to some strength. In early March he was taken by stretcher to the railroad station where they made the overnight trip to Mexico City.

This time, instead of the favorite Hotel Monte Carlo, the couple splurged on two sunny rooms on the top floor of the fashionable Imperial Hotel on the Paseo de la Reforma. Lorenzo was still spitting blood

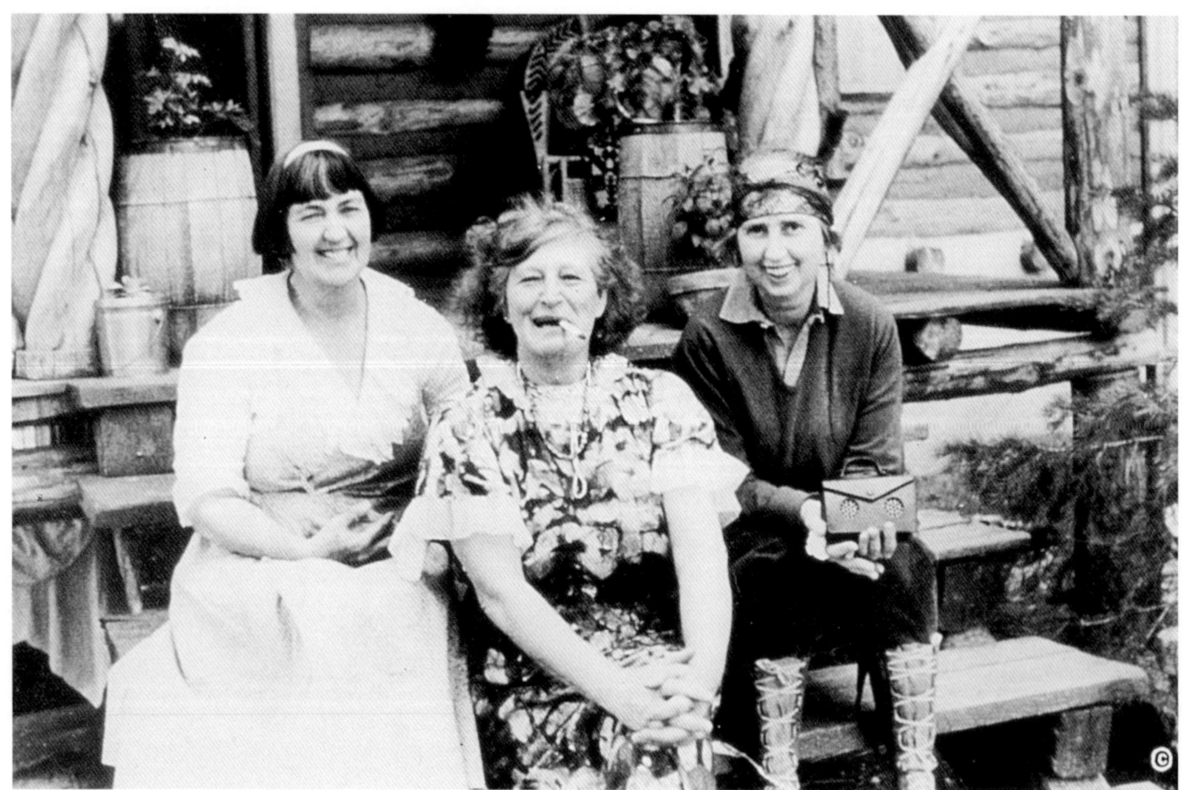

Mabel Dodge Luhan, Frieda Lawrence, and Dorothy Brett on the steps of the Kiowa Ranch house, 1935.

daily, and Frieda arranged an appointment with Dr. Sydney Ulfelder, head of surgery at the American Hospital.

Ulfelder's verdict was simple and inescapable: Lawrence was in the advanced stages of tuberculosis. Ulfelder told him he had one or two years to live. The doctor advised Lawrence to return to New Mexico as soon as he felt strong enough to travel.

Lawrence looked so pale and sickly that he used rouge to give his complexion some color. The four-day train ride from Mexico City to El Paso was hellish; he and Frieda shared a small compartment with a Mexican family of nine. At the border he was detained for a day while health inspectors debated whether to let the consumptive back into the United States. Finally they granted him a six-month visitor's visa. He knew it was the last ticket to America he would receive.

New Mexico Farewell

Witter Bynner was stunned to see how much Lorenzo had aged. The impassioned conversations and the brilliant flashes of insight from the depths of the blue eyes were still fresh memories. But now, the great writer appeared exhausted and defeated. Painter Andrew Dasburg and his wife, actress Ida Rauh, drove the Lawrences from Santa Fe to Taos. They skipped Mabel's and went straight to their sanctuary in Kiowa Ranch, New Mexico, where they first spent a few days recuperating at Hawk's Del Monte Ranch. The sweet breezes of spring were soothing to their tired souls.

Back at Kiowa Ranch, Lawrence set about transforming his cabin into a veritable sanitarium. He reclined on the porch every morning, enjoying the milk from his beloved black-eyed cow, Susan, and eggs from his eleven hens.

As his strength returned slowly, he insisted on working around the ranch, milking Susan and helping dig an irrigation ditch. Frieda was tickled with Lorenzo's progress:

How thrilling it was to feel the inrush of new vitality in him; it was like a living miracle. . . . How grateful he was inside him! "I can do things again, I can live and do as I like, no longer held down by the devouring illness." How he loved every minute of life at the ranch! The morning, the squirrels, every flower that came in its turn . . . all assumed the radiance of a new life.

Defying the conventional wisdom prescribing absolute rest, Lawrence began writing. Among his works that summer were a play he wrote called *David* with Ida Rauh in mind for the leading actress, and several essays on the philosophy of the novel. In one of them he reaffirmed his belief in the novel as the supreme art form:

One can live so intensely with one's characters and the experiences one creates or records, it is a life in itself, far better than the vulgar thing that people call life.

Dorothy Brett managed to stay near her idol, lodging that summer at Del Monte Ranch. (Frieda refused to have her any closer). Brett taught him how to target shoot, and he developed his skill enough to kill a porcupine. His remorse led to the essay "Reflections on the Death of a Porcupine."

Conspicuously missing that summer was the company of Mabel and Tony. They stayed away, wounded by Lawrence's personal and literary attacks. In fact, they never saw each other again. Both Mabel's and Lawrence's dreams of artistic utopia had evaporated into the Taos heavens. By late summer Lawrence had recuperated, and it was time to leave America. D. H. Lawrence gazed upon his beloved Kiowa Ranch for the last time on September 10, 1925. Near the end of his life, he paid tribute to his adopted New Mexico in an essay published in *Survey Graphic* magazine at Mabel's request in December 1928:

For a greatness of beauty I have never experienced anything like New Mexico. All those mornings when I went with a hoe to the Canyon, at the ranch, and stood in the fierce, proud silence of the Rockies, on their foothills, to look far over the desert to the blue mountains, blue as chalcedony, with the sagebrush desert sweeping grey-blue in between the vast blue amphitheatre of lofty, indomitable desert, sweeping round to the ponderous Sangre de Cristo mountains on the east, and coming flush as the pine-dotted foothills of the Rockies! What splendour!

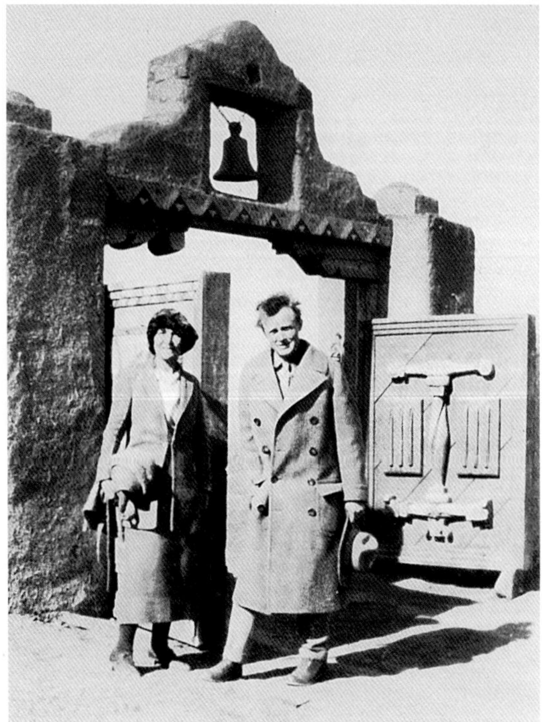

Ida Rauh and Andrew Dasburg at the gate to Mabel's estate, about 1925.

D. H. Lawrence in America : Postscript

D. H. Lawrence died of tuberculosis on March 2, 1930, in Vence, France. To the end he had hoped to return to New Mexico, writing to Mabel on January 6, 1930:

Ida [Rauh] says she has written you about our coming to Taos in the spring. I think, if I felt safe about it, I would have the energy to get up and start, and I feel that once I got there, I should begin to be well again. . . .

We talk and make plans: plans of coming back to the ranch and having places near one another—and perhaps get going with a few young people, building up a new unit of life out there, making a new concept of life. Who knows!

Frieda returned to Taos in June 1931 with her new lover Angelo Ravagli (whom she married in 1950). Soon followed a slew

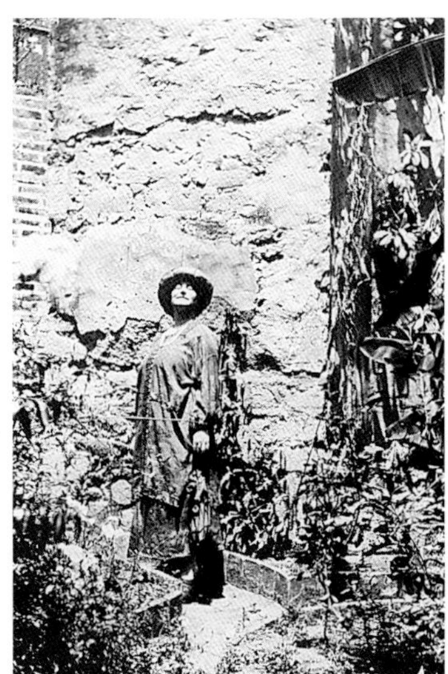

Frieda Lawrence in Mexico, 1923.

of Lawrence biographies, including Mabel Dodge Luhan's *Lorenzo in Taos* (1932), Dorothy Brett's *Lawrence and Brett* (1933), and Frieda's own account *Not I, But the Wind . . .* (1934).

Frieda settled into Taos life, along with Mabel and Brett and O'Keeffe, becoming one of the legendary sirens of northern New Mexico. In a letter to Lawrence scholar Eliot Fay in 1953, Frieda noted:

In our old age Mabel and Brett and I are friends. Our fights are over. I always liked Mabel better than Lawrence did. I was never jealous of either of them but they thought I was. I had no reason to be. Brett came too close to Lawrence's and my life together. But I was jealous of Lawrence's sister Ada and Lady Ottoline. Of course I cannot be as detached from all this as an outsider can be, this was and is my life.

Her last twenty-five years in Taos were happy ones, and Frieda graciously welcomed the never-ending stream of Lawrence worshippers, including Tennessee Williams in 1938, who described himself to Frieda as a young writer and admirer of her late husband's and much like him: "nomadic, restless, and uncertain." Georgia O'Keeffe described Frieda in a letter to Alfred Stieglitz:

I can remember very clearly the first time I saw her, standing in a doorway there, with her hair all frizzy, wearing a cheap red calico dress that looked as if she'd wiped the frying pan with it. She was not thin and not young, but there was something wonderful about her. . . . She was very beautiful. Oh, Frieda would come into this house with that huge voice of hers. "Georgia!" Her voice would fill the house. She stayed on the top of the heap. I really liked her.

Frieda suffered a massive stroke on August 8, 1956, the day before she was to visit her dear friend Hal Bynner on his seventy-fifth birthday. She died three days later. At her funeral service, a young writer read the Lawrence poem "Song of a Man Who Has Come Through." It contains a verse she adopted as her own mantra:

Not I, not I, but the wind that blows through me.

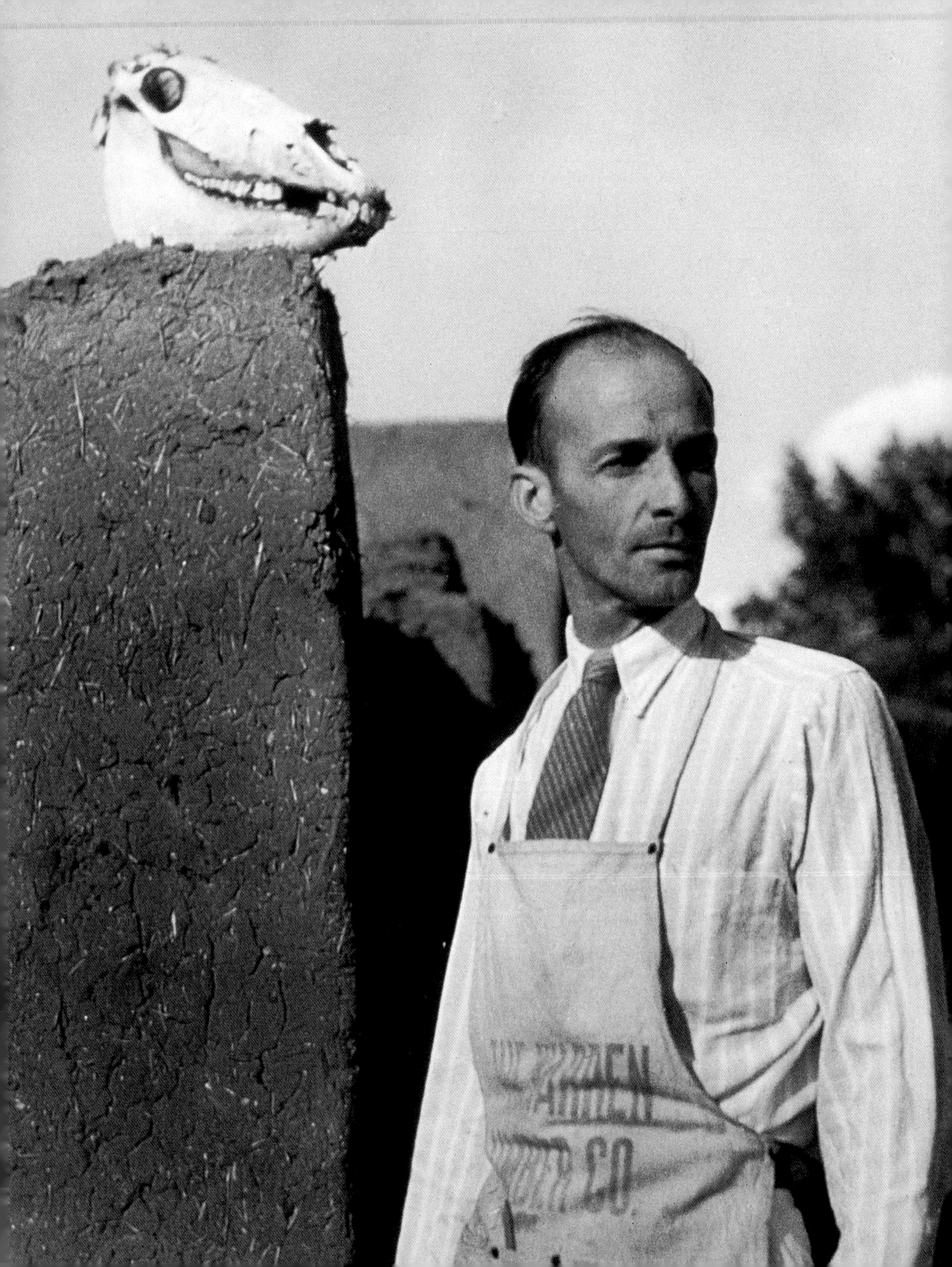

Spud Johnson: The Laughing Horse

He was called "Spud" from childhood and throughout his adult life—a visually appropriate nickname that later was affectionately transformed to "Spoodle" by D. H. Lawrence. Spud emerges from the bohemian veils of Taos history more as an amusing character from a novel, short story, or play than an actual person, although he was actually a vital figure in the cultural milieu of New Mexico for over forty years until his death in 1968.

Thin and unassuming, Walter Willard Johnson discovered his literary ambitions after his seventh-grade teacher in Greeley, Colorado, praised his essay about a house finch. It was an early and inspired career choice that Spud pursued with dedication, editing his high school newspaper and contributing bits of journalism to the local newspaper. Spud would prove to be a pesky gadfly, attracted to controversial people, events, and issues, interpreting them in print in wry and witty ways.

Enrolling at Colorado State Teachers College and later at the University of Colorado, Spud took English and writing classes to the virtual exclusion of everything else in the curriculum. By 1920 he had outgrown the small-town attitudes and constraints of Boulder and moved on to Berkeley. There he enjoyed the unorthodox poetry class of Witter Bynner, stimulated by the literary lions Bynner invited to class. Spud emerged from the class as Bynner's favorite pupil. The well-connected Bynner, who in the early 1920s was considered one of America's *next* great poets, found a job for Spud as a librarian in the exclusive Bohemian Club on San Francisco's Nob Hill. Disgusted by the bland student publications on the Berkeley campus, Spud and two other literary subversives decided to launch a new publication dedicated to presenting progressive points of view regarding literature, arts, social criticism, and even campus politics. It was called *The Laughing Horse.* With a loan of fifty dollars from Spud, the first 500 copies of *The Laughing Horse* appeared on the Berkeley campus in April 1922. When the fledgling literary magazine turned a tiny profit and was noticed by a few of the Bay Area's daily newspapers, the irreverent student editors were jubilant.

The same spring, Spud made a fateful decision. He dropped out of Berkeley, refused to take the military training required of all male students, and decided to return home to Colorado. That summer of 1922, Spud's dilemma coincided with Witter Bynner's collapse and recuperation in Santa Fe (while he was on a lecture tour), and Spud was persuaded to detour to New Mexico. The familiar bohemian magic worked its spell, and Spud was also bewitched by the "City Different."

Bynner fulfilled many crucial roles in Spud's young life: literary mentor, lover, father figure, and employer, among others. The two men eagerly spent the summer socializing, meeting other literary personalities, such as Alice Corbin, and traveling to nearby pueblos. They spent most of July in residence at Mabel's Los Gallos estate in Taos, where Spud

Spud Johnson in 1932.

was to become a fixture in later years.

Bynner acquired what Spud called an "adobe hut" that consisted of three rooms. By "bunking in the studio," Spud and Witter could accommodate guests in their bedroom, which they were unexpectedly asked to do on the night of September 10, 1922. Coming home from a Tom Mix movie, Spud was surprised to find Witter entertaining a dinner party that included Mabel Dodge, Tony Luhan, and Mr. and Mrs. D. H. Lawrence. Maybe Spud was auspiciously seated between David Herbert Lawrence, affectionately known as Lorenzo, and Harold Witter Bynner, for that would be his social position thereafter. Stubborn as his nature, Spud would frustrate both writers by not favoring one over the other with his allegiance and support.

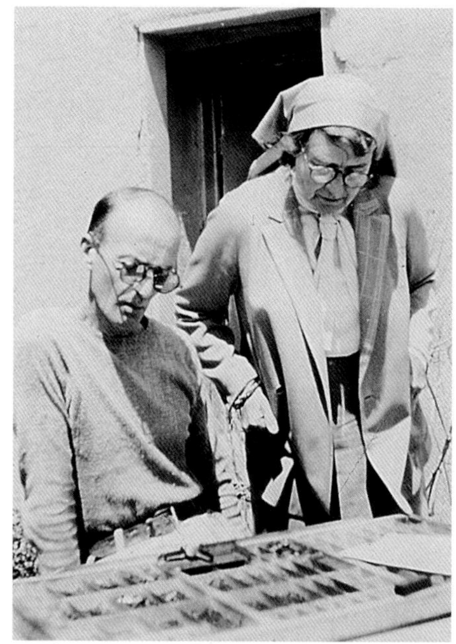

Spud Johnson and Mabel Dodge Luhan review type at Spud's house, 1950s.

Frieda and David Lawrence genuinely liked their hosts. Although David Lawrence and Bynner would carry on literary and philosophical tempests, Spud secretly thought the two giant egos loved each other. Lawrence's affection for Spoodle never wavered, but Bynner felt betrayed when Mabel hired Spud away as her secretary and publicist in 1927.

Spud seized the opportunity in front of him; he asked Lawrence to contribute to the next issue of *The Laughing Horse*. Already internationally famous, Lawrence would lend instant prestige to the fledgling magazine. Surprisingly, Lawrence responded with a review of Ben Hecht's book *Fantazius Mallare* that was published in the fourth issue of *The Laughing Horse*.

The incident was a watershed in Spud's career and for the growing reputation of *The Laughing Horse*. Years later, Spud reflected that "Lawrence's review we had printed with all the 'objectionable' four-letter words left out—but the presence of dashes made it seem even more 'obscene' than if we had left them in!" Berkeley officials were not amused. Declaring *The Laughing Horse* obscene, they tried to suppress its publication and distribution, which, of course, rallied prominent artists and writers to defend the magazine. Most importantly, the publicity raised the stature of *The Laughing Horse* to one of the literary world's notable "little magazines."

Witter and Spud developed close friendships with the Lawrences while they were in residence at Mabel's, and later trudged through deep snow in January to visit them at the Del Monte Ranch. By March 1923, the two couples were making plans to head for the Mexican border and points south.

D. H. Lawrence's first trip to Mexico accompanied by Witter Bynner and Spud Johnson has become an important saga of the Lawrencian myth, having been well told by Lawrence himself in *The Plumed Serpent,* a vast and ambitious novel published in 1926 that nearly killed him. Bynner published his slightly acidic reflections on Lorenzo and Mexico in 1951 as *Journey with Genius.* Under the pen name "Bud Villiers," which was his character in *The Plumed Serpent,* Spud offered the essay "D. H. Lawrence in Mexico," which was published in 1930, the year of Lorenzo's death.

Spud's account of the vacation is self-effacing, humorous, entertaining, and perceptive regarding the talents he was traveling with, including Frieda. He remembered the following:

> *The days we spent there, some are sharply etched in memory. . . . [T]here was the day we discovered [the great illustrator Miguel] Covarrubias in a sort of Greenwich Village cafe on the Calle de la Republica de Cuba; and the day I went to the hospital followed by a shower of Lawrencian invectives for having drunk too much tequila; and the day Mrs. Lawrence discovered the strawberry shortcake at Sanborn's.*

THE HORSE FLY

Smallest and Most Inadequate Newspaper Ever Published

Vol. I, No. 2. *Taos, New Mexico* *July 16th, 1938*

CAN MABEL'S TRIAL CONTINUE WITHOUT PLAINTIFF, JURORS AND WITNESSES?

Dr. Charles D. Kantor's $50,000 slander suit against Mabel Dodge Luhan, will be resumed in District Court here early Monday morning, but apparently without a jury, without witnesses, and without the plaintiff! But anyhow not without an audience.

"I was very much surprised and disappointed to read in the paper that the jury has been dismissed," said Mrs. Luhan in an interview last night. "None of my lawyers told me a thing about it! What's the use of having so many lawyers, if they won't tell me of developments in my own case?"

Indications are that Kantor's attorneys will file a plea for dismissal on Monday, but court will convene and it will be argued, nevertheless. Defense attorneys intimate they will not accept dismissal save "with prejudice." A dismissal "without prejudice" might be a loophole for a later suit, they claim.

Accident Victim To Leave Hospital

Mrs. Robinson Jeffers, who has been under treatment at the Holy Cross Hospital all week as a result of a gun-shot wound in her left side, self-inflicted while cleaning a pistol last Saturday night, is reported much improved. She expects to leave the hospital tomorrow.

RAYMOND OTIS

The many Taos friends of Raymond Otis, beloved Santa Fe novelist, were both shocked and grieved to hear of his untimely death on Wednesday night. Not only have his friends lost a staunch and faithful ally, but the world is poorer from the loss of a gallant and beautiful spirit.

Precinct Primary In Syrian Saloon?

An unofficial A.P. report, states that there are two complete sets of delegates to the Taos County Democratic Convention to be held here Monday: one all-wet set elected by the Walk-Out Party in the Younis Bar, late Wednesday night.

Children's Book Benefit at Harwood Sunday

NEW EXHIBIT IN GALLERY

Music-starved Taosenos have a treat in store for them at the Harwood Foundation Library on Sunday afternoon, July 17, at 4 p.m., when they will have the opportunity to enjoy an hour of vocal and instrumental music; and at the same time contribute to a most worthy cause: The Children's Book Fund.

The program will include a group of songs by Miss L. Langston, soprano, who has been broadcasting over the radio from Phoenix, Arizona; selections by Eduardo Rael, well-known Taos baritone; and several numbers by Mr. David Middleton, an accomplished pianist, nephew of Mrs. Joseph Fleck, and son of the famous writer, Scudder Middleton.

A silver offering will be taken for the Children's Book Fund—and it has been announced that Tony Tarleton will take contributions for this fund from any who cannot attend the concert, but who would like to help buy books for the children.

SECOND EXHIBITION

On Sunday, also, the second 1938 exhibition of the paintings of Taos artists will be opened to the public in the new gallery directly above the Library. This is likely to be even better than the last one.

Note the headline of a July 1938 edition of The Horse Fly.

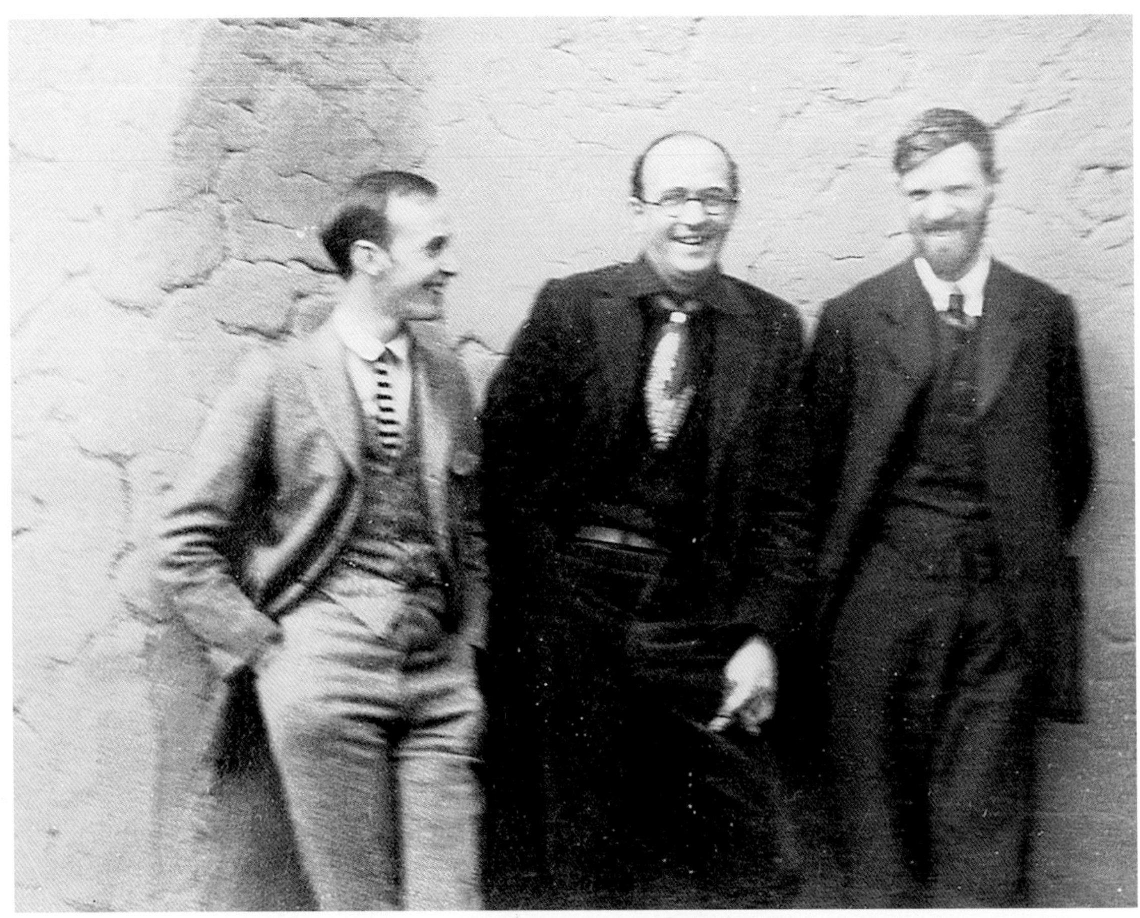

Spud Johnson, Witter Bynner, and D. H. Lawrence at Bynner's house in Santa Fe shortly before their Mexican adventure in 1923.

THE HORSE FLY

Vol. I, No. 5. *Taos, New Mexico* *August 6, 1938*

Come to Good Old Taos For the New Revolution!

Miss Myra Kingsley, famed New York astrologress and horoscopist, was to have been the guest of Mrs. Mabel Luhan this week, but she got lost en route. She says there is to be another bloody American Revolution in 1942 (according to the stars) and that she is looking for a New Mexico hide-out to which she may escape at that time. Perhaps she found such a hermitage, somewhere down the canyon. Or maybe she's decided not to arrive in Taos until the cataclysm, and is making a four-year detour on the new hypothetical Tingley highway in the hills above Pilar.

The 'Review' Has Bud Sahd as Editor

Peter (Bud) Sahd, son of P. A. Sahd, and brother of—well, all the other Sahd boys and girls—took over the "Taos Review" this week as its new editor. Here's best of luck to him from *The Horse Fly.*

Sahd is a graduate of the University of New Mexico, and has been interested in writing for some years, practising the craft while teaching school. He is at the moment writing a play in his spare time.

Taos Council Plans OIL LAMPS As Street Lights

NUDE PROWLER SPURS OFFICIALS INTO ACTION

To avoid the prohibitive cost of expensive electric equipment and current, yet to provide much-needed illumination, the village Council is now planning installation of oil lamps as street lights.

The argument at the last council meeting was brief. Taos streets are dark and rough, quite often full of mud-holes; a nude man terrorized our women-folk only last week; Taos electricity is expensive; and Taos Village is poor. Ergo: kerosene.

The plan is to have attractive lanterns designed by local artists, executed by local tin- and black-smiths, then donated by our more affluent citizens or clubs as memorials. Thus, a 'Dr. Martin Light' at the corner of Bent & Pueblo; a 'Dunton Lantern' in the Loma plaza, et cetera.

This should not only solve the town's double problem of illumination with economy; but will certainly be unique and, if well done, most attractive as well.

We're for it!

Lockwood Goes Chinese On Us

If you're interested in the unusual and experimental in art, one of the most amusing paintings now on exhibit in Taos, is included in the new show at the Heptagon gallery. It's a water-color by Ward Lockwood, depicting a late spring snow; and not until you approach to within a couple of feet of it, do you see that the artist has supplied the picture with a text. Running along below the clouds, among the branches of trees, across foothills, as much a part of the design as the brush-strokes themselves, is a description of the scene and of the occasion of its painting. Just like a Chinese painting, with its poem in ideographs. And yet Ward says he wasn't imitating the oriental idea, only giving an explanation because it seemed to be needed. Better go in and see it.

Taos Voices

ELLIS DE LONG is now announcing for KOZ, Denver; & ARCH KEPNER is one of the new announcers over WQXR, New York City, said to be one of the best and most independent stations in the country. EDUARDO RAEL is in Denver, hoping for a radio-opportunity, but he has not yet been heard from.

COMPARATIVE STATEMENT OF CONDITION OF FIRST STATE BANK OF TAOS, NEW MEXICO

Resources:	Aug. 1, 1937	Aug. 1, 1938
Due from Federal Reserve Bank	None.	$ 42,610.37
Cash and sight exchange	$ 94,779.80	110,461.01
U.S., Other bonds and securities	153,331.67	112,358.18
Fixtures & other Real Estate	4,300.00	3,800.00
Loans and Discounts	180,508.11	185,366.22
Total	$ 432,919.58	$ 454,595.78
Liabilities:		
Capital Stock	$ 25,000.00	$ 25,000.00
Surplus Fund	7,500.00	12,500.00
Undivided Profits	1,904.63	2,160.41
Reserves	5,362.50	4,250.00
DEPOSITS	393,152.45	410,685.37
Total	$ 432,919.58	$ 454,595.78

Member Federal Reserve System - Member Federal Deposit Insurance Corporation

Another edition of The Horse Fly *from August 1938.*

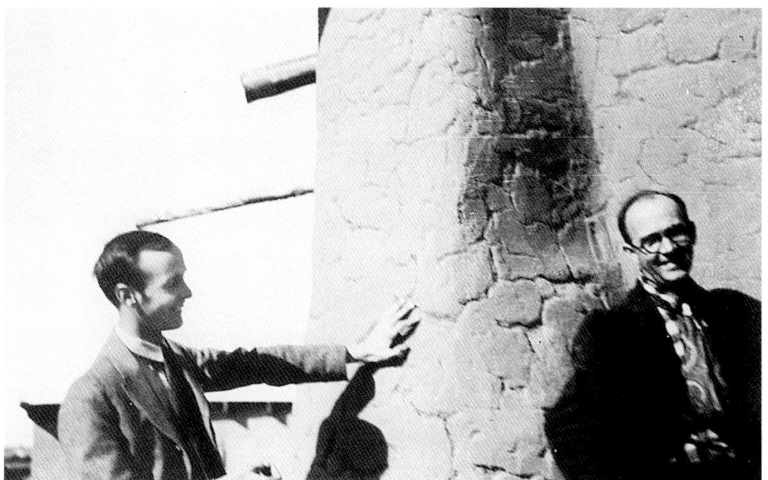

Spud Johnson and Witter Bynner, 1923.

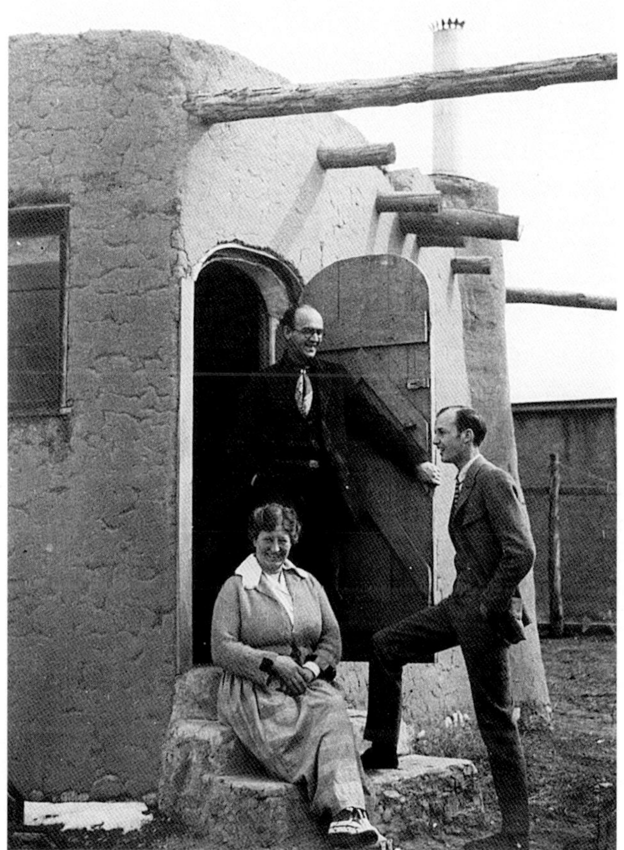

Witter Bynner, Spud Johnson, and Frieda Lawrence at Bynner's house, 1923.

Once arrived at Lake Chapala near Guadalajara, Spud describes the slightly surreal spectacle of two famous authors viciously attacking each other by night and pleasantly walking along Chapala's beaches or back streets by day, enjoying the sleepy Mexican resort village. As Lawrence's traveling secretary, Spud secretly snickered at Lorenzo's scathing portraits of his friends Mabel and Bynner and even poked fun at himself.

Other times we walked on the beach of the lake or the pier when week-end crowds gave a semblance of gayety. We laughed at the fi-fi boys—or rather the others did, always with sly digs to the effect that I was also a fi-fi boy, which injured my pride tremendously. But my reputation as such became fixed when it was known that I sometimes joined the dancers on the Sunday night sidewalks in front of the cafes.

For Spud, the Mexican adventure ended beautifully and poetically, on a boat in the great lake of Mexico during the early days of June. With Lawrence and Frieda and the boat crew (Bynner left the party early due to illness), Spud's vessel drifted on, "slow as the little islands of water hyacinths." At night on the still waters of Chapala, the thick warm air trembled with the boisterous frontier ballads of the Mexican crew or the sentimental English songs Lawrence bellowed out from his sad childhood.

Back in Santa Fe, Spud and Bynner slowly grew apart. Spud had matured in his own right as a poet and personality, and Taos seemed to suit his style better than Santa Fe. Besides, Mabel was generous to him and didn't grate on his nerves like she did on everyone else—he wasn't competing with her. By 1927 Spud had decided to stay in Taos and become Mabel's secretary and publicist. For Bynner this was the last straw. By "stealing" his protégé and lover, Mabel had struck at Bynner's pride. He retaliated in 1929 with his scathing play about Mabel called *Cake*, inscribing his copy to Mabel: "Cast your bread on the Witter, and it comes back Cake."

Meanwhile, Spud continued his sundry literary projects. Initially planned as a monthly, *The Laughing Horse* evolved into a quarterly review by the mid-1920s, with Spud as its sole editor. By 1927 Spud purchased his own foot-operated printing press and went into business as "Willard Johnson, Pamphleteer, Laughing Horse Press, Taos, New Mexico."

Spud's own writing projects were unconventional and far-ranging, including a stint during the fall of 1926 as a staff writer for the emerging *New Yorker* magazine. Spud easily adapted to *New Yorker*'s urbane style and readership, and the great editor Harold Ross warned him not to tell anyone where he was really from!

In the late 1920s and '30s, Spud toiled devotedly to keep his publication alive and vibrant. He literally handcrafted each issue—printing, collecting, folding and stapling each copy by himself or sometimes with friends' help—in his three-room adobe house. After the initial Bay Area issues, *The Laughing Horse* became a southwestern literary journal with a few exceptions, such as the special issues on Mexico, censorship, and D. H. Lawrence. The last issue of *The Laughing Horse* appeared in 1939. As publications, the issues of *The Laughing Horse* were semipermanent in nature and highly disposable. Few have survived and are much sought after by collectors. A Taos bookstore recently featured rare original issues of *The Laughing Horse* for sale at $400 each!

Spud enjoyed the parade of notable guests that wound its way through Mabel's salons and guest houses during the "glory" years. In particular, he became a favorite of Georgia O'Keeffe, Thornton Wilder, Lincoln Steffens, and Leopold Stokowski. In a letter to his friend Gina Knee, he described a memorable Christmas:

Brett and I went to Abiquiu Christmas Eve and spent a very pleasant two days with Georgia O'Keeffe. To be more exact, I commuted between Taos and Abiquiu over the holiday. After dinner on the 24th, we lit Christmas trees (one inside, one out in the patio), built the traditional 9 bonfires on the cliff-edge outside, drank mulled wine, and gossiped cozily before the fire, went to midnight mass in the nearby church. On the 25th we drove to Taos to see the Deer Dance, returning to Abiquiu for turkey dinner that night. And on the 26th, Brett and I returned home.

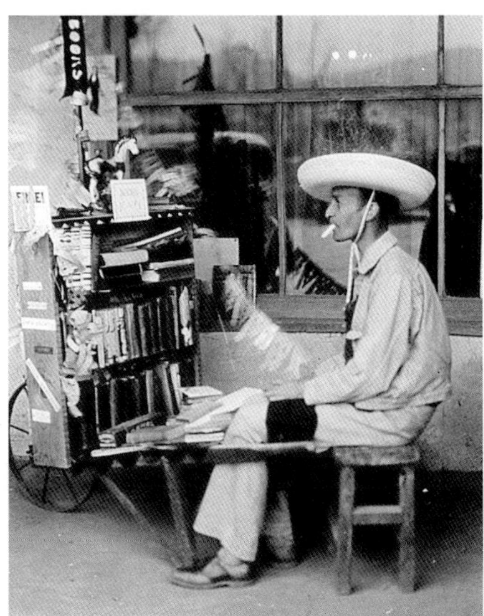

Spud Johnson and his portable book cart, circa 1935.

With the demise of *The Laughing Horse* in 1939, Spud turned his attentions to a humorous spin-off, *The Horse Fly,* a one-sheet rag billed as "The Smallest and Most Inadequate Newspaper Ever Published." Extremely labor intensive and very low budget, *The Horse Fly* taxed Spud's resources. He produced exactly fifty-two weeks' worth before writing its obituary in the final issue. *The Horse Fly* later became a column in the county newspaper. On several occasions, both in Santa Fe and Taos, Spud contributed many precious columns on local affairs, personalities, and visiting dignitaries that endeared him to the public.

Spud passed on in 1968, a few years after Mabel died and the same year as Witter Bynner's death. He was loved dearly by his close friends and from afar by his readers. His own homosexuality made it difficult, if not impossible, for him to find a lifelong companion in remote northern New Mexico. In Taos he ultimately settled on his love of the place and its legends. It was enough to sustain the lover of horses and words.

The "back room" in Spud's house is Rembrandtesque: all brown and black and white, from the hand press and the trays of type, the stove, the benches, the loom (where some day, we suppose serapes will be woven, fusing together into odd patterns against the white walls), the dim old ceiling made of ancient cedar strips laid on beams, which comes weightily close to one's head, and the dirt floor, which provides a constant veil of fine dust which softens every outline and subdues every surface. A few numbers of past "Laughing Horses" that were born in this room, rest on shelves in their assorted colors. The room has dark corners; it has warmth, vitality, and the sense of being that places have where someone works and likes it.

Mabel Dodge Luhan, "Spud's House,"
from Winter in Taos, *1935*

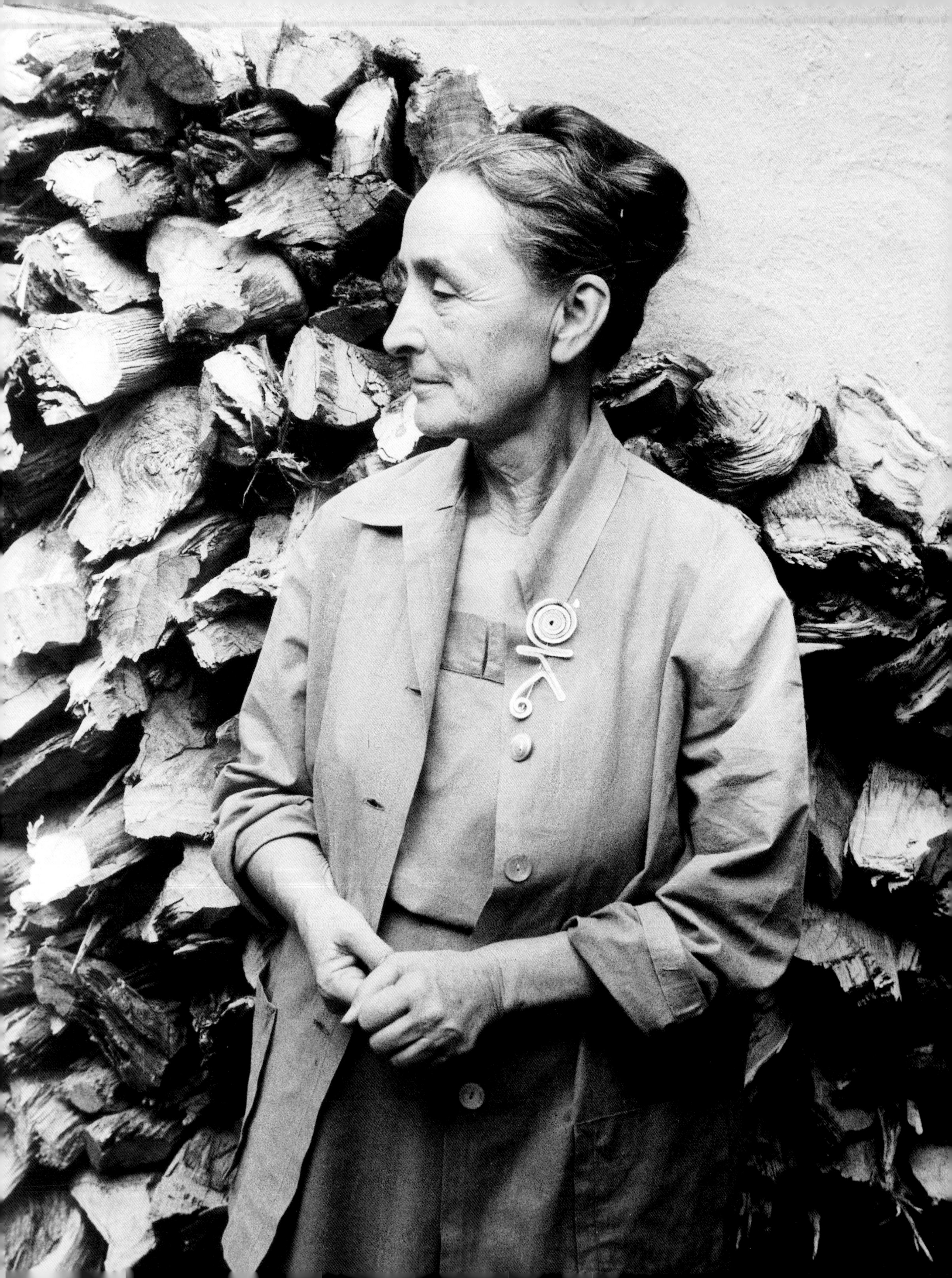

Flowering of O'Keeffe

A Woman on Paper

Georgia O'Keeffe had shaken the foundations of New York's art world long before her fateful visit to New Mexico in the summer of 1929. From commonplace beginnings in Wisconsin and Virginia, Georgia emerged as a young woman with an almost fully realized personality and tenacious will. An expert seamstress, she meticulously crafted her simple and elegant dresses and tunics during high school and throughout her life. Her trademark black-and-white wardrobe was developed from her youth, which instantly set her apart from all other women.

Throughout her life, O'Keeffe glowed as an enigmatic beauty. Her willowy features, ivory skin, and exquisite hands (they were long and tailored, noticed by everyone) were a dramatic contrast to her austere clothes. As much as any other woman in the history of art, Georgia O'Keeffe possessed the hypnotic presence of a Mona Lisa. Willful, mostly serious, a serene but somehow volcanic presence, highly charged, O'Keeffe could also bless her intimate world with a soft smile, which formed slowly and deliberately on her lips as if it were a flower blooming.

Early in 1916, close friend and confidante Anita Pollitzer received a package of drawings in New York from Georgia, who was then a teacher at Columbia College for women in South Carolina. The bold charcoal abstractions pulsated with energy. Impulsively Anita took the powerful works to Alfred Stieglitz at Gallery 291. Stieglitz had earned a solid reputation as a champion of modernist artists and also pioneered the introduction of the European avant-garde artists in America.

By then in his early fifties, Stieglitz was a commanding bespectacled and mustachioed figure who loved to "hold court" in his gallery and elsewhere. The polemics of art and the artist's utter devotion to the expression of truth and beauty formed Stieglitz's passion. He had met Georgia briefly in his gallery during one of her excursions to New York. But when he unrolled the sheaf of Georgia's drawings in Anita's presence, he instinctively appreciated the extraordinary. "At last, a woman on paper!" he blurted, either vocally or subconsciously (the legend is not clear). Certainly Stieglitz could feel the feminine energy of the art, and so could everyone who gazed upon Georgia's rapidly maturing sensitivities.

By 1918 Georgia and Alfred had begun their mating dance. Her first show at Gallery 291 in the late spring of 1916 had caused a sensation; most critics and viewers were not sure how to react to the rich charcoal drawings of abstract yet fleshy forms, evocative of fertility and sexuality. Men squirmed and women gasped.

In the fall of 1916, Georgia departed for a teaching job at West Texas State Normal

Georgia O'Keeffe in Abiquiu, 1950s.

College in Canyon, Texas. Her confidence was buoyed by Stieglitz's enthusiasm for her work, and the curious stares and questions from faculty members, students, and townspeople had little or no effect. She worked harder than ever, knowing that Gallery 291 was waiting. So, too, was Stieglitz.

His marriage of twenty-four years was stale, and his finances were tenuous. Georgia's star glowed faintly but distinctly for Stieglitz far beyond the western horizon. He mounted another impressive spring showing of her work in 1917, and she sold a watercolor for $400. Georgia could feel his desperation in his letters, and in late May she boarded a train for a brief vacation in the city. Alfred's spirits soared when Georgia arrived, and he asked her to pose for photographs (Stieglitz has been called the "father of modern photography"). Georgia was deeply flattered and charmed by Stieglitz.

For Georgia, the break with a teacher's life in academia was becoming inevitable. Canyon, Texas, had become rabid with patriotic fervor for World War I, and Georgia's antiwar sentiments did not go unnoticed. The fall of 1917 and winter of 1918 were wrenched with Georgia's misgivings, misunderstandings with townspeople and faculty members, and influenza. She took a leave of absence from the college in late February and never looked back. After convalescing during the spring of 1918 in Waring and San Antonio, Texas, O'Keeffe was ready to return to Stieglitz in June.

Finally, their mutual admiration grew into passionate love. Georgia moved into Stieglitz's two-room brownstone at 114 East Fifty-ninth Street, where the hot July days were spent making love, talking, and taking photographs. Alfred began a fifteen-year study of Georgia O'Keeffe's body, moods, and her soul, which he called her "whiteness," producing more than 300 photographs and one of the most unique collaborations in the history of art. Georgia's intensity was essential to Stieglitz's art:

He wanted head and hands and arms on a pillow in many different positions. I was asked to move my arms in many different positions. I was asked to move my hands in many different ways also my head and I had to turn this way and that. There were nudes that might have been of several different people. . . . There were large heads, profiles and what not. . . . I was photographed with a kind of heat and excitement.

Later that summer, the couple traveled to the Stieglitz retreat at Lake George in upstate New York, establishing a migratory pattern of winters in Manhattan and summers on the lake that they would follow for the next ten years. Alfred was still married, but Georgia was championed by the matriarch Hedwig, and the Stieglitz clan soon became accustomed to Georgia's reclusive privacy and unorthodox habits.

Stieglitz's estranged wife Emmy was not inclined to forgive, however. Income from her family had enabled Alfred to live

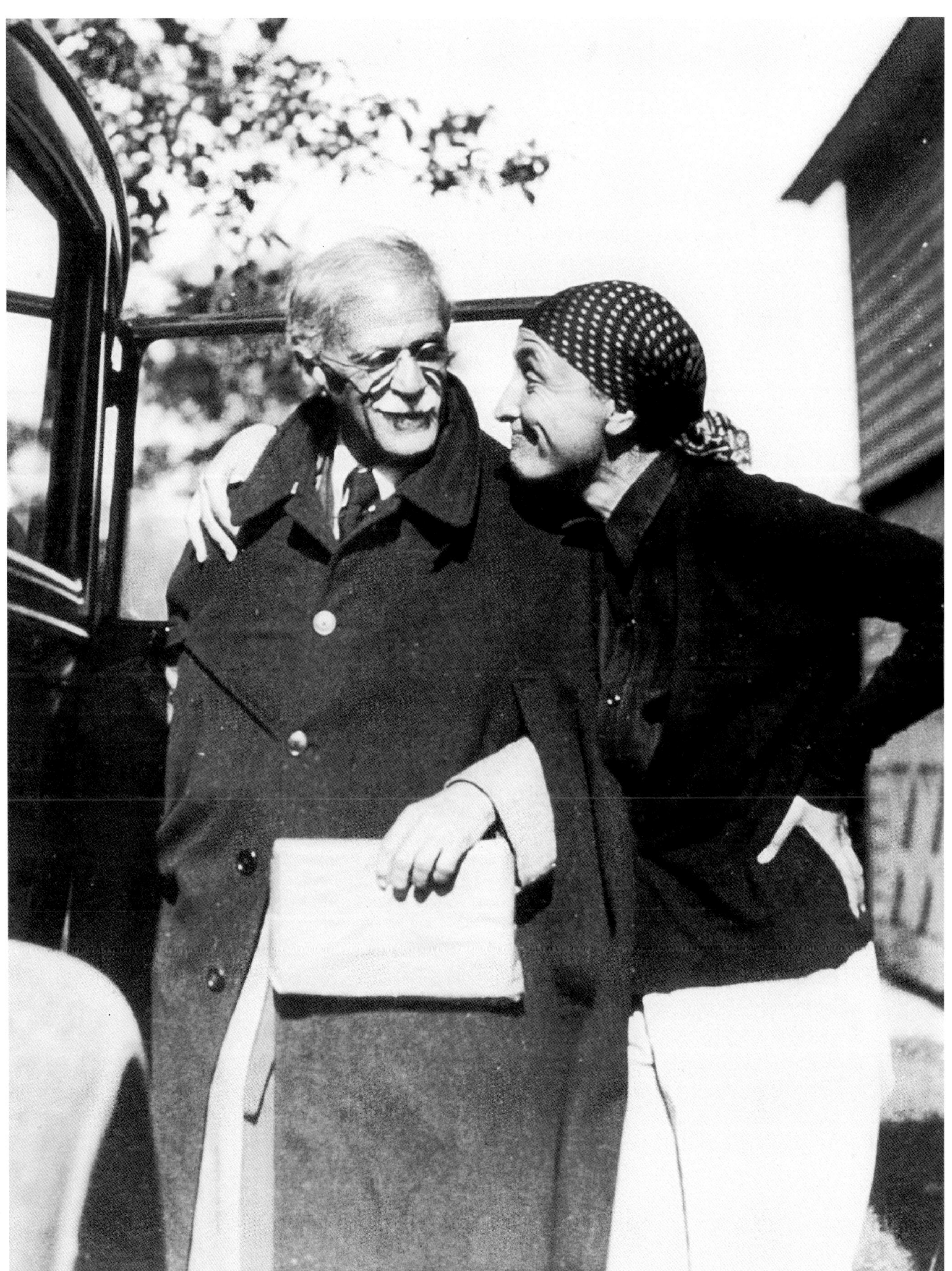

Alfred Stieglitz and Georgia O'Keeffe banter at Lake George, New York, upon her return from New Mexico in September 1929.

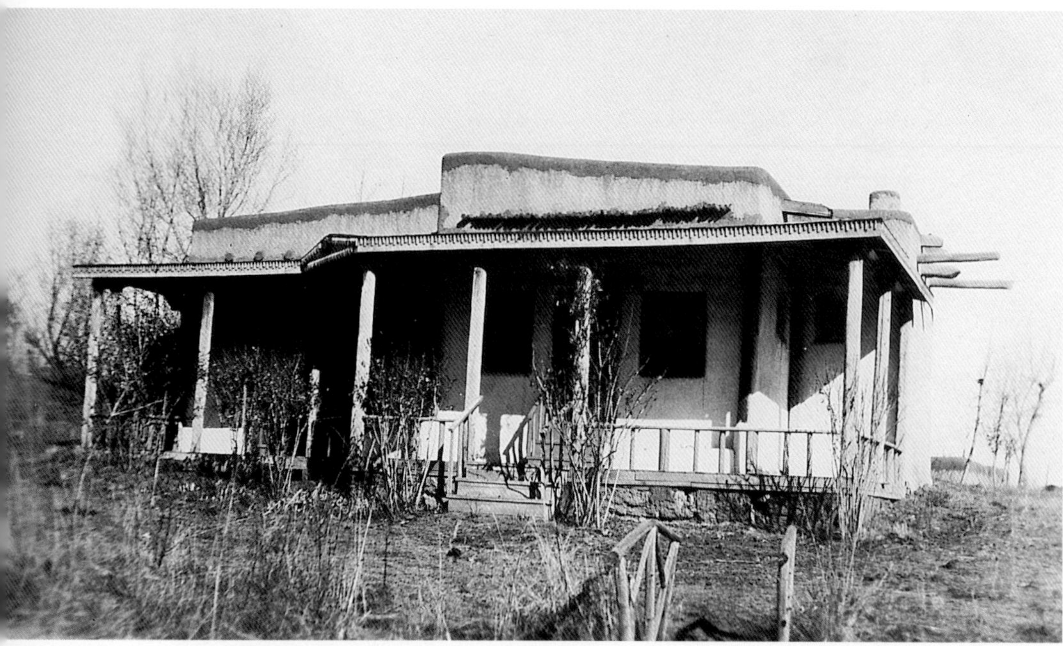

The Pink Studio, Mabel Dodge Luhan estate, Taos, about 1925.

uncompromised as a high priest of photography and modern art. Now Alfred and Georgia must forage for survival. Fortunately, Alfred's brother Lee stepped in to offer the couple an apartment. Through it all, Georgia maintained her laser-like concentration and composure, continuing to paint and develop her unique vision.

A Portfolio of Blossoms

One of the couple's closest friends during this early blissful period was Paul Strand, a disciple of Stieglitz who was quickly becoming a master photographer in his own right. Strand had been part of Stieglitz's stable of modernists at Gallery 291. Georgia had been attracted to Strand emotionally and physically as well as artistically. His closely focused, meticulously cropped photographs profoundly impressed her.

Georgia herself was evolving out of the phase of abstraction that had so befuddled audiences and critics with the overtones of feminine forms, colors, and implied sexuality. Her attention was becoming intent on directing her powerful emotions on simple but tangible forms—plums, grapes, pears, and apples—all meditatively and sensuously rendered.

She had become attracted to calla lilies, whose large brilliant blossoms and beautifully tapered foliage seemed a logical progression in form from the abstractions. But Georgia, perhaps co-opting some of Strand's vision, presented the great lilies close-up so that they filled and overflowed the boundaries of the canvas. The new O'Keeffe flowers were startling and potent. Later in 1928, a small set of six O'Keeffe calla lily panels was sold by an astonished Stieglitz to an American collector living in France for $25,000. That sum, equivalent to about $250,000 today, was the highest sale on record for a living American artist.

Throughout the mid-1920s, O'Keeffe's annual shows had become sensations in New York. She had greatly expanded her flower repertoire, increasingly attracted by dark or black blossoms as if to reflect her own somber wardrobe. Dark pansies, petunias, and purple-black irises were her favorites. The glorious flower paintings emerged as Georgia's personal life was stabilizing. Alfred had finally been granted a divorce by Emmy, and he and Georgia were unceremoniously married in December 1924.

After 1925, however, the dynamics of Alfred and Georgia's marriage began to subtly shift. Increasingly, Georgia's art had become a force to be reckoned with. She had become accepted by the New York art world as one of the leading modern artists, and her sales had helped keep Stieglitz and his gallery afloat.

Her flower paintings had touched a nerve in the public consciousness, and audiences and critics alike were reacting strongly to the erotic forms of the blossoms. In a decade of sexual awakening, O'Keeffe's art was celebrated as the visual counterpart to the frankly sexual literature of D. H. Lawrence. Influential critic Lewis Mumford observed that Georgia "has invented a language, and she has conveyed directly and chastely in paint experiences for which language conveys only obscenities. Without painting a single nude, without showing a part of the human body, she has magnificently embodied passion, sexual life, womanhood, as physical elements and as states of mind."

Manhattan Towers

In the fall of 1925, assured by increasing sales, Stieglitz and O'Keeffe moved to the new Shelton Hotel, a thirty-four-story building at Lexington Avenue and Forty-eighth Street on Manhattan's East Side. Georgia's choice of the Shelton was eminently practical: she would not have to cook or clean house in the managed building. From the couple's sparsely furnished two-room suite on the twenty-eighth floor (typically painted neutral gray so as not to distract the artist from her colors), Georgia could devote her entire waking hours to art. Within the next five years, O'Keeffe would complete a series of skyline and skyscraper paintings to complement her oeuvre of flowers, shells, and abstractions.

Though life and work in the Shelton were fully under Georgia's control, her relationship with Stieglitz was being tested. In some important ways, the pair were opposites. Georgia required absolute privacy and control of her environment to do her art; Stieglitz enjoyed collaboration and the

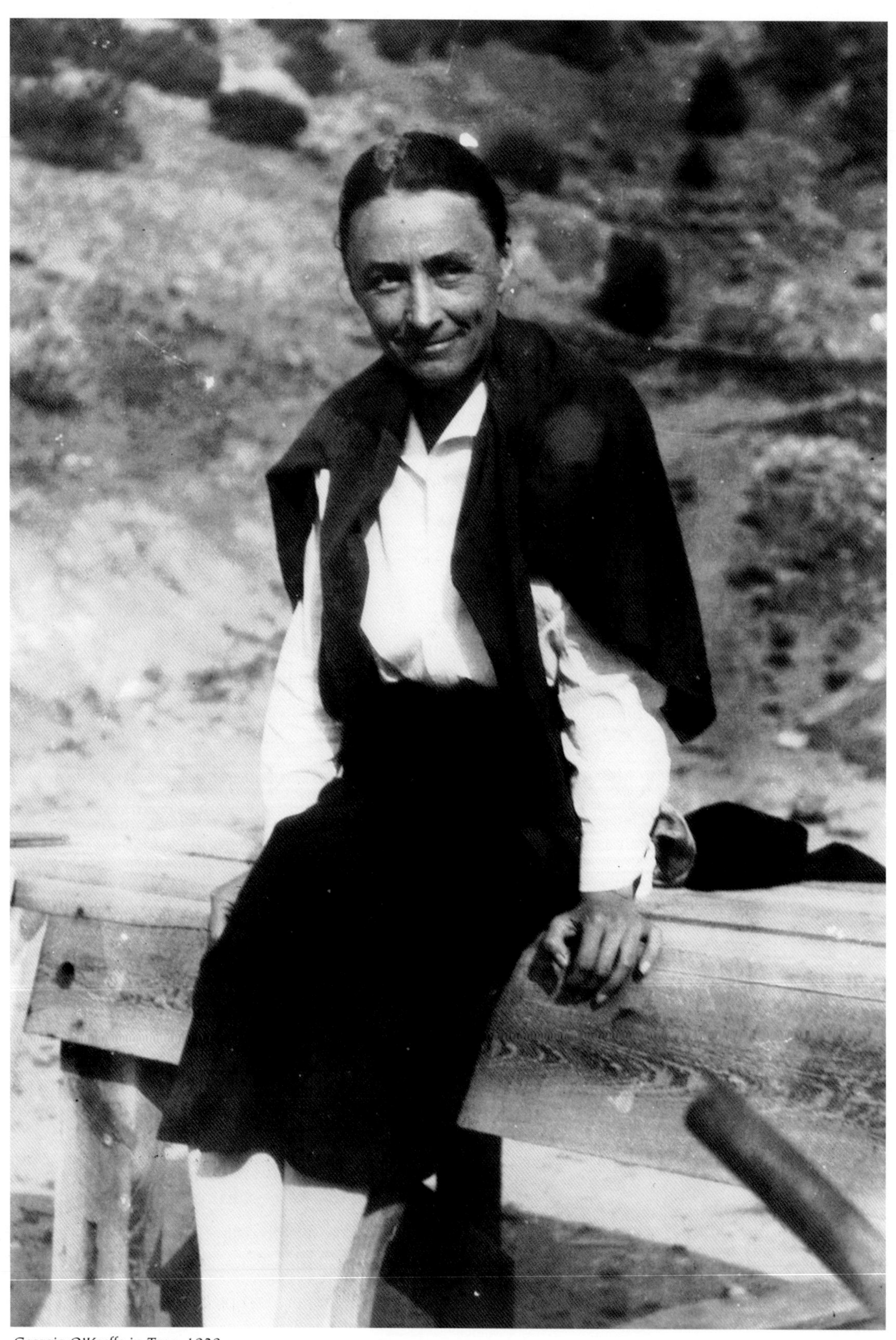

Georgia O'Keeffe in Taos, 1929.

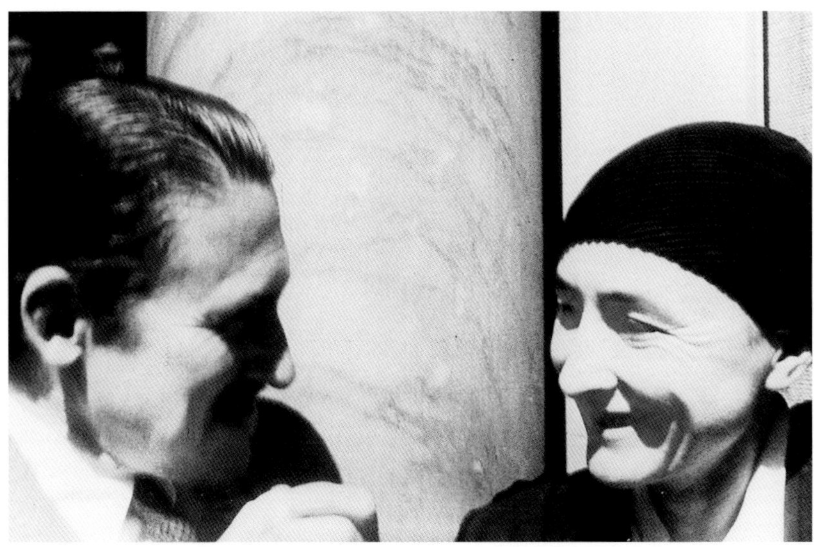

Georgia O'Keeffe and an unidentified friend at the Museum of Modern Art, 1932.

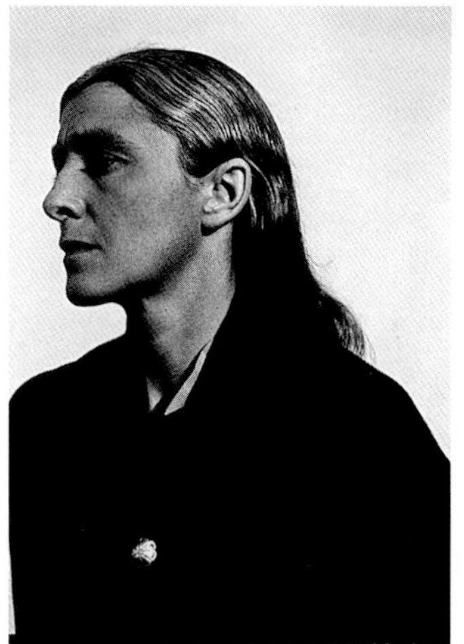

Rebecca "Beck" Strand, wife of photographer Paul Strand and close friend of Alfred Stieglitz and Georgia O'Keefe.

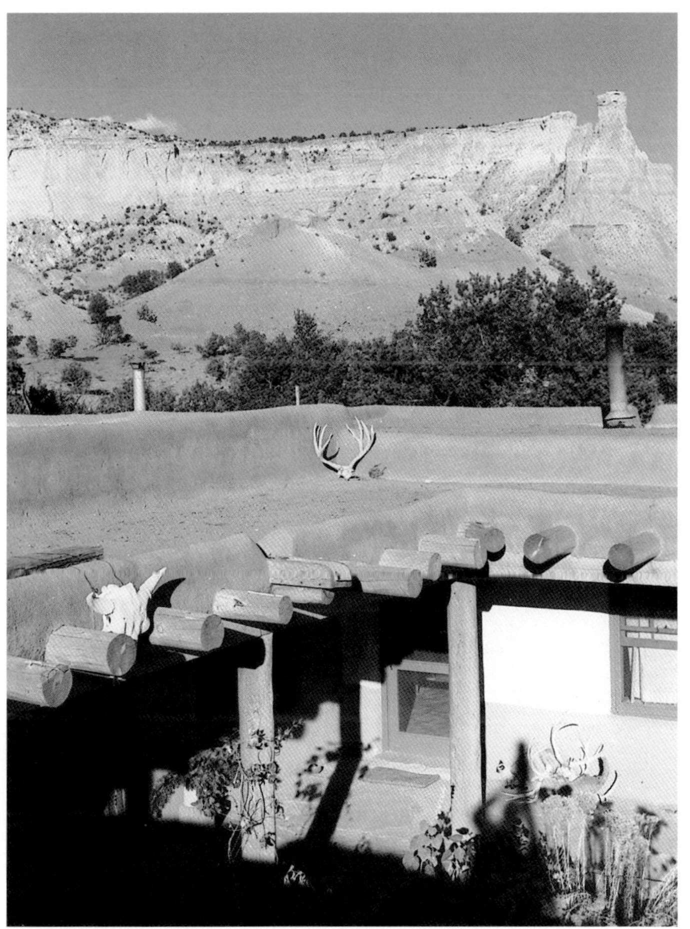

Georgia O'Keeffe's house in Ghost Ranch, New Mexico, as it appeared in the 1950s.

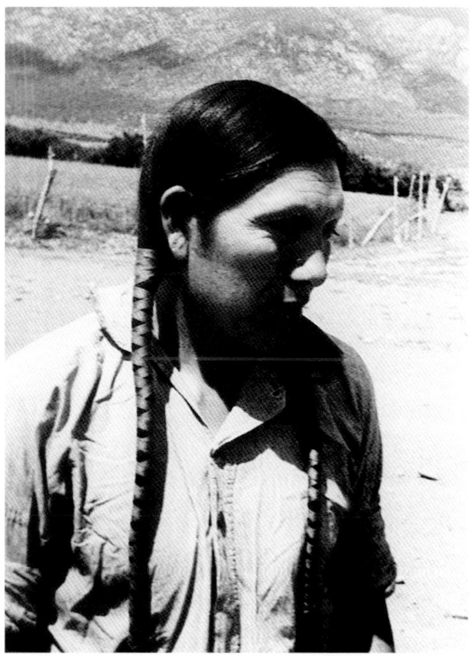

Trinidad, Taos Pueblo Indian, about 1930.

company of other artists. Georgia was intensely private and shunned the limelight she increasingly attracted; Stieglitz basked in attention and adulation of others. Inevitably, it was the annual retreat to Lake George that began to accentuate their differences.

In spite of his urbanity and artistic sophistication, Stieglitz was a provincial New Yorker, never having ventured far from the Manhattan–Lake George axis (except for trips to Europe in his youth). In actuality, Alfred was a control freak who didn't much care to have his daily or annual routines altered. Georgia began to find the Lake George summers stifling with boisterous nosy Stieglitzes, foggy clammy weather, and too much greenery. By 1928, she despaired for a lack of inspiration and new themes for her painting. She was restless and longed for the vast prairie sky she had loved and painted in Texas.

Alfred's health became a serious concern in the fall of 1928. The sixty-four-year-old photographer suffered a heart attack and was confined to bed. Georgia and her sister Ida nursed Alfred lovingly, but it was nearly impossible for Georgia to paint. At forty-one years old, Georgia was reaching her creative peak but felt trapped. To friends she appeared depressed and exhausted.

That winter Dorothy Brett stayed at the Shelton for an extended visit. Dorothy had followed D. H. Lawrence to Taos in 1924 and had come to know O'Keeffe from her occasional trips to New York. A painter herself, Brett had gained Georgia's affection. Brett remembered fondly her breakfasts with Stieglitz and O'Keeffe at the Shelton's cafeteria:

The famous breakfasts began . . . Stieglitz with his silver hair like an aureole round his head; his serene face; lovely, shapely lips; strange dark eyes . . . slight and small . . . composed and dignified. Georgia, her pure profile against the dark wood of the paneling, calm, clear, her sleek black hair drawn swiftly back into a tight knot at the nape of her neck; the strong white hands, touching and lifting everything, even the boiled eggs as if they were living things—sensitive, slow-moving hands.

More importantly, Brett was the harbinger of change for O'Keeffe. Mabel Dodge Luhan and her husband Tony had also visited New York during Georgia's winter of discontent. Mabel had offered Georgia a studio in Taos anytime she wished to come, and the lure of the West grew larger for Georgia as the light faded on 1928. The following spring Georgia resolved to go to New Mexico, and Stieglitz, wisely, didn't hold her back.

The Mountain Beckons

After her disappointing winter show of 1929 (even the critics noted that O'Keeffe's work seemed to be in transition), Georgia began methodically packing clothing and art supplies for the overland odyssey to New Mexico. She coaxed Rebecca Salsbury Strand, Paul's wife, into joining her for the adventure, which helped calm Stieglitz's anxieties. Beck Strand was strikingly handsome—regal and leonine, flashing sapphire blue eyes and white-blond hair. High spirited and playful, Beck showed her independence at times by donning mannish clothing. She would help steer Georgia through her midlife rite of passage. On April 27, the two women boarded a train bound for Santa Fe.

Almost immediately upon their arrival in Santa Fe on April 30, Georgia and Beck purchased Harvey motor-coach tickets to see the corn dance at San Felipe Pueblo. Although they had arrived in New Mexico unannounced, Georgia recognized Tony Luhan and Mabel at the corn dance, and Mabel took over.

The Strands had been guests at Mabel's estate in Taos before, and Beck knew how domineering Mabel could be. Strong-willed Georgia was probably too worn out and awe-struck by the exotic scenery to put up much resistance. The next morning, the group left La Posada Hotel and snaked through the Rio Grande canyons en route to Mabel's Los Gallos (The Roosters) enclave.

Mabel settled Georgia and Beck into guest bedrooms within the Big House, but after three weeks, the two women relocated to the Pink House, where they would enjoy more privacy. Georgia also was given a separate adobe studio on the property. Almost immediately, Georgia was overwhelmed, declaring joyously, "Well! Well! Well! This is wonderful. No one told me it was like *this!*"

For most tourists venturing up to the high plains of Taos (7,500 feet), the perception of vision is enhanced by the pure sunlight and thin air. One can suddenly see clearly, vividly, and far, far away to Pedernal

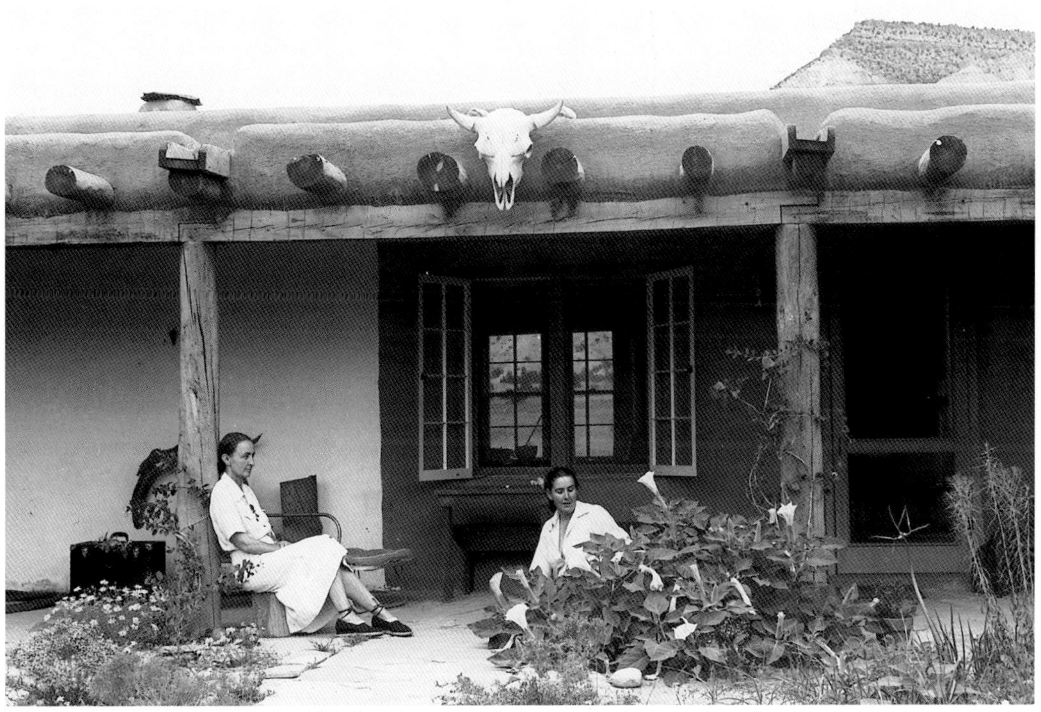

Georgia O'Keeffe and an unidentified friend in the courtyard of Georgia's Ghost Ranch residence, circa 1950s.

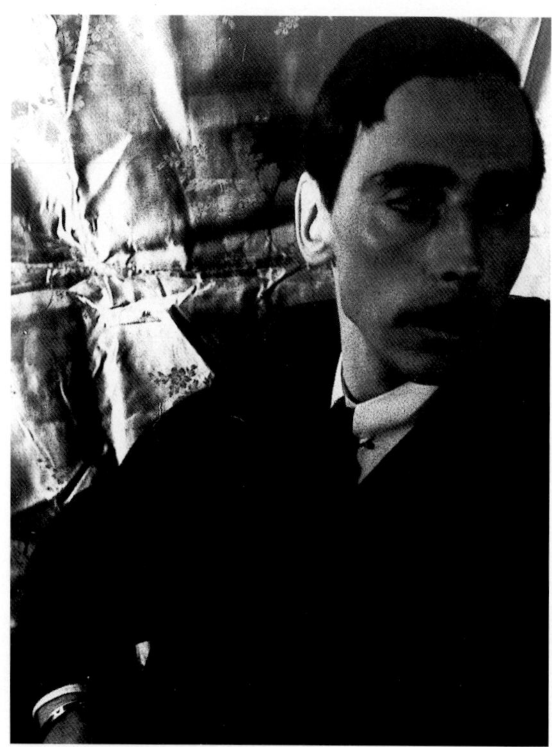

Santa Fe writer Oliver La Farge, December 1933.

Peak (a noble and solitary saddle-horn mesa that became a favorite O'Keeffe haunt) some sixty miles distant. For a person possessed of O'Keeffe's visual powers of focus and emotional empathy, the New Mexico landscape was overwhelming and exhilarating. Georgia's first impressions render Taos as "a high, wide, sage-covered plain. In the evening, with the sun at your back, it looks like an ocean, like water. The color up there is different . . . the blue-green of the sage and mountains, the wildflowers in bloom. It's a different kind of color from any I'd ever seen—there's nothing like that in north Texas or even in Colorado. And it's not just the color that attracted me either. The world is so wide up there, so big." From May 1929 until her death on March 6, 1986, at the age of ninety-eight, Georgia O'Keeffe never satiated her passion for the sage-and-juniper-dotted earth of Taos country and fought heroically to render its incomparable beauty with each new canvas.

A Mustang Set Free

Not only were Georgia's senses piqued by the high desert, her spirits seemed to soar higher with each passing day in Taos. She allowed herself new freedoms and behaviors now that she was removed from Stieglitz's protective eye. Georgia became more spontaneous, and she played.

Everyone at Mabel's was astonished when, the day after arriving, Georgia declared that she would learn how to drive. Tony and Beck would be her instructors. Tony's first lesson ended abruptly when Georgia, forgetting to brake, nearly drove through Mabel's massive wooden gate. He declared Georgia incapable of the fine coordination necessary to navigate a motorcar and asked Beck to continue the lessons. A week later, Georgia bought a black Ford sedan for $678; she would master it! All summer, various friends risked their safety teaching the "demon driver" from New York how to drive.

Georgia and Beck bonded, egging each other on with increasingly carefree and wild behavior. Daily routines included long walks, horseback riding, touring in Georgia's new car, and girlish bantering. Once while washing the Ford, Georgia teased Beck by hinting at a striptease, and the pair finished the job naked, laughing and squirting each other with water.

Another morning, at Mabel's breakfast table they teased John Marin (the great watercolor artist who was also visiting that summer) with their confessions of nude sunbathing the previous afternoon. As Marin flushed his embarrassment beneath a serious disdain, the two women pounced on him. His stuffy attitude became a target. "If you don't look out, I'll kiss you!" Georgia warned him one night. Beck instantly chimed in, "Yes, we'll both kiss you," and they playfully pecked him about the head as he finally let down his guard and laughed along.

Nights provided yet another opportunity for frolic. One evening, Beck and Georgia startled everyone at Mabel's by showing up for dinner dressed to the nines; Georgia even put on makeup and a fancy hat. Another enchanted evening, Georgia and Beck went out dancing in the village at a town-hall dance, escorted by Andrew Dasburg and his friend Bob Smith. By evening's end, the two women had taken a spin on the dance floor together. Beck was thoroughly enjoying the "new" Georgia, writing to others that O'Keeffe was "eating like a man" and even "smoking a cigarette every once in a while."

Meanwhile, amidst all the fun with Beck, Georgia was finding her groove again artistically. Nearly everything she saw that summer made a lasting impression, but above all she was inspired by the deep passion of the land. The buildings, hills, mountains, trees—all seemed possessed or endowed with feeling. Catholic crosses of the Penitentes spoke volumes to O'Keeffe; she was not familiar with a landscape scarred by human emotion and spiritual longing.

That summer of 1929, Georgia O'Keeffe produced her first of many New Mexico masterpieces. Beck's own sensitivity influenced Georgia by her response to the vast power and drama of the sky, her fascination with the plastic flowers that lay scattered across New Mexico graveyards, and her appreciation of the crosses. All of these themes would become favorite O'Keeffe motifs.

The following February, O'Keeffe exhibited her New Mexico work in Manhattan amid much excitement and anticipation. Included in the collection of twenty-seven paintings (nineteen from New Mexico) were pictures of saints, kachina dolls, crosses, the famous Ranchos de Taos church, Taos Pueblo, and landscapes. Among them, the *Lawrence Tree, Black Cross New Mexico,* and *Ranchos de Taos Church* would become among the most popular of Georgia's works. Critic Henry McBride responded enthusiastically and insightfully: "Georgia O'Keeffe went to Taos, New Mexico, to visit Mabel Dodge. . . . Naturally something would come from such a contact. But not what you would think. . . . Georgia O'Keeffe got religion. What Mabel Dodge got I have not yet heard." McBride also saw clearly the essential new direction in Georgia's work. "It is intellectually thrilling to find Miss O'Keeffe adopting so quickly the Spanish idea that where life manifests itself in greatest ebullience there too is death most formidable."

Georgia and Mabel

While Georgia was enjoying her stay at Los Gallos immensely, she soon came to appreciate her hostess's capricious ways. Georgia had remarked to many, including Stieglitz, how generous Mabel had been to offer her a house and studio for the summer. With the passing of the summer, however, Mabel and Georgia would cross swords over Tony Luhan.

Georgia had instantly admired Tony. His quiet reserve, silent composure, and sparse and elegant appearance were reflections of O'Keeffe's own standards. Tony had been a generous guide for Beck and Georgia's adventures, helping them with horseback rides and camping trips and showing them his favorite places near Taos.

In June Mabel left on a trip to Buffalo for a hysterectomy, and she was particu-larly vulnerable and sensitive. Tony still maintained his pueblo household, and after Mabel left, he moved back in with his former wife. While Mabel was away in New York, she and Georgia carried on a letter correspondence that was full of revealing insights concerning their marriages. Compulsively jealous, Mabel wrote threatening letters to Tony (which Georgia read to him), and Georgia tried to mediate a difficult situation. Mabel had even suggested that Tony and Georgia were having an affair.

Georgia and Mabel shared common concerns about their husbands. Alfred Stieglitz and Tony Luhan were both charismatic and attractive men (though in contrasting ways) and were fond of women. Both men had enjoyed romances with other women during their marriages to Mabel and Georgia. Georgia had suffered silently through Stieglitz's indiscretions. She reacted by maintaining control over her own emotions and resisting trying to dictate to Alfred with whom he could and couldn't spend time. Mabel reacted volcanically to reports of Tony's wanderings.

Mabel's threats of divorce that summer were causing emotional turmoil at Los Gallos, and Tony's mood became increasingly gloomy with Mabel's prolonged absence. Finally Georgia counseled Mabel in a letter, "For God's sake—don't try to squeeze all the life out of him. I know from experience that it isn't a pleasant situation."

It was advice she could also have sent to Stieglitz. After ten years of his loving though firm paternalistic control of Georgia's life, she was breaking free, and he agonized over it daily. Alfred sent dozens and dozens of heartfelt pained letters to Georgia that summer, wondering when she was ready to come back to New York.

Mabel finally returned home in August, and Tony's affections and attention swept away the thunderclouds of midsummer. But Georgia and Mabel had come to know each other perhaps more intimately than either cared to. They were both strong, willful, and highly competitive. Within a few days of Mabel's presence at Los Gallos, Georgia knew it was time to go home. She quickly packed and slipped away in late August without saying good-bye.

O'Keeffe returned to New York a changed woman. She had discovered in the remote mountains of New Mexico a special place of her own whose colors, moods, scenery, and emotions matched her own finely tuned personality. A playful and vibrant Georgia had broken out of Stieglitz's corral as if a mustang set free on the *chamisa* (sage) plains of Taos.

Alfred was overjoyed to see Georgia, and everyone remarked on her blissful spirit and suntan. Photographs of the couple at Lake George after her return show a beaming Georgia. Even her dimples, which she always tried to hide, were on full display.

Georgia had begun a separate life apart from Stieglitz. By the following summer of 1930, the couple had resigned themselves to this new reality. She returned to Mabel's place in 1930 for another painting season, but the magic of 1929 had vanished. Without Beck and with Tony under Mabel's hawk-like gaze, Georgia retreated from the usual social scene at the Big House and concentrated on her work. Georgia had personally felt the manipulative and petty side of Mabel and determined after she began to make her annual visits to New Mexico to maintain a healthy distance. For O'Keeffe, however, her days spent at the Pink House would always be gilded with the nectar of self-discovery. A letter to Mabel in August 1929, written in Georgia's sensuous and flowing handwriting, reveals the wonder of it all:

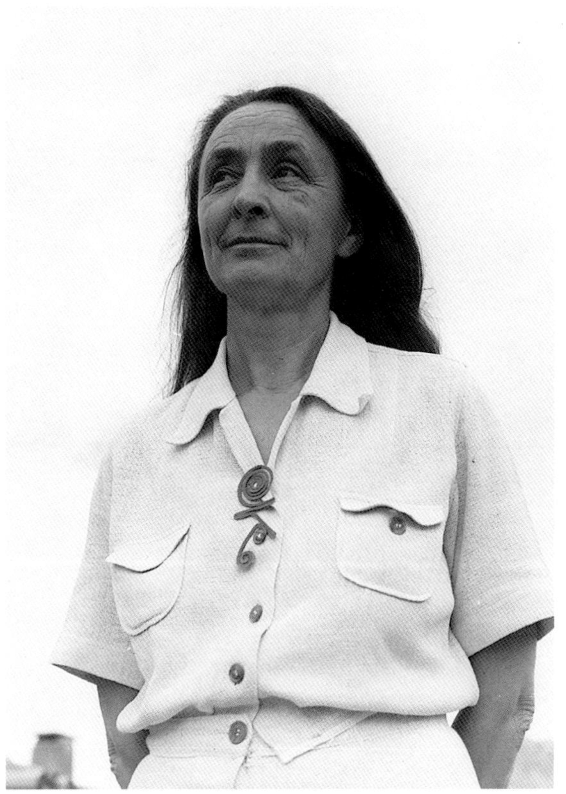

Georgia O'Keeffe, circa 1950s.

Dear Mabel,

It is 5 a.m.—I have been up for almost an hour—
Watching the moon grow pale—and the dawn come—I
walked around in the wet grass by the Pink House—one
bright—bright star—so bright that it seems like a tear in
its eye—The flowers are so lovely—I came over here to
the studio—so I could see the mountain line so clear
cut where the sun will come—
It seems so perfect that I wonder—is it just a dream
I make up—

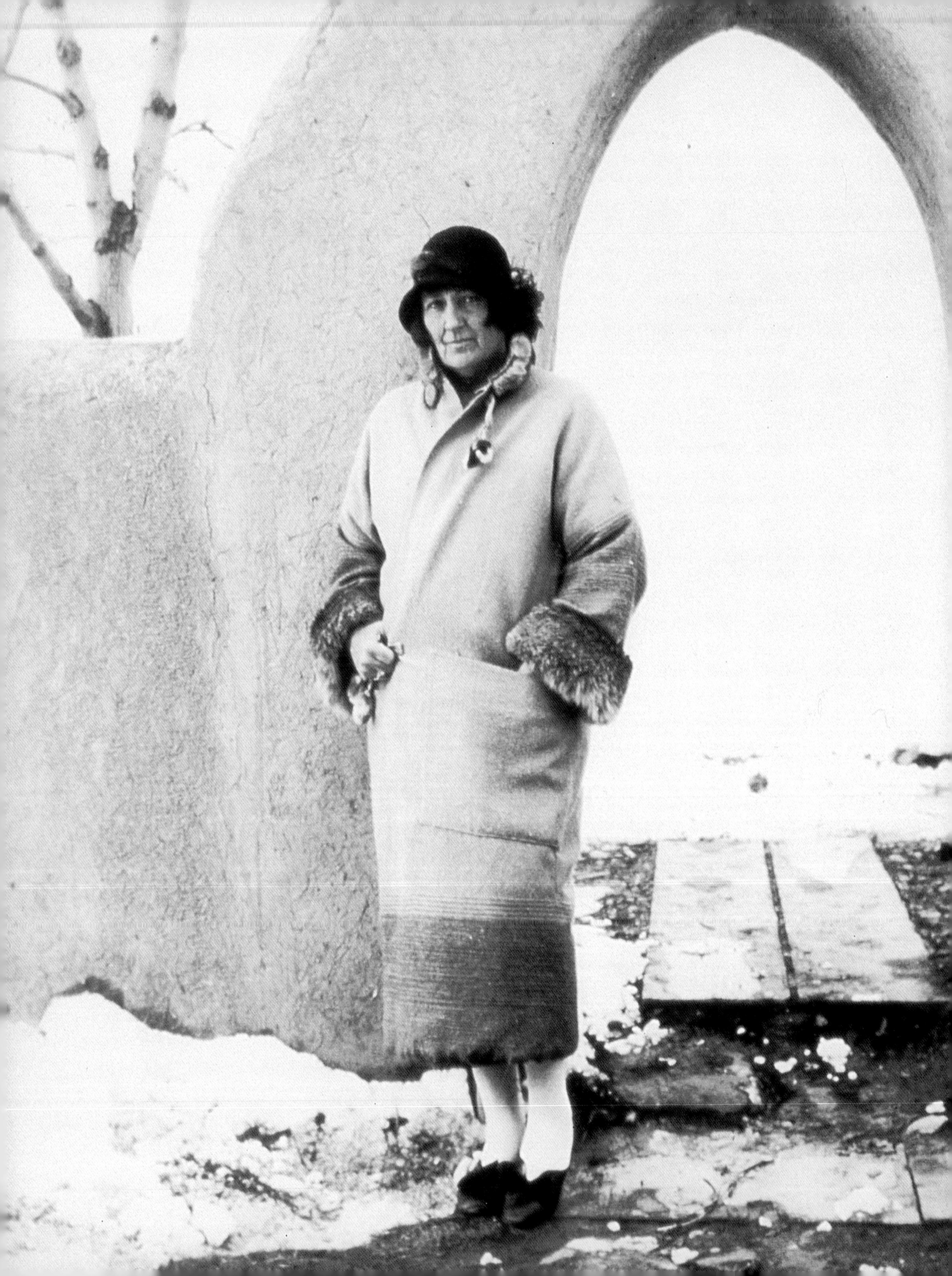

Carmel and Taos: Autumn of the Mountain

The 1920s at Mabel Dodge Luhan's Los Gallos estate in Taos had witnessed an extraordinary gathering of hugely talented people, most of them searching for ultimate truth or creative expression. Mabel's haven beneath the mountain had inspired some of America's greatest artists to produce their best work or gain flashes of brilliant insight.

One of these surely was Willa Cather, who had been pondering a southwestern novel since her visits to New Mexico in 1912 and 1925. By 1927, when she returned again for the summer, the genesis for *Death Comes for the Archbishop* was already well developed. As Mabel recalled years later in a newspaper column:

> *Willa Cather came and remained to write* Death Comes for the Archbishop *in the Pink House and had to finish it in Santa Fe where she had recourse to the archives in the old governor's palace. She and [her lover] Edith Lewis had a peaceful life in the little house doing their own housework. In the afternoons Tony would take us on long drives over Taos valley and she learned many old legends from him that enriched her book.*

Through the eyes of her fictional French priest Father Latour (based upon Archbishop Jean Baptiste Lamy), Cather brilliantly describes the essence of the New Mexican landscape, a wild and pure beauty that inspired the innermost wells of a person's vitality—a beauty that caused the dying French bishop to recall that "in New Mexico he always awoke a young man."

The frenzied pace of industrialization, urbanization, and modernization that had held most of the eastern seaboard of America in its sway had fascinated many intellectuals with its possibilities for a "new age" and had also repelled others. By the Roaring Twenties the forces of change were advancing over the land at a frightening pace. Some feared the alienation of modern man from nature, and as a consequence, from his inner self. D. H. Lawrence, of course, was a prophet warning against the machine age and machine-like

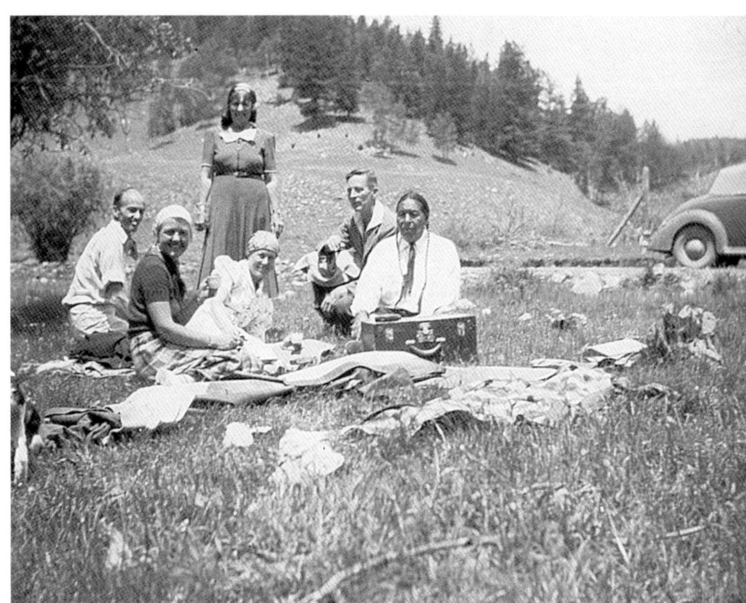

A Taos picnic includes (left to right) Spud Johnson, Una Jeffers, Mabel Dodge Luhan (standing), unidentified woman, Robinson Jeffers, and Tony Luhan, about 1935.

Mabel, dressed for a Taos snowfall, about 1935.

people, but he was not alone.

Besides Cather, Lawrence, and Georgia O'Keeffe, all of whom had found redemptive power in the New Mexican landscape, young Ansel Adams would also find his way. Ansel had been visiting New Mexico since 1927 but was still torn between a career as a photographer and a concert pianist. He first became acquainted with Taos through Mary Austin, and the spectacle of the mountain and its valley deeply moved him. He described the scene in a letter to his wife, much as a painter would:

A marvelous snowy range of mountains rises from a spacious emerald plain and this little Old World village nestles closely to the hills. Adobe—bells—color beyond imagination—and today, the heavens are filled with clouds.

In 1929 Adams returned to Taos on a photographic assignment for the Sierra Club. That summer he was in residence at Mabel's along with John Marin, the great watercolorist, and Georgia O'Keeffe. In contrast to the literary giants Mabel had attracted earlier in the decade, Los Gallos was now hosting three of America's most powerful and perceptive sets of eyes.

As 1929 had proven to be a profound revelation for O'Keeffe, so too it was a watershed year for Adams. With Mary Austin, he embarked on a collaborative interpretation of Taos Pueblo. Thanks to Tony and Mabel's assistance, he gained access to the restricted village and produced a luminous portrait of everyday life at the pueblo, drenched by the rays of the midsummer sun.

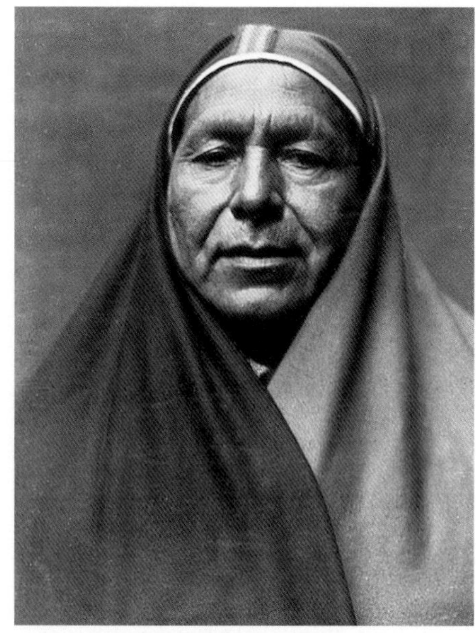

Tony Luhan, about 1930.

A year later Ansel Adams met Paul Strand at Mabel's. Strand had grown out of Stieglitz's shadow by 1930 to become one of the country's leading photographers. Strand's photographs stretched the boundaries of light contrast, clarity of vision, and the technique of composition and cropping that had also influenced O'Keeffe. After meeting Strand, Ansel's commitment to photography was complete.

Though Adams was sensitive and critical of Mabel's personality shortcomings, he recognized her genius for enabling other artists and writers to flourish. In her he recognized a generous hostess, lively intellect, and kindred spirit. In a 1937 letter to Mabel on the occasion of her book *Edge of Taos Desert*, he wrote, "Not unlike you, when you first came to Taos, I am confronted with the problem of finding a real way of life, and real and vital simplicity."

Ansel Adams and Georgia O'Keeffe symbolically bridged the transition from one decade to another at Los Gallos estate. The 1920s in America were filled with great optimism and achievement. Prosperity swept the land and many artists felt its benevolence. With the stock-market crash in 1929, the "blue skies, nothing but blue skies" mood quickly clouded over. Even the blue skies over Taos Mountain and Los Gallos turned somber.

Now in her early fifties, Mabel began to reflect upon her incredible life and all the "bohemian legends" she had met and nurtured. It was truly an amazing constellation. With Spud at her side busily and effectively promoting her achievements and cultural contributions, Mabel had achieved a national reputation and notoriety as an extraordinary salon hostess. After D. H. Lawrence's death in March 1930, she was inspired to tell her stories publicly (although she had already begun recording her thoughts on paper years earlier). In her expansive, flowing handwriting, she wrote and wrote and wrote, producing volumes of memoirs. Several books were published in rapid succession, including *Lorenzo in Taos* (1932), *Intimate Memories: Background* (1933), *Intimate Memories: European Experiences* (1935), *Winter in Taos* (1935), *Intimate Memories: Movers and Shakers* (1936), and *Edge of Taos Desert: An Escape to Reality* (1937).

Mabel's autobiographical devotion awed many of her friends, including Dorothy Brett, who also released her memoirs of Lawrence in 1933. Brett observed that:

When she started to write her memoirs, she wrote incessantly without stopping, day after day, lying on her sofa with a copy book and pencil. She poured herself untiringly into those books. The energy and concentration was boundless, until all of a sudden the book was finished and Mabel resumed normal life—which was energetic enough, Heaven knows.

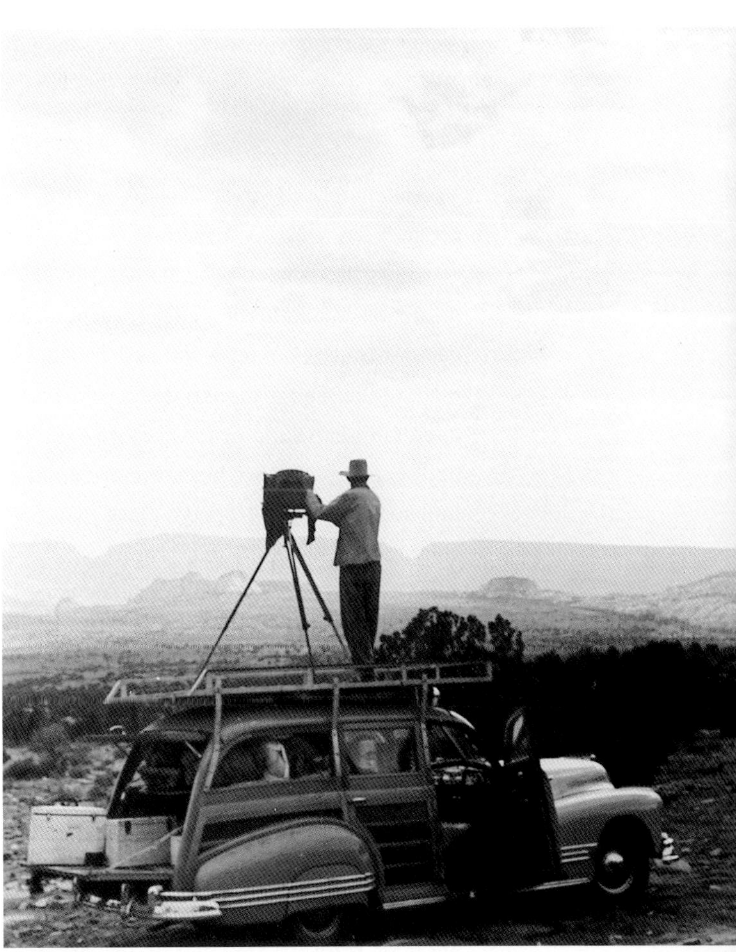

Ansel Adams in a photo shoot near Rainbow Lodge, New Mexico, 1944.

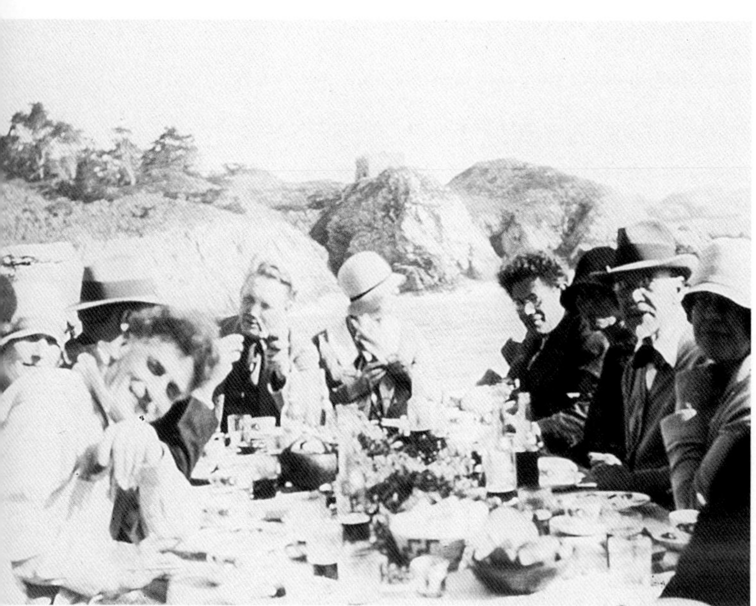

A Carmel, California, al fresco dinner party includes (left to right) three unidentified diners, Sinclair Lewis, Molley O'Shea, another undentified member, Ella Young, Lincoln Steffens, and Mabel Dodge Luhan.

Meanwhile, life at Los Gallos carried on, in many ways as intriguing in the 1930s as the previous decade. Despite her attraction to and lusting after (psychologically or otherwise) powerful and creative men, Mabel had demonstrated a tolerance and emotional support for homosexuals of both genders. Besides her secretary Spud Johnson, Mabel developed a close relationship during the 1930s with Thornton Wilder, winner of the 1928 Pulitzer Prize for his novel *The Bridge of San Luis Rey.* In her declining years, Mabel recalled Wilder's slight and bashful stutter with great fondness.

Earth Knower: Maynard Dixon

During the summer of 1931, Mabel lent her large studio to Maynard Dixon, one of the Bay Area's leading artists and a man of great insight and empathy for the primal simplicity of the western landscape and its people. Dixon and his wife, photographer Dorothea Lange, had motored to New Mexico with their two small boys in tow. Once arrived in Taos, the Dixon family settled into a small adobe house about one-half mile out of town.

Taos offered Dixon a real sanctuary from the pressures of San Francisco and also his troubled marriage to Lange. The simplicity of life in Taos suited Maynard's personal unfettered tastes, and his deeply held spiritual convictions were reaffirmed by the religious customs of New Mexico. He responded by producing over sixty paintings and many more drawings, sketches, and studies during the eight months he lived in Taos. In particular, he painted one of his masterpieces, *Earth Knower,* a dramatic portrait of a blanketed Indian seemingly sculpted out of the raw earth that formed background scenery.

By 1931 the country was firmly in the clutches of the Great Depression, and many Taos residents were struggling to get by. Dorothea Lange remembered:

There I saw, for the first time, this thing—living by barter. Indians, Mexicans, poor whites, natives—all would come to that square in Taos on Saturday afternoons and bring their produce, their red beans and pinto beans, their pinyon nuts, their dried corn, some weavings, flour, eggs, lamb, hides, and there they bartered. When it began to get dark, they were still bartering.

Though life in Taos in the early 1930s was a challenge for the Dixon family, they were all impressed by simple acts of love. Their neighbors at Taos Pueblo often dropped by the small adobe house for impromptu dances, such as eagle and buffalo ceremonies and the social round dance where everyone joined in.

Christmas 1931 became forever etched in Dan Dixon's memory. As a youngster of six, he trudged out into the deep snow with his father, Maynard,

to cut down our Christmas tree. It was a juniper that grew where the mountains dropped down to the edge of the frozen fields. Dorothea took a photograph of us as we carried it back to the house, and we decorated it with painted bits of wood, and feathers, and tinted pine cones, and other ornaments that Maynard contrived to make it something to celebrate. There wasn't a single store-bought object on it.

In January it was time for the Dixons to return to San Francisco, where Maynard faced an uncertain future with little money in the bank. On the way home through Socorro, Deming, Phoenix, Yuma, and Los Angeles, they passed countless destitute men hitchhiking on the road, on their way to a better future somewhere, anywhere. The brutal scenes of poverty shook both Maynard and Dorothea. "Is this my country?" he moaned.

Music of the Cosmos

For other charmed souls, the 1930s continued to promise undreamed-of opportunities. Such a fortunate man was Leopold Stokowski, then the flamboyant conductor of the Philadelphia Symphony Orchestra. Stokowski had gained a huge following in America for popularizing classical music and making it accessible to his audiences. His fame had drawn the wrath and criticism of serious musicians who felt Stokowski was watering down the classics for the masses.

Stokowski first met Mabel in 1931 when he and the great Mexican conductor Carlos Chavez converged on Los Gallos for a summer visit. Both Stokowski and Chavez were excited by the artistic possibilities of

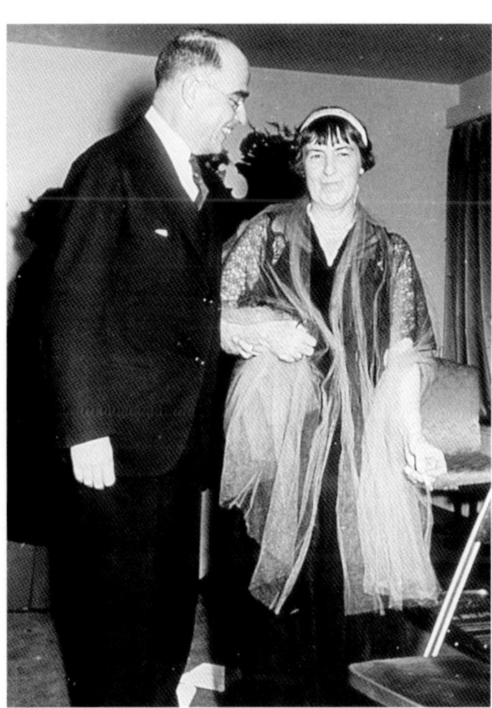

Thornton Wilder and Mabel Dodge Luhan, about 1935.

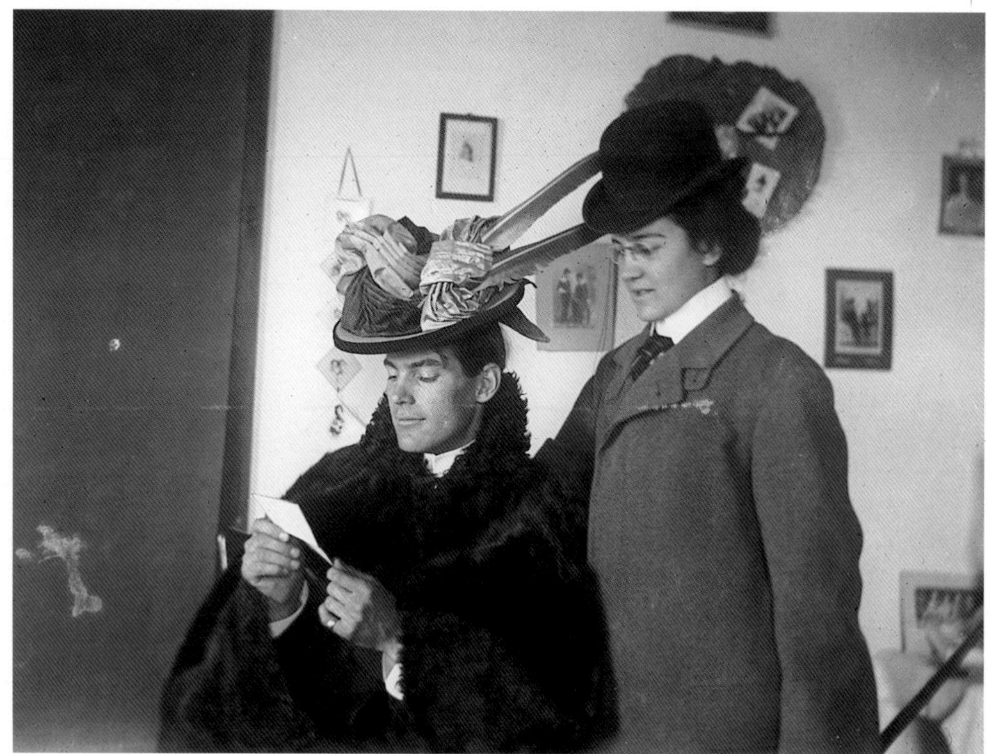

Archaeologist and Pueblo scholar Kenneth Chapman and his wife, Kate, dressed for a Santa Fe costume party, 1920.

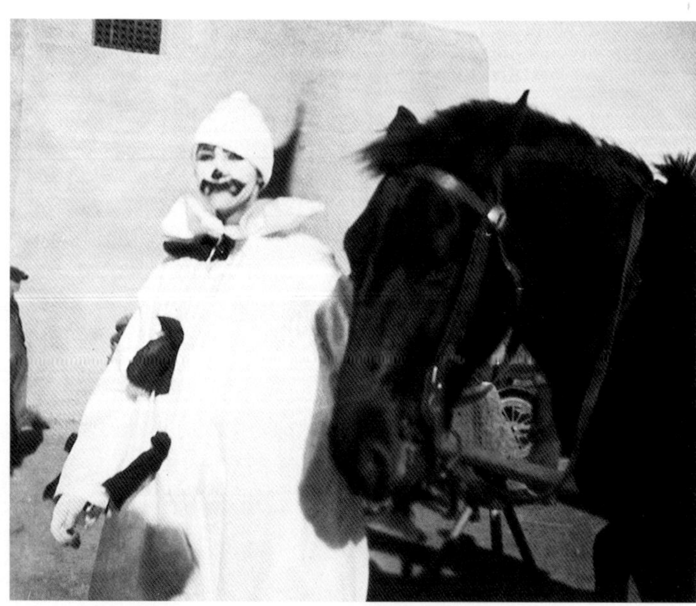

Helen Greene Blumenschein, artist and wife of Ernest L. Blumenschein, dressed in costume for a Taos Fiesta parade, 1930s.

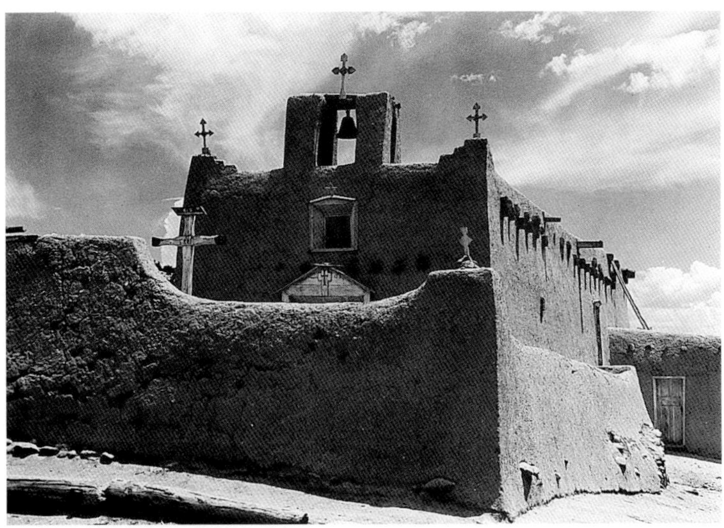

Northern New Mexico church, perhaps San Lorenzo Chapel, Picuris Pueblo, 1930.

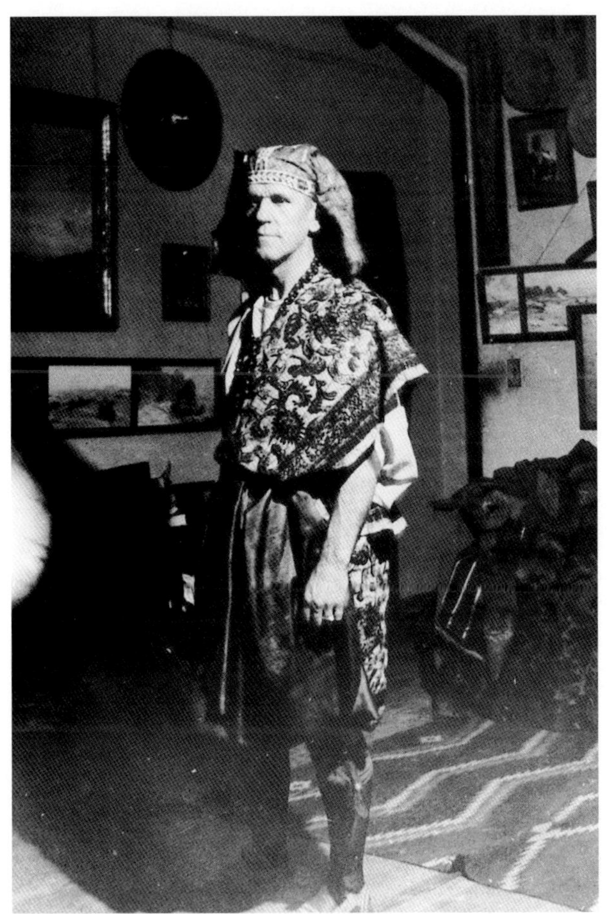

Santa Fe artist Gerald Cassidy, dressed in Egyptian costume for a party, about 1925.

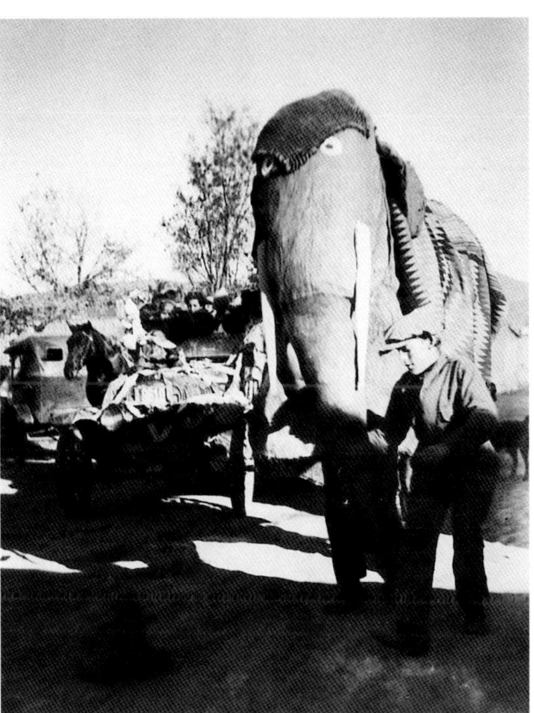

A papier-mâché elephant made an appearance at a Taos Fiesta parade in the 1930s.

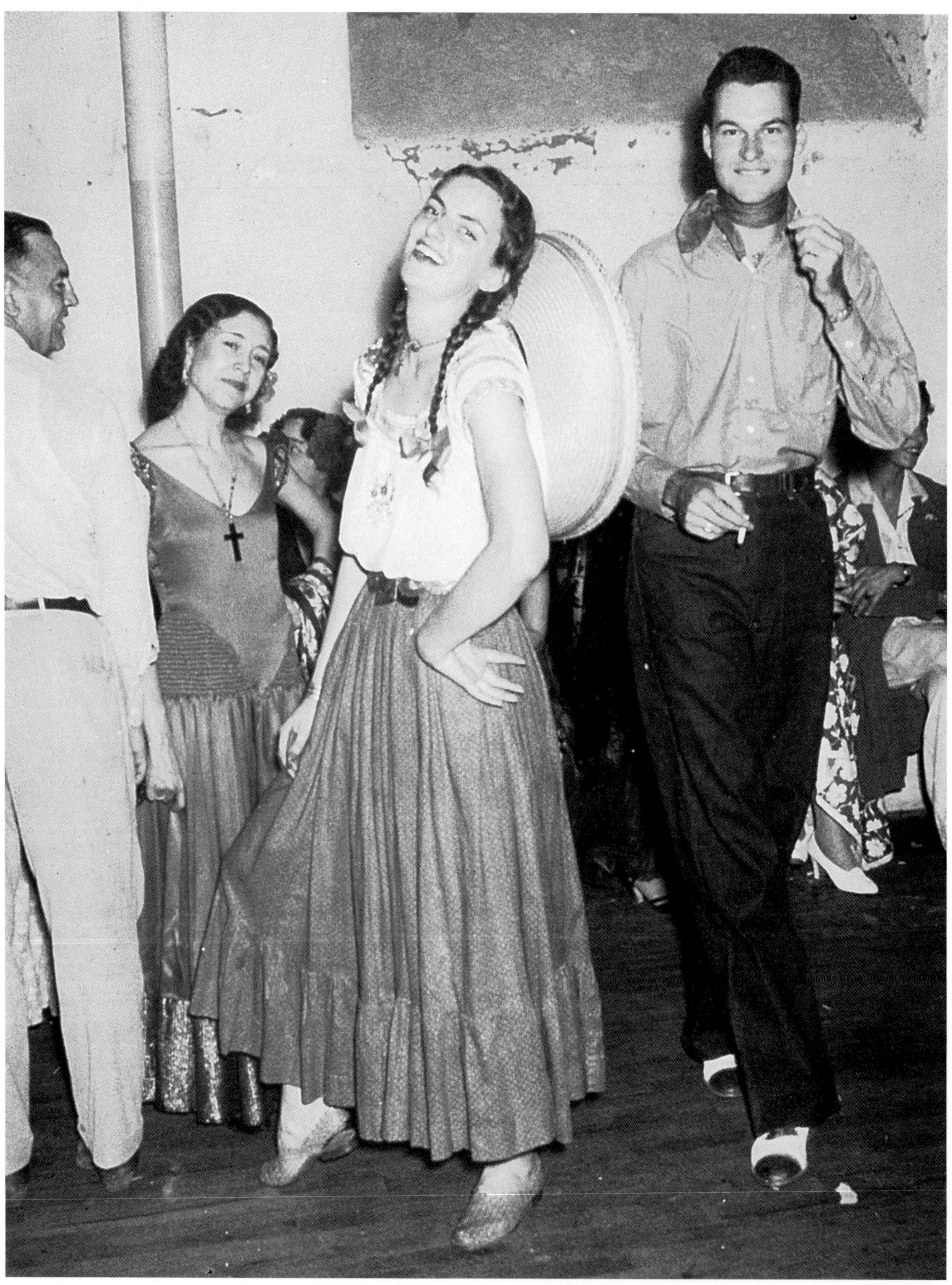

nontraditional, non-western music of indigenous people. Both hoped that folk music of the Americas, Africa, and Asia could be fused with classical melodies to create "world" or "cosmic" music. Theirs was an ideal that still resonates today. Stokowski was captivated by the ceremonials he witnessed, and the deep baritone chanting of the Taos men vibrated within his heart chakra.

Because of his own musical talents as a singer (many of Mabel's guests remarked on Tony's singing during long afternoon drives), Tony Luhan and Stokowski formed a quick and deep friendship forged of mutual admiration. Tony recognized Stokowski's genuine desire to record Pueblo music on wax records so he could transcribe it. With Spud Johnson's assistance and Tony's intervention at the Taos Pueblo, Stokowski attempted to record the guttural music, but to no avail. He wasn't satisfied with his squeaky recordings. Nevertheless, Tony and the Taos Pueblo hosted a huge feast in Stokowski's honor.

Like Lawrence had hoped, Mabel still wished to create an ideal center where creative men and women could develop a new model of living—a utopia. Through Stokowski and Carlos Chavez, she saw a new connection was possible with artists south of the border. Together with Tony and Spud, Mabel made the long trip to Puebla and Oaxaca in February and March of 1932 and could see for herself the inscrutable paradoxes of Mexico. A Taos-Mexico connection began to obsess her.

Mabel made a concerted effort in March 1932 to recruit Diego Rivera and Frieda Kahlo to her "center." Stokowski responded to Mabel in a letter dated March 13, 1932:

Will you ask Diego or shall I? Somehow I feel better if you would ask him. I am crazy with too much work but as soon as I have time I want to study and think about your idea about a bridge between cultures.

On March 24, Stokowski agreed to hand-deliver a letter to Diego Rivera from Mabel. Rivera and Frieda Kahlo never visited Mabel at her Los Gallos estate, which effectively killed her idea of a cultural center, but she maintained her friendships with Carlos Chavez and Stokowski.

Throughout the 1930s, "Stoky" continued his seasonal visits to Taos, and his charms won him many friends and admirers, including Dorothy Brett, who gushed:

Through the glass doors walked this amazing, fantastic creature. Tall and slim, with ash-blond hair and one of the most finely chiseled, sensual faces I ever saw, he walked right out of a fairy tale. I just gasped. With all the charm in the world and with perfect understanding of the effect he produced, he bowed, and we were swept into the living room.

Another Stoky admirer turned out to be Greta Garbo. Stokowski had quit his job with the Philadelphia Symphony in 1934 and set his sights on Hollywood. (He would later take a turn as the conductor of Mickey Mouse's orchestra in Walt Disney's

Clarence Thompson, a friend of Mabel's, and an unidentified young woman enjoy a Taos fandango, about 1925.

animated classic *Fantasia* in 1940.) Stokowski would also make tabloid headlines in 1938 concerning his "torrid" affair with "The Face"—Garbo.

From Mabel's scrapbooks, pasted over with news clippings and *Photoplay* magazines, now housed in Yale's Beinecke Rare Book Library, one can sense the excitement of Garbo's visits to Taos and Los Gallos on the arm of Leopold Stokowski. He had endured an agonizing and very public separation from his wife and family during his budding relationship with the Swedish film goddess. But true to her nature, Garbo proved too elusive for Stokowski to pin down. They broke up in 1938 and he turned his attention to heiress Gloria Vanderbilt. On December 31, 1938, he wrote Mabel a sentimental letter:

At the present time G is busy preparing a new picture. But later she would like to follow your generous suggestion in Taos.

I am always remembering the romantic old roads off in the desert that we went to one day—where people used to ride horses and carriages in the old days. They seem to be full of the life of the past still—and are much more alive than what is happening on the modern cement roads.

Carmel and Taos

In California the small coastal community of Carmel had served, for the West Coast, much the same cultural role that Taos and Santa Fe had for the Southwest. After 1900 the Carmel colony had fostered a strong literary group that included in its early years novelist Jack London, satirical writer Ambrose Bierce, naturalist John Muir, and writer Mary Austin. After the early founders had died (about World War I) and Austin had moved on to Santa Fe in 1924, Carmel continued to flourish, attracting new talents such as Sinclair Lewis, Lincoln Steffens, Langston Hughes, John and Molly O'Shea, Robinson Jeffers, Edward Weston, and John Steinbeck.

Like Mabel Dodge Luhan, Mary Austin grew restless after the Great War (World War I) ended. Privately, she felt that Carmel had already been ruined with its discovery by tourists, and she lamented,

The moment that rumors of Carmel's fame as an "art colony" became general, the place was doomed. Bric-a-brac shops were established, along with exquisite tea rooms; costly homes were erected on the highlands; hospital hotels were erected for the benefit of rich alcoholics. . . . The nouveau riche came in hordes and built . . . homes . . . determined to live the Bohemian life and to devote at least one afternoon a week to "art."

After wandering a few years looking for a new home, Austin settled in "the City Different" in 1924, and the cross pollination of the two major western artists and writers colonies began in earnest.

Spud Johnson and Witter Bynner maintained their Berkeley connections, and Mabel kept in close touch with her old New York salon friends. The complex alliances often intertwined, as they did in the winter of 1928–29, when Spud returned to San Francisco for the winter. There he assisted Lincoln Steffens, a political writer and one of the stars of Mabel's New York salons, in editing his autobiography. It was easy for Spud to coax a humorous political essay out of Steffens on the 1928 presidential election for *The Laughing Horse*.

Perhaps the visit to Taos of Ansel Adams in 1929 inspired Mabel to head west to California in the spring of 1930 for a vacation. There she met poet Robinson Jeffers and his wife, Una. By 1930 Jeffers had emerged as one of America's leading and most controversial poets. His great poems—"Tamar," "The Women at Point Sur," and "Roan Stallion"—revealed a distrust of man's rational powers and transcendent faith in the power of love and nature to lift mankind to a higher consciousness. Jeffers felt that sometimes violent or tragic events were necessary to shake loose a spiritual revelation or cosmic awakening. In these convictions Jeffers was closely related to D. H. Lawrence.

As Lawrence lay dying in Europe, Mabel transferred the thwarted aspirations she had harbored for Lawrence—to give a voice to Taos—onto Jeffers. In courting Robinson Jeffers to come to New Mexico, she demonstrated that she had learned valuable lessons from the Lawrence fiasco. Her zealous southwestern idealism had ultimately repelled Lorenzo, and Mabel was determined not to make the same mistake with Jeffers. She would court his wife, Una, and their two young sons instead.

Thanks to an inheritance from a cousin, Robinson Jeffers was able to devote himself at an early age to poetry. His own depressing estimation of humanity and its tendencies towards banal existence led him to build a stone fortress, which he called "Tor," at the tip of Monterey Peninsula. Jeffers's "Tower Beyond Tragedy" was an utterly romantic and self-indulgent work of architecture, in some ways reminiscent of Mabel's Los Gallos estate. But while Mabel welcomed the world to Taos, Jeffers fiercely guarded his privacy, protected by his gatekeeper wife, Una.

Like many of the remarkable women Mabel had come to know in her life, Una Jeffers was highly educated and intelligent and extremely protective of her husband.

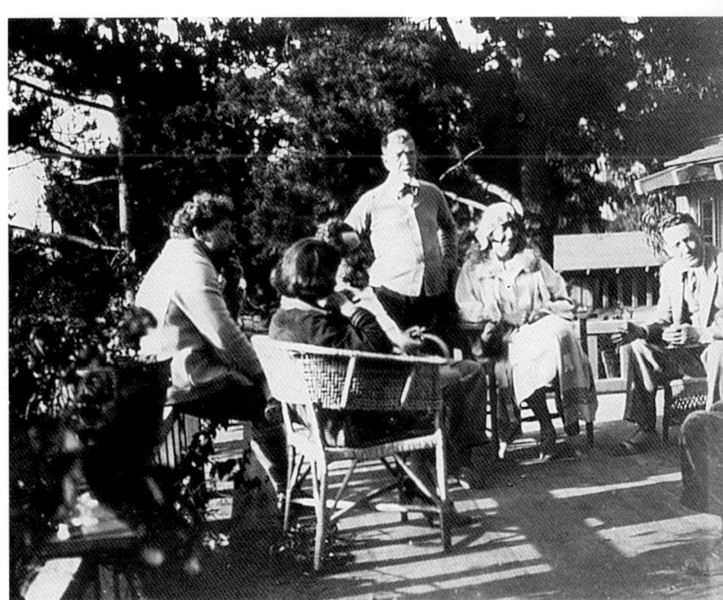

Lincoln Steffens (standing) presides over a Carmel tea party, which includes Mabel Dodge Luhan and Edward Weston, 1930s.

Mabel marveled at how completely Una "possessed" her genius husband even more than Frieda had owned Lorenzo. Both Frieda and Una had been credited by many critics with inspiring their husbands to achieve greatness, but Una had given Robinson even more—the children and fatherhood that the Lawrences were unable to realize. Unlike the calm and brooding Robin, however, Una could exhibit flashes of rage and jealousy that Mabel had seen too much of in D. H. Lawrence.

After their initial meeting, Mabel shared drafts of her memoirs of the Lawrences (later published as *Lorenzo in Taos*, 1932) with Una and Robinson. The Carmel couple was tantalized by the insider gossip of the great English writer and his free-spirited German wife. The Jeffers's were incredulous at Mabel's glowing praises of Taos and northern New Mexico, and even though they both had resolved not to leave Tor House, they were beginning to ponder a trip to Taos Mountain.

Una and Mabel began an intimate and intense letter correspondence that finally produced a visit by the Jeffers family to Taos in the summer of 1933. The two families traded visits between Carmel and Taos nearly every year until tragedy struck in 1938. In New Mexico, Jeffers and his sons enjoyed horseback riding and idyllic picnics into the mountains on Tony's Indian ponies. In Carmel, the group savored

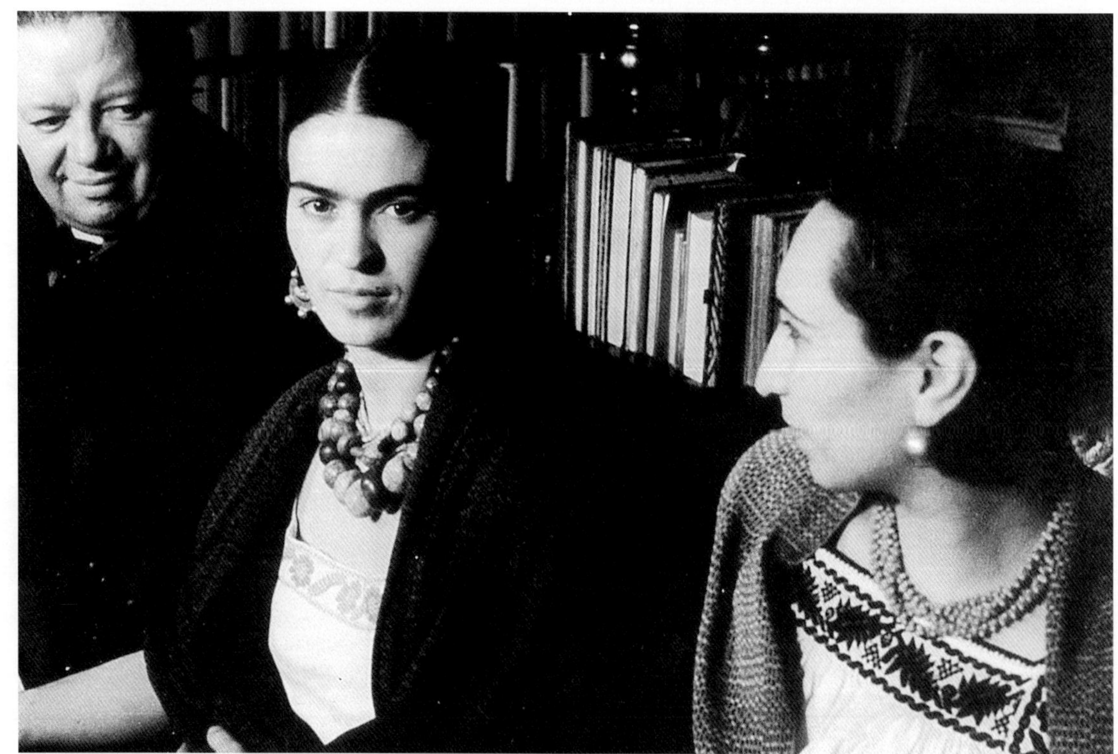

Mexican artist Diego Rivera and Frieda Kahlo (center), shown here with an unidentified woman, were contacted by Mabel to join her Taos colony in 1932. They never did.

spectacular picnic lunches beside the roaring ocean. Ella Young remembered the marvelous company and spectacle:

Everyone had to descend about a hundred steps cut in the rocks. Arrived, one might be on a desert island. No sound of a motor-horn, no glimpse of a roadway or of a house. A sound of the sea makes itself felt, the sea advancing in great waves and churning among the rocks. Far off, on Lobos magnificently thrust upon the horizon, there is the barking of sea lions. . . .

Sinclair Lewis is raying out the wittiest and most fantastic remarks. John O'Shea replies in kind. Lincoln Steffens is even more dazzling. So lightning quick is thrust and riposte in this rapier play of wit that I find myself bewildered by it. . . .

Tony, tired of it all, is standing on a rock. He stands majestic in a scarlet serape. The sea curls in waves behind him, sapphire-blue except where churning foam transfixes it to chalcedony.

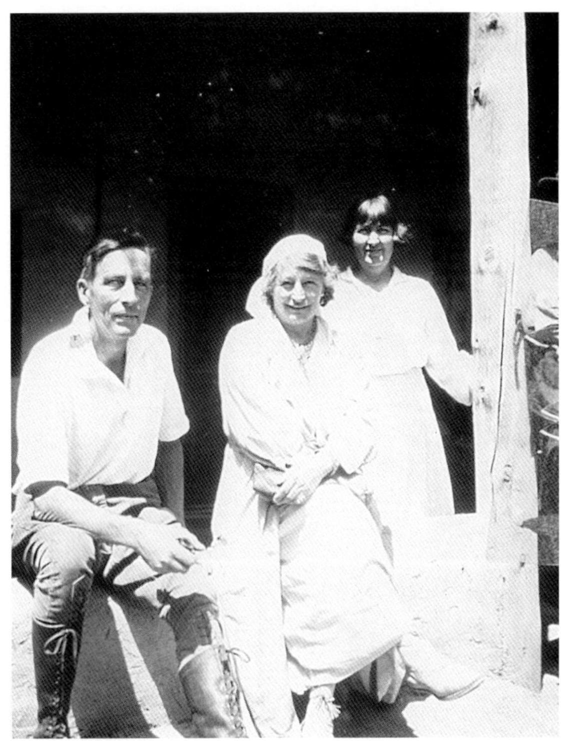

Robinson Jeffers, Frieda Lawrence, and Mabel enjoy a summer moment together at Los Gallos, about 1935.

By 1937 both Mabel and Robinson Jeffers had felt their creative wellsprings running dry. Mabel had exhausted herself writing volumes of memoirs, and Jeffers was desperately searching for new themes for his poetry. In the winter of 1937–38, Mabel retreated to New York City for psychotherapy sessions with her longtime analyst, Dr. A. A. Brill. The sessions restored her self-confidence, and she returned to Taos in high spirits for a new summer season of hospitality. She urged Robinson to come; she would gladly share her insights with him.

Adopting a page from Frieda Lawrence's philosophy, Mabel felt that Robinson needed to be sexually recharged in order to be creative. In residence that summer at Los Gallos was a lovely young woman, a refugee of a broken marriage to a Yale professor (who had suggested a ménage à trois with his mistress). In the hurt and beautiful young pianist, Mabel saw a remedy for Jeffers's writer's block. Mabel maneuvered the poet and the pianist closer together until sexual attraction took over.

Once Una heard of the affair, she went ballistic, frantically searching through Robinson's drawers for his handgun. Once she found it, she fled to Mabel's upstairs bathroom, placed the gun on her chest, and fired. The .32 caliber bullet narrowly missed her heart.

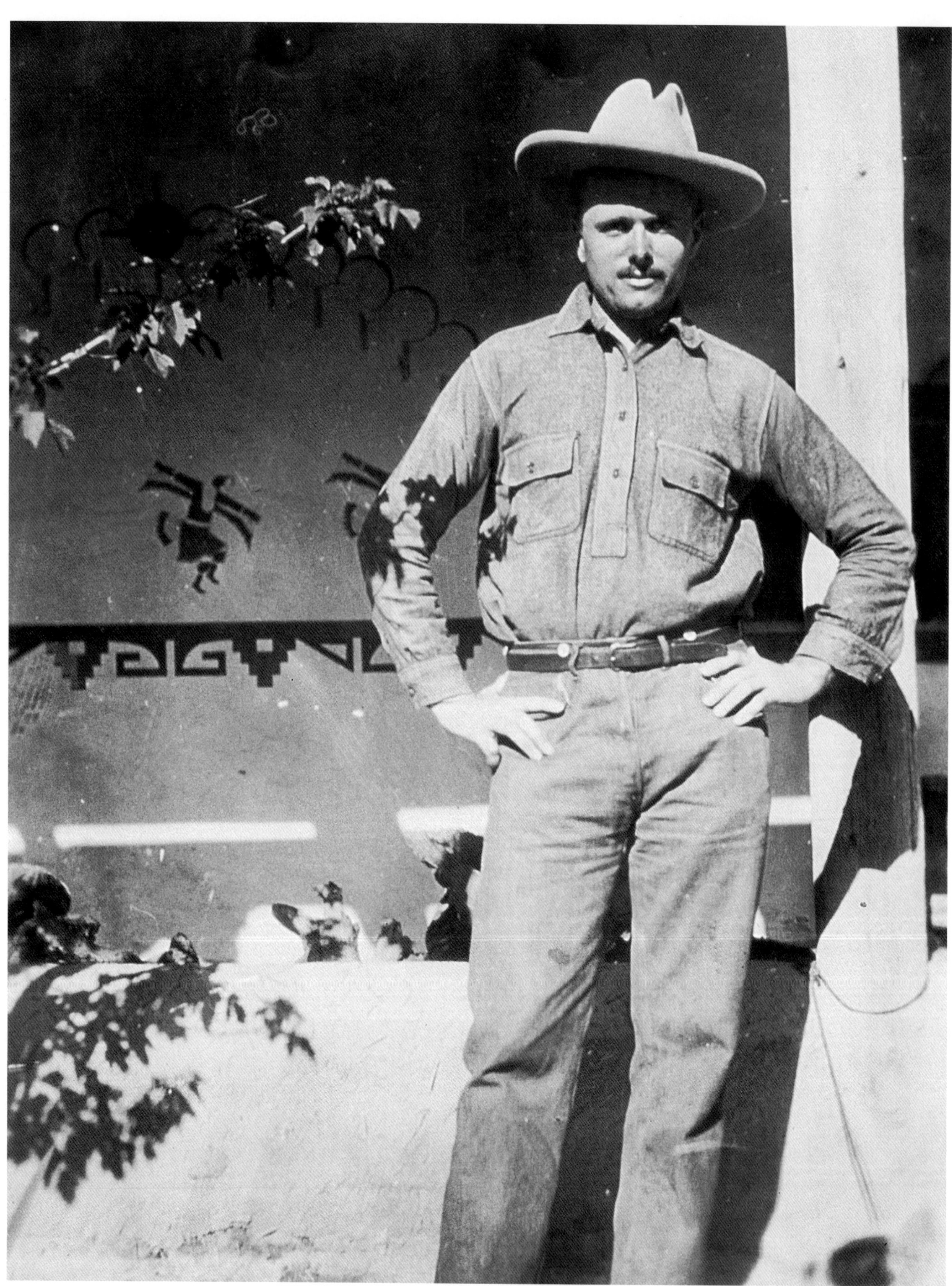

Mexico's great conductor Carlos Chavez enjoyed retreats at Mabel's estate during the 1930s. There, he collaborated with Leopold Stokowski on theories and projects.

The stunned guests included Thornton Wilder and his sister Isabel, who concluded that "Mabel was encouraging that affair. . . . She was an incorrigible meddler, you know." For her part, Mabel chided Una for causing a scandal and disrupting her house guests by attempting suicide. Mabel had neatly washed her hands of any personal responsibility in the affair that nearly caused Una her life and almost broke the Jefferses' marriage apart.

Fortunately Robinson and Una Jeffers repaired their partnership. The summer of 1938 could have been scripted by Jeffers himself, fond as he was of Greek tragedies and the situations of emotional violence that caused human beings to behave in unpredictable and tragic ways. He and Una had also come to know all too personally an archetype of feminine willfulness and manipulation in the shrew of Los Gallos.

The Jeffers incident eclipsed Mabel's dreams to endow Taos with its literary voice. In her own stormy legacy, however, she did that herself, perhaps not in her own writings but in the human dramas that unfolded upon her stage at Los Gallos. The sublime message of "cosmic consciousness," as demonstrated by the Indians and the land, proved as elusive for Mabel to capture as the flames of a campfire. But the hard lessons and foibles of people yearning for higher truths have remained imbedded in Mabel's saga for us to see and from which to learn.

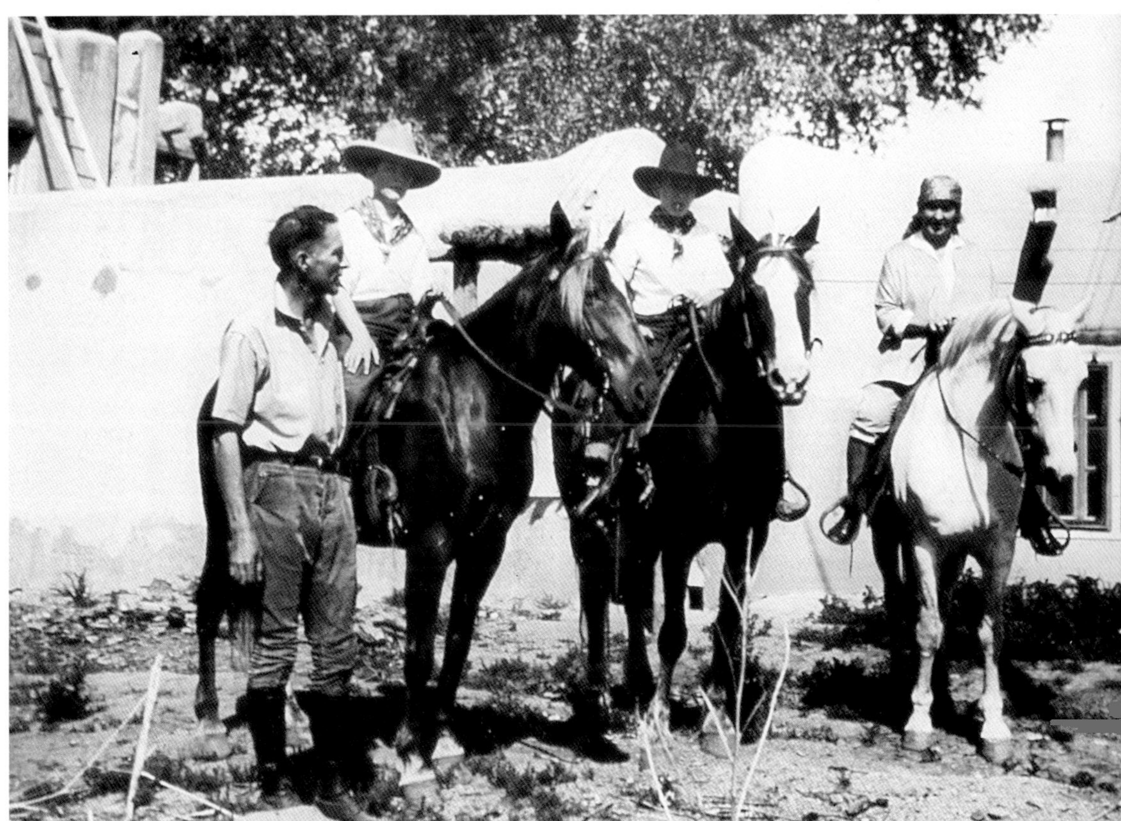

Robinson Jeffers and his sons enjoyed carefree summer vacations horseback riding at Mabel's before tragedy struck in 1938.

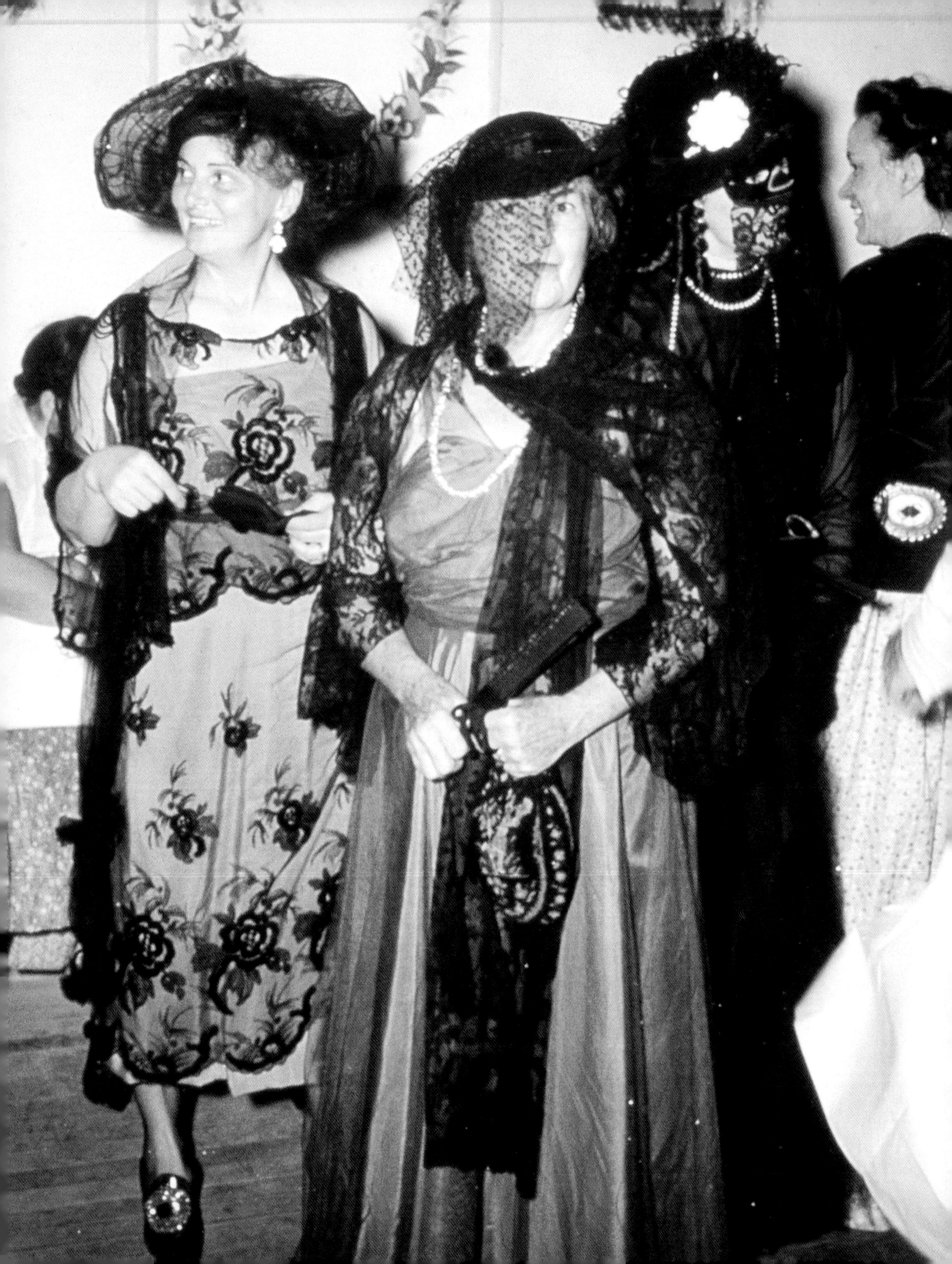

Sunset on the Mountain

By the end of the 1930s, global politics and the Great Depression had combined to cast an ominous pall in every corner of the globe. Once again the world was bracing for war. As Mabel turned sixty in 1939, she, too, was bracing for unprecedented changes in her life.

During the war years, life at Los Gallos became a daily rude awakening for Mabel. Gone were the superstar guests, as they, too, struggled to find safe havens or join the war effort. Gone were the young men of Taos Pueblo, off to serve the flag in remote countries; they would bring back modern sensibilities and demand new lifestyle changes (such as plumbing and electricity) from the elders. Gone were the carefree days of leisure, of writing and reading by morning, of long afternoon drives with Tony, of holding court at dinner or evening gatherings. Mabel's "days of wine and roses" at Los Gallos were gone, sweet memories made bittersweet by the fact that she had to work to sustain her cherished *bella vita*.

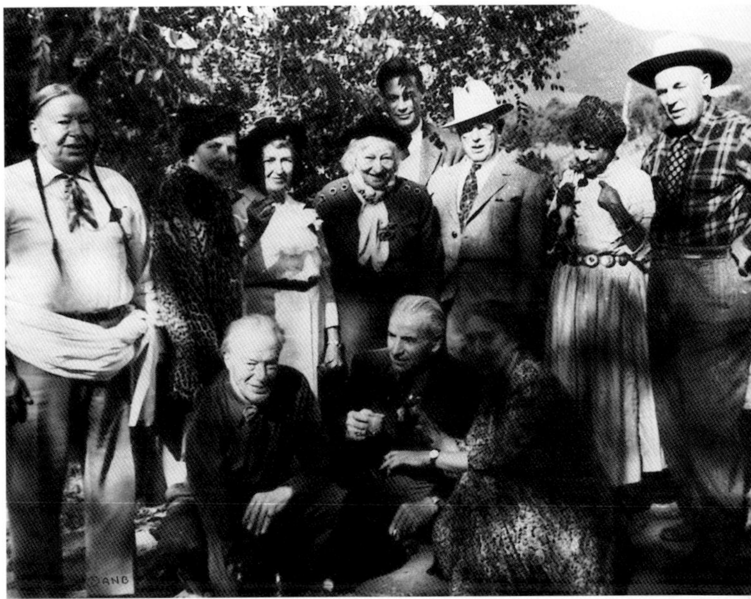

Well-known Taosenos: (standing, left to right) Tony Luhan, Mabel's cousin Angie, Mabel Dodge Luhan, Frieda Lawrence, Frank Waters, Leon Gaspard, Evelyn Gaspard, and an unidentified man; (sitting, left to right) John Young-Hunter, Angelino Ravagli, and Eve Young-Hunter.

The harsh reality facing Mabel was that she would have to survive without servants, maids, and cooks. Mabel's servants were earning salaries making widgets for the war machine instead of the much lower wages she paid. With no help, Mabel and Tony moved out of the Big House and into the much smaller two-story one. For the spoiled and pampered Mabel it was traumatic: "The weight upon us was enormous. All those *things!* And that big empty kitchen where I couldn't find anything!" She admitted she was unaware how inconvenient her guest houses had been all those years. Smoky woodstoves, no electric icebox, steep ladders to climb, but no one had complained!

For the first time in her life, Mabel had to cook her own meals. True, she had baked bread for Lorenzo, but he had tasted it and thrown it into the fire! During those painful first strange meals, Tony would make excuses to be away during supper time. Gradually, Mabel and Tony found a way to cope. Tony would cook breakfast, and Mabel would coax her guests to bring in main entrees to dinner from one of Taos's restaurants.

Mabel Dodge Luhan (center) at a Taos costume party, about 1940.

Delivery service was another much-lamented loss at Los Gallos. Now Mabel had to plan ahead. With gas rationing in force, she couldn't ring the butcher shop or hardware store and have what she wanted delivered when she needed it. So many errands get in the way of *real* living.

Finally Mabel began to appreciate a lifestyle she had never known:

What are we women getting today that we missed in the years before? A certain reality of purpose for one thing. Instead of living fantasies, fantasy of gracious living that was mostly done for us by our servants, now we have to cook, clean, run on essential errands, and in doing these things we finally perceive that living is doing something and not ordering it done or thinking about it. If we get a meal together onto the table, we experience a pleasure in it that is more than the eating of it. What we have lost in grace and graciousness, we seem to have gained in another kind of satisfaction.

Mabel was now a prisoner of her lifestyle in her own mansion. Scarce gasoline prevented the cherished weekend trips to Albuquerque, where she loved to stay in the grand Alvarado Hotel by the rail yards and watch the swallows flit by her window. Even the thin pure air of Taos was not enough anymore. Some days she just wanted oxygen!

After the war, Mabel found her second (or third or fourth) wind and produced a handsome illustrated retrospective book, *Taos and Its Artists,* in 1947. In it her mood mellowed, and she was able to pay tribute to the great Taos Society Artists founders as well as the legendary creative talents of her own circle. She maintained her passion for the mountain she had embraced as her own:

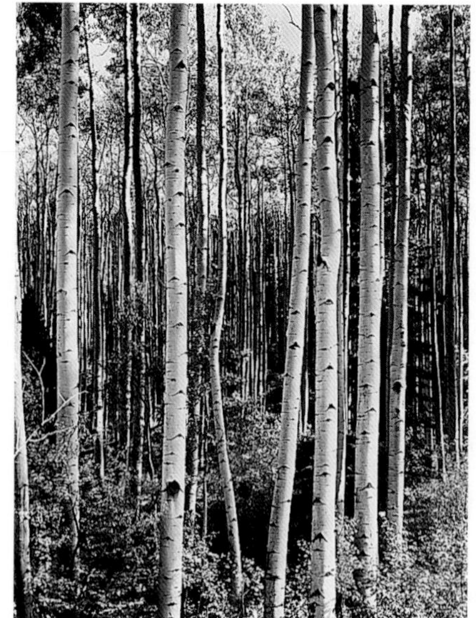

Eyes of the Forest, *photograph by Laura Gilpin.*

This is the provocative landscape that stirs the emotions. Tender and strong, sometimes darkening dramatically, the half-circle of mountains surrounds the somnolent desert and embraces the oasis that is named Taos, a name whose origin remains unknown.

Most writers and critics agree that by World War II the dynamic creative energy and sense of community of the Taos and Santa Fe colonies were declining. The war had redirected everyone's priorities; no longer were many artists seeking to escape but, rather, join in the invigorating power of American supremacy and postwar prosperity. Postwar Americans were obsessed with conformity, urbanization, suburbanization, and the country's industrial might, which seemed to produce a new marvel daily.

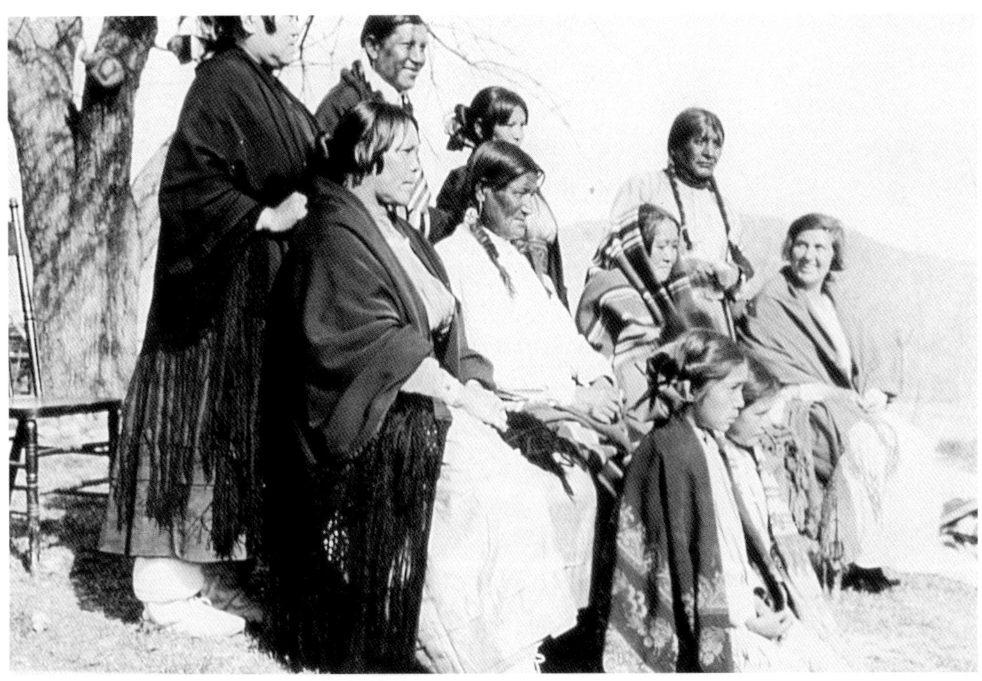

Mabel Dodge Luhan (far right) with a group of Taos Pueblo women, about 1920.

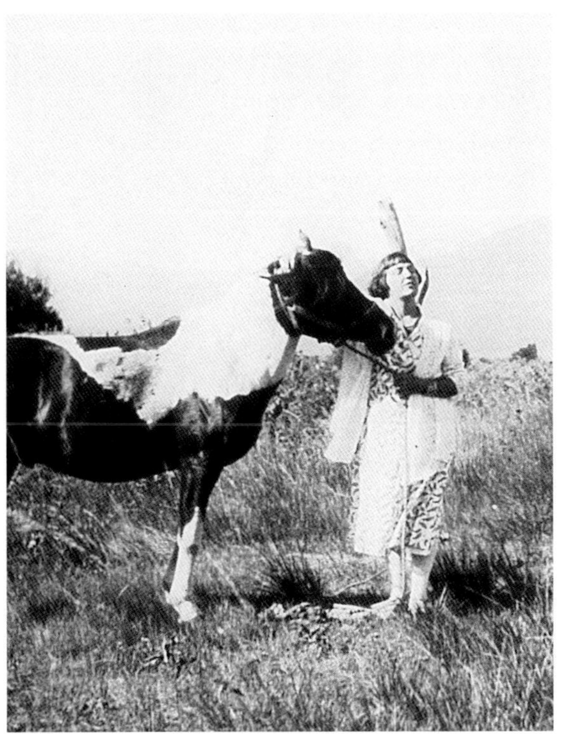

Mabel and her pony on the high desert plains of Taos, about 1920.

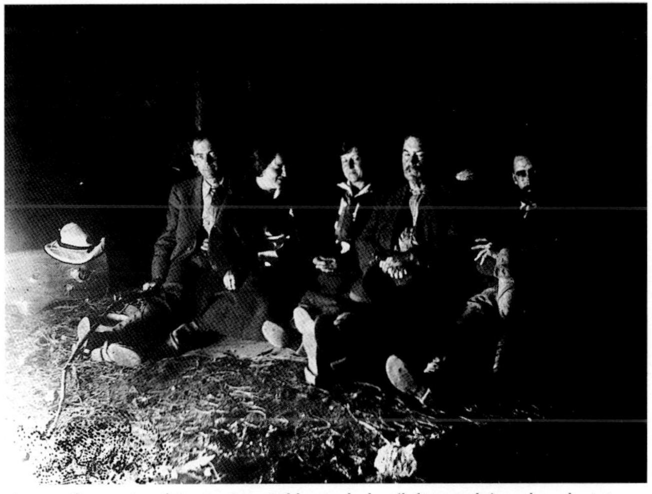

A campfire party of Santa Fe notables includes (left to right) archaeologist and scholar Kenneth Chapman, his wife, Kate, an unidentified woman, patron Frank Springer, and artist Carlos Vierra, circa 1920.

What would Lorenzo think of television? When Mabel mourned the passing of *her* era, she often thought of the red-bearded Englishman, as she did in a newspaper column written on June 5, 1949:

Old Taos has gone, this present-day Taos does not thrill the visitors as it used to. What they find here now they can find (and avoid) in almost any state in the union. Business, busyness, a lot of activity ending up in nothing. . . .

I imagine Lorenzo if he should unfortunately awaken from his long sleep, coming into our neon lighted village any night of the week! How he would turn away and hasten back to his dreams!

Within a few years, Mabel's own preeminence and glamor would be overshadowed by Millicent Rogers, a blond and svelte former model who decided to maintain a home in Taos in the 1950s. Much married and much enriched by her career and husbands, Millicent proved gracious to her socialite predecessor, and Mabel made a conspicuous presence at Millicent's parties. At one, Mabel and Hal (Witter) Bynner nervously encountered each other and decided they were getting too old to remain hostile any longer.

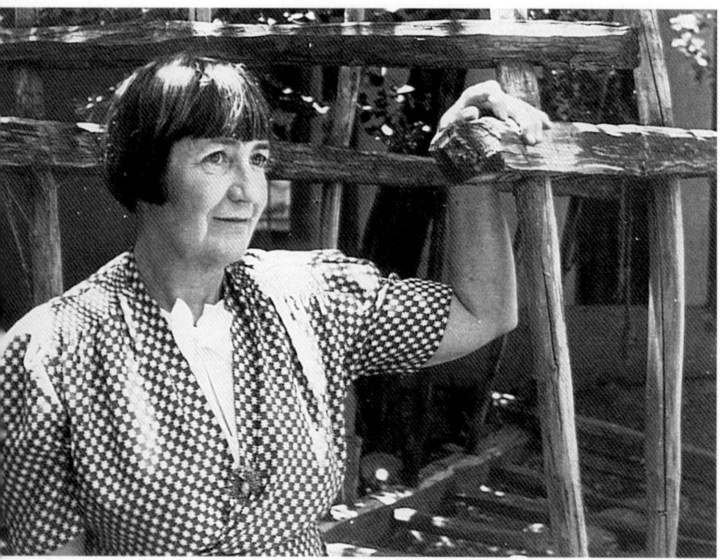

Mabel, posing for Vogue *magazine photographer Irving Abbe, late 1930s.*

Mabel and Frieda and Dorothy Brett resolved their differences as well, and in their old age each had become an icon—"The Three Muses of Taos." Writer Paul Horgan liked to say that the Santa Fe and Taos colonies revolved socially around the "Mabellites" and the "Friedonians," but when Frieda passed away in 1956, Mabel was left with her memories.

Mabel died in 1962 at the age of eighty-three. During her last years senility and fading eyesight left her disoriented. At times she didn't even recognize Tony, and scenes from her Buffalo childhood haunted her. At her funeral Tony cried out that the sun had dropped out of the sky, which was the loudest statement anyone had heard him make after all those years.

Dorothy Brett recalled Mabel's funeral vividly, painting a picture of the lonely casket beneath a shade tree in the Kit Carson cemetery. The mahogany casket is showered with sprays of scarlet, orange, and white gladiolus, Mabel's favorites. Four nuns in white tunics are praying near her grave. Ironically, Mabel claimed not to have known many Catholics in her lifetime. She remained a contradiction to the end of her days beneath the mountain.

Tony died a year later. He was buried in the Taos Pueblo cemetery within the ruined walls of the old church. He was returned to his people, the mysteries of the pueblo, and its sacred mountain that Mabel tried so hard to fathom.

Photographic Credits

Photographs from the Mabel Dodge Luhan Collection, Bienecke Rare Books and Manuscript Library, Yale University, appear on pages 11 upper left (photo by Ernest Knee) and lower right (photo by Carl Van Vechten), 12, 13, 14, 15, 16 upper, 17 upper and lower right, 18 upper, 19 upper and lower, 24 lower right, 25 lower right, 27 (photo by Ernest Knee), 28 lower, 29 upper, 38 upper left, middle right, and lower left and right, 46 lower (photo by Carl Van Vechten), 58 lower, 61, 63. 64, 65 lower right, 66, 69, 71 upper and lower right, 73, 74, 76, 80, 82, 84 upper, lower left and right, 85 lower left and right, 86, 89, 91, 93 lower right, 102, 104, 106, 108, 110, 111, 112 lower, 115, 116, 117, 119, 120, 123 upper left and right and lower right, 126 (photo by Carl Van Vechten), 130, 131, 132, 134, 135, 137 upper (photo by Ernest Knee) and lower right, 138, 141, 142, 143, 144, 145, 146, 148, 149 upper and lower left, and 150.

Photographs from the Museum of New Mexico (note: negative numbers, when available, follow page numbers in parentheses) appear on pages 20 (60955), 21 (4253), 22 (130157), 23 (60536), 24 upper (59944), 25 upper and lower left (31189), 28 upper (135188), 29 lower left (22671), 35 (40403), 36 (40373), 38 upper right (20787) and middle left (17011), 39 (7318), 43, 44 lower, 45, 46 upper, 47 upper right, middle, and lower left, 48 upper, 50, 51, 52 upper, 53 upper right and left, 54 upper, 56, 58 upper, 59, 62, 76 (50969), 77, 122 (9763), 123 (165657), 125, 129 (165648), 133 (6986), 136 (28483), 137 lower left (91574), and 149 lower right (28502).

Photographs from the Kit Carson Historic Museum Collection appear on pages 11 upper right, 17 lower left, 26, 29 lower right, 32 upper and lower, 34 (photo by Will Connell), 37, 39 lower, 40, 41, 79, and 136, 137 lower right, 147.

Photographs from the Witter Bynner Foundation appear on pages 63 lower, 65 upper right and left, lower left, 91 upper, 92 upper, 93 middle and lower left, 96, 107, 112 upper, and 113 upper and lower.

Photographs by Elmo Baca appear on pages 6, 8, 9, 10 upper, 11 lower left, 42, 47 upper left and lower right, 49, 53 lower, 77, 78, 81, 83, 85 upper left and right, 90, 92 lower, 94, 99, 100, and 103.

Photographs from the private collection of Elmo Baca appear on pages 10 lower, 18 lower, and 24 lower left.

All other photographs are from private collections.

Bibliography

Bynner, Witter. *The Way of Life According to Lao Tzu.* Putnum's Sons, 1944.

——— Journey with Genius. John Day, 1951.

Cather, Willa. *Death Comes for the Archbishop.* Knopf, 1927.

Coke, Van Deren. *Taos and Santa Fe: The Artists' Environment 1882–1942.* University of New Mexico, 1963.

Eisler, Benita. *O'Keeffe and Stieglitz: An American Romance.* Doubleday, 1991.

Eldridge, Charles C., Julie Schimmel, and William H. Truettner. *Art in New Mexico, 1900–1945: Paths to Taos and Santa Fe.* Abbeville, 1986.

Everett, Patricia R. *A History of Having a Great Many Times Not Continued to Be Friends.* University of New Mexico, 1996.

Fay, Eliot. *Lorenzo in Search of the Sun.* Bookman Associates, 1953.

Fiore, Kyle, and Martha Weigle. *Santa Fe and Taos: The Writers Era, 1916–1941.* Ancient City Press, 1982.

Gibson, Arrell Morgan. *The Santa Fe and Taos Colonies.* University of Oklahoma, 1983.

Gronowicz, Antoni. *Garbo: Her Story.* Simon and Schuster, 1990.

Hahn, Emily. *Mabel.* Houghton Mifflin, 1977.

Henderson, Alice Corbin, editor. *The Turquoise Trail,* 1927.

LaFarge, Oliver. *Santa Fe.* University of Oklahoma, 1959.

Lawrence, Frieda. *"Not I, But the Wind . . .".* Southern Illinois University, 1934.

Lisle, Laurie. *Portrait of an Artist: Biography of Georgia O'Keeffe.* Seaview Press, 1980.

Lummis, Charles F. *The Land of Poco Tiempo.* University of New Mexico, 1966 (reprint); 1884 (first published).

Maddox, Brenda. *D. H. Lawrence: The Story of a Marriage.* W. W. Norton, 1996.

Moore, Harry T., and Warren Roberts. *D. H. Lawrence and His World.* Viking, 1966.

Morrill, Claire. *A Taos Mosaic: Portrait of a New Mexico Village.* University of New Mexico, 1973.

Nestor, Sarah, and Edna Roberston. *Artists of the Canyons and Caminos.* Peregrine Smith (Gibbs Smith, Publisher), 1976

Robinson, Roxana. *Georgia O'Keeffe, A Life.* Harper and Row, 1989.

Rudnick, Lois Palken. *Mabel Dodge Luhan: New Woman, New Worlds.* University of New Mexico, 1984.

———. *Utopian Vistas.* University of New Mexico, 1996.

Sagar, Keith, editor. *D. H. Lawrence and New Mexico.* Peregrine Smith (Gibbs Smith, Publisher), 1982.

Schwart, Ted, and Sherry Clayton Taggett. *Paintbrushes and Pistols.* John Muir Publications, 1990.

Turner, David T., director. *Artists of the Twentieth Century New Mexico.* Museum of New Mexico, 1992.

Udall, Sharyn R. *Spud Johnson and Laughing Horse.* University of New Mexico, 1994.

Waters, Frank. *Masked Gods.* Ballantine, 1970 (reprint); 1950 (first published).

Whitman, Walt. *Leaves of Grass.* 1855 (first published).